S0-AED-162

Larousse
Best Recipes Ever

Larousse
Best Recipes
Ever

Veronika Müller
and
Mechthild Piepenbrock

Photography by C.P. Fischer

Larousse Co., Inc.
New York

This edition published in the United States by
Larousse Co., Inc.
572 Fifth Avenue
New York, N.Y. 10036

English edition published by
The Hamlyn Publishing Group Limited
London . New York . Sydney . Toronto
Astronaut House, Feltham, Middlesex, England
© Copyright The Hamlyn Publishing Group 1982
All rights reserved. No part of this publication may be
reproduced, stored in a retrieval system, or transmitted
in any form or by any means, electronic, mechanical,
photocopying, recording or otherwise, without the
permission of The Hamlyn Publishing Group Limited.

First published under the title
Spass am Kochen — Freude beim Essen
© Copyright BLV Verlagsgesellschaft mbH, München 1980

L.C. 82–08 1525
ISBN 0-88332-282-X

Photography by C. P. Fischer, assisted by
Anneliese Kompatscher-Hoppe and Michael Henkelmann
Photograph on page 19 by Paul Kemp

Phototypeset by Page Bros (Norwich) Ltd, Norwich, England in 9pt Times
Printed in Italy

Contents

Introduction

If you delight in gourmet food, you will enjoy cooking and preparing it, and it is for people who really enjoy good eating and find cooking fun that this book has been written. Just a glance at the beautiful photographs will show you that it is packed with imaginative recipes for every occasion and will provide countless ideas for different meals throughout the year. There are many classical dishes and original recipes created specially as well as a wide choice of wholesome family fare for every day.

To make it easy to plan a complete menu, the chapters are arranged in the classic order of a meal. There are recipes to suit every taste using a variety of fresh produce whether homely vegetables in hotpots and casseroles or luxuries such as lobster or asparagus for those really special occasions. Let yourself be inspired by the splendid photographs — every recipe is illustrated in full color to show you how to present the food so that it looks as delicious as it tastes. What is at first a feast for the eyes is transformed in the kitchen to a feast for the palate.

We, the two authors and the photographer, have taken much time and care in putting together this unique collection of recipes and we would like to take this opportunity to thank all those who helped in the preparation of this book. We hope you will now feel fired with enthusiasm, eager to try out the recipes, and that you will enjoy everyday cooking as much as entertaining and cooking for festive occasions, or simply just cooking for fun.

Veronika Müller
Mechthild Piepenbrock
C. P. Fischer

Appetizers
for Special Occasions

Appetizers

Stuffed avocados

Serves 4

2 large, ripe avocados
2 tablespoons lemon juice
1 (16-oz) can palm hearts or
*   artichoke hearts, drained*
4 firm, ripe tomatoes, peeled if liked
small bunch parsley, reserve a few
*   sprigs for garnish if liked*
2 hard-cooked eggs, shelled and
*   chopped*
1 small onion, peeled and finely
*   chopped*
2 tablespoons green peppercorns in
*   brine, drained and juice reserved*
*   for the dressing*

Dressing

2 tablespoons dry white wine
few drops hot pepper sauce
1 tablespoon tarragon or cider
*   vinegar*
¼ cup olive or walnut oil
1 clove of garlic, peeled and crushed
pinch of salt
pinch of sugar
4 sprigs of lemon balm or parsley to
*   garnish (optional)*

Halve the avocados lengthwise and
carefully remove the seeds. Sprinkle
with lemon juice.

Cut the palm hearts or artichoke
hearts into ½-in slices. Quarter the
tomatoes, remove the seeds and
stalks, and chop them. Chop the
parsley, then mix with the chopped
eggs and onion. Spoon this mixture
into the avocado halves. Sprinkle
over a few peppercorns.

To make the dressing, whisk
together the reserved peppercorn
juice, white wine, hot pepper sauce,
vinegar and oil. Add the garlic, salt
and sugar.

Spoon a little of the dressing over
each filled avocado. Garnish with
lemon balm or parsley sprigs if
liked.

Melon and Parma ham cocktail

Serves 4

1 medium-sized honeydew melon
3 tablespoons dry sherry
¼ lb Parma ham, thinly sliced
freshly ground black pepper
1 small head of lettuce, washed and
*   shaken dry*

To finish

1 tablespoon lemon juice
1 cup heavy cream, stiffly whipped
few lightly crushed peppercorns

Cut the melon in half and scrape out
the seeds and threads. Using a
melon baller or teaspoon, scoop out
balls of melon flesh. Do this over a
bowl to catch the juice. Put the balls
and juice into a large bowl, pour the
sherry over, cover and chill in the
refrigerator for 2–3 hours.

Strain the melon balls, reserving
the liquid. Turn very lightly with the
slices of ham, separated from each
other, and season to taste with
pepper.

Cut the lettuce leaves into thin
strips, then put into 4 small glass
dishes or bowls. Arrange the melon
mixture on top.

Beat the reserved melon liquid
and lemon juice into the whipped
cream; spoon this over the melon
mixture. Sprinkle with a few crushed
peppercorns. Serve at once.

Bacon and olive kabobs

Serves 4

¼ *cup olive oil*
¼ *teaspoon dried rosemary*
¼ *teaspoon dried basil*
16 stuffed olives
½ *lb slices of bacon*
freshly ground black pepper

Beat the oil with the dried herbs, cover and stand for about 15 minutes to allow the flavors to develop.

Thread the olives alternately with the bacon slices, which should be loosely folded, on long metal skewers. Brush all over with the flavored oil, then cook under a hot broiler for 10–15 minutes, turning the skewers from time to time so that the bacon cooks evenly and becomes crispy. If necessary, baste from time to time with the flavored oil.

Serve hot, with a little pepper sprinkled over, together with slices of hot French or garlic bread.

Cheesy prune kabobs

Serves 4

½ *lb prunes, soaked and pits removed*
6 tablespoons dry sherry
½ *lb Edam or mild Cheddar cheese*
3 tablespoons oil
freshly ground black pepper

Put the prunes in a bowl, pour over the sherry, cover and leave for about 4 hours.

Meanwhile, cut the cheese into ½ × ½ × ¾-in cubes. Stuff each prune with a piece of cheese, then thread them onto long metal skewers about six at a time. Brush over the prunes with the oil and cook under a hot broiler until the cheese starts to melt. Sprinkle with a little pepper and serve hot with crusty bread if liked.

Note Very moist prunes may not soak up all the sherry. In that case pour the remainder over the skewers after cooking.

Variation
For a change, substitute pitted fresh dates, or dried ones soaked in sherry as above, for the prunes. Or use port instead of sherry.

Stuffed prunes make tasty accompaniments to pork chops, liver or kidneys.

11

Appetizers

Savory crêpes

Makes about 15

According to the filling, crêpes may be served as an entrée or dessert.

Basic plain batter
1¼ cups all-purpose flour
pinch of salt
1 cup milk
2 eggs
butter for frying

Basic rich batter
1¼ cups all-purpose flour
pinch of salt
½ cup milk
½ cup light cream
1 egg plus 2 egg yolks
butter for frying

Sift the flour and salt into a large mixing bowl. Make a well in the center.

Whisk together the milk, cream if using, eggs and egg yolks, if using. Pour into the well in the flour and gradually whisk in the flour to form a smooth batter. Cover and leave to stand for 30 minutes.

Heat a pat of butter in the crêpe pan until hot. Pour off any surplus.

Pour or spoon in about a tablespoon of batter. Swirl it around quickly, then cook for about 1 minute till golden underneath. Flip over with a spatula or toss and cook the other side till golden.

Tip onto a hot plate and keep warm. Repeat until all the batter is used up. Use as recipes below.

Caviar filling

Enough for 15 crêpes

1 quantity of Rich Batter (see above)
¾ cup sour or heavy cream
1 (3½-oz) jar Danish black lumpfish caviar
3 tablespoons sliced almonds
1 tablespoon lemon juice

Make the crêpes as in basic recipe above and keep warm.

Softly whip the cream, then fold in the lumpfish caviar, almonds and lemon juice.

Spread the filling over the crêpes, fold in four and arrange on a heated serving plate.

Tongue filling

Enough for 15 crêpes

1 quantity of Plain Batter (see above)
½ cup wiped and coarsely chopped mushrooms
1 shallot or small onion, peeled and finely chopped
1 tablespoon butter
¼ lb cooked tongue, cut in thin strips
1 tablespoon Madeira or dry sherry
2 teaspoons finely chopped parsley
salt and pepper

Make the crêpes as in the basic recipe above and keep warm.

Cook the mushrooms and onion in the butter until soft. Set aside.

Toss the tongue in the Madeira or sherry, add the parsley and season to taste. Stir into the mushroom mixture and heat through gently.

Spread each crêpe with a little of the filling, then fold in half or in four and arrange on a hot serving plate. Serve at once.

Camembert fritters

Serves 4

*4 portions of Camembert cheese,
  each weighing 1½ to 2 oz
2 tablespoons flour
1 egg, beaten
3 tablespoons soft white breadcrumbs
oil for deep frying*

*Garnish
4 sprigs of parsley
¼ cup canned whole-berry cranberry
  sauce to finish (optional)*

Scrape each Camembert portion
very lightly and carefully with a
knife, but without removing the
rind. Roll each one in flour, then in
the beaten egg, and then in the
breadcrumbs, pressing them on well
with a small knife to coat evenly.
Chill 30 minutes.

Heat the oil to 340°. Put in the
cheese pieces, without allowing them
to touch, and cook till golden brown
(about 2–3 minutes). Lift them out
with a slotted spoon onto paper
towels to drain.

Meanwhile plunge the parsley into
the hot oil for a few seconds until
crisp, lift out with a slotted spoon
and drain on paper towels.

Serve the fritters on heated plates,
garnished with the fried parsley and
with a spoonful of cranberry sauce
over each, if liked.

Deep-fried stuffed pears

Serves 4

*4 firm but ripe pears
¼ cup pear liqueur or dry sherry
3 oz Roquefort or other blue cheese
3 tablespoons ground or finely
  chopped hazelnuts or walnuts
3 tablespoons flour
1 egg, beaten
1½ cups soft white breadcrumbs
oil for deep frying*

Peel the pears without removing the
stalks and halve them lengthwise.
Scoop out the core to leave a small
hollow in each half. At once dip the
cut surfaces into the liqueur or
sherry.

Mash the cheese with a fork, then
mix into the rest of the liqueur or
sherry. Stir in the nuts.

Fill the pear hollows with the
cheese mixture. Carefully reshape
the pears by pressing them together.
Roll the pears in the flour, then in
beaten egg, then in the
breadcrumbs, pressing them on well
with a flat-bladed knife to coat
evenly.

Heat the oil to 325°. Dip a frying
basket in and out of the oil, then
put in the pears, without them
touching. Lower them into the oil
and fry 5–8 minutes, according to
size, until crisp and golden brown.
Lift out and drain on paper
towels. Serve immediately.

Note Fried stuffed pears are equally
delicious served as a dessert. Try
sprinkling over a few drops of pear
liqueur or sherry just before serving.

Appetizers

Onion quiche

Serves 6

2 cups all-purpose flour
pinch of salt
½ cup butter, chilled
1–2 tablespoons iced water

Filling
¼ lb bacon, finely chopped
2 large onions, peeled and finely
  chopped
3 tablespoons butter
salt and freshly ground black pepper
½ to 1 teaspoon caraway seeds
2 eggs
¾ cup sour cream
grated nutmeg

Make the pastry by sifting the flour
with the salt into a large mixing
bowl. Make a well in the middle.
Flake the butter and rub in until the
mixture resembles fine breadcrumbs.
Put the iced water into the well.
Work quickly either with your hands
or with a fork, to form a smooth
dough. Wrap the dough in plastic
wrap and chill for 30 minutes.
  Preheat the oven to 400°. Roll out
the dough on a floured surface and

use to line an 8-in fluted quiche or
flan pan. Prick all over the bottom
of the pastry case with a fork.
  Fry the bacon in a large pan until
the fat runs. Add the onion and the
butter and cook gently, stirring
frequently, until the onion is soft
and transparent. Remove from the
heat, cool the onion mixture a little
and season with salt, pepper and
caraway seeds to taste.
  Spread the onion mixture over the
pastry. Whisk together the eggs and
cream, season to taste with salt and
nutmeg and pour over the filling.
  Bake in the heated oven for 30–
35 minutes until golden brown on
top and set. Serve while still hot, cut
in wedges.

Variations
Cauliflower Line the pastry case with
a large cooked cauliflower broken
into florets mixed with ½ cup diced
cooked ham. Top with 2 eggs beaten
with ¾ cup sour or light cream and 1
cup grated cheese.

Leek and cheese Cover the bottom
of the pastry case with 1 cup grated
cheese. On this put ½ lb crisply fried
and crumbled bacon, then top with
2–3 lightly cooked sliced leeks.
Season with freshly ground black
pepper to taste and top as for Onion
quiche.

Mushroom and ham Cover the
bottom of the pastry case with 2
cups thinly sliced mushrooms cooked
with 1 peeled and chopped onion in
3 tablespoons butter, and mixed
with ½ cup diced cooked ham and 2
tablespoons finely chopped parsley.
Season with salt and freshly ground
black pepper to taste. Top with 2
eggs beaten with ¾ cup light cream,
and sprinkle with 2–3 tablespoons
finely chopped chives and a
generous pinch of paprika.

Red pepper dip

Serves 4–6

5 medium-sized red peppers
2–3 cloves of garlic, peeled and
*   crushed*
salt and freshly ground black pepper
1 teaspoon vinegar or lemon juice
2–3 tablespoons olive oil
1–2 tablespoons chopped chives to
*   garnish*

Wash and dry the peppers. Place under a hot broiler for about 8 minutes, turning them from time to time, until the skins are well blistered and charred. Remove them carefully, cover with a damp cloth and leave for a few minutes. They will then peel easily.

   Peel off the skin, and when cool, halve the peppers, deseed and finely chop. Put in a bowl and mix with the garlic; season to taste with salt, pepper, vinegar or lemon juice. Then stir in as much olive oil as the peppers will absorb.

   Cover and chill. Sprinkle over the chives and serve with pieces of wholewheat bread or pumpernickel to dip into it.

Taramasalata

Serves 4–6

½ lb cooked or canned pressed cod's
*   roe or 1 (8-oz) jar red caviar*
1 onion, peeled
5 slices of white bread, each ¾-in
*   thick*
5 tablespoons milk or water
1 clove of garlic, peeled and crushed
½ cup olive oil
juice of 1 large lemon or 2 limes
salt and freshly ground black pepper
ripe olives to garnish

Place the roe in a large mixing bowl and mash well. Grate the onion finely. Remove the crusts and soak the bread in the milk or water for a few minutes then squeeze dry.

   Add the onion, bread and garlic to the roe. Beat together, adding the oil alternately with the lemon or lime juice a little at a time. Beat until smooth and creamy. Alternatively process all the ingredients in a blender or food processor till smooth. Season to taste with salt and pepper. Garnish with olives and serve with hot buttered toast.

Eggplant dip

Serves 6

3 medium-sized eggplants, washed
salt
1 cup olive oil
2 cloves of garlic, peeled and crushed
white pepper
1 tablespoon lemon juice
2 tablespoons roughly chopped
*   parsley*

Preheat the oven to 350°.

   Prick the eggplants all over with a fork and bake for 40–45 minutes until the skins wrinkle. Remove from the oven and cover with a damp cloth until cool and the skins can be peeled off easily.

   Scoop out the flesh and squeeze in a clean cloth to remove any excess liquid. Mash the flesh. Whisk in the salt, then the olive oil, drop by drop, until completely absorbed. Finally beat in the garlic. Alternatively process all the ingredients in a blender or food processor. Season to taste with pepper, lemon juice and a little extra salt if necessary. Stir in the parsley and chill.

Appetizers

Party patty shells

Makes 6 patty shells

1 (8-oz) package frozen puff pastry
   patty shell, thawed
1 egg yolk

Preheat the oven to 400°.
   Roll out the dough to a thickness
of about $\frac{1}{4}$ in on a floured surface.
Using a 3-in plain cookie cutter, cut
out 12 rounds. Then, using a
2-in plain cutter, cut out the center
of six rounds to give you six rings
and six lids.
   Brush around the edges of the
large rounds with a little cold water.
Place the rings of pastry on top,
pressing gently to seal them
together.
   Dampen a large cookie sheet.
Place the pastry rounds and the lids
on it, spacing them well apart.
Brush the pastry with a little beaten
egg yolk. Bake in the heated oven
for about 15 minutes or till risen and
golden. Take out, cool slightly, then
transfer to a hot serving platter if
serving at once, or to a wire rack to
cool.

Creamy avocado filling

Enough for 6 patty shells

$\frac{1}{2}$ cup fresh or frozen peas
1 large, ripe avocado
3 tablespoons lemon juice
3–4 tablespoons heavy cream
1–2 tablespoons finely chopped dill
   or parsley (optional)
salt and pepper

Garnish (optional)
$\frac{1}{4}$ cup red salmon caviar
lemon wedges

Cook the peas till tender in boiling
salted water, drain and process in a
blender or food processor.
   Halve the avocado lengthwise,
remove the seed and scoop out the
flesh. Process in a blender or food
processor with 2 tablespoons of the
lemon juice. Then blend in the
puréed peas and cream till thick and
creamy. Stir in the herbs if using,
and season to taste with salt and
pepper and the rest of the lemon
juice.
   Spoon a little of this filling into
the patty shells, top each with a
spoonful of red caviar. Serve with
lemon wedges, if liked.

Kidney ragoût filling

Enough for 6 patty shells

$\frac{1}{2}$ lb lamb kidneys, halved lengthwise,
   skinned and cored
$\frac{3}{4}$ cup milk
$\frac{1}{4}$ cup butter
1 small onion, peeled and finely
   chopped
2 tablespoons flour
$\frac{3}{4}$ cup chicken stock or broth
$\frac{1}{4}$ cup light cream
salt and pepper
$\frac{1}{2}$–1 teaspoon prepared mustard
$\frac{1}{2}$ cup diced cooked chicken, or cut
   into strips
2 tablespoons chopped pistachio nuts

Soak the kidneys in the milk for 30
minutes. Drain and dry on paper
towels, then cut the kidneys into
thin slices.
   Heat 2 tablespoons of the butter
in a pan and fry the kidney slices, a
few at a time, for 1–2 minutes,
removing and setting aside each
portion as it cooks. Cook the onion
in 1 tablespoon of the butter till
crispy. Set aside.
   Melt the remaining butter in the
pan, add the flour and cook for 1
minute till straw-colored. Add the
hot stock beating well till combined.
Bring to a boil, stirring all the time,
then reduce the heat and simmer for
1 minute. Stir in the cream. Remove
from the heat and season with salt
and pepper and mustard to taste.
   Add the chicken and kidney slices
to the sauce, and let it barely
simmer for 4–5 minutes. Add the
pistachio nuts.
   Spoon a little of the filling into
hot patty shells, sprinkle with the
onion and put on the lids. Serve at
once on a heated plate.

Ham and mushroom filling

Enough for 6 patty shells

1 cup wiped and thinly sliced button
   mushrooms
3 tablespoons butter
1 (8-oz) can asparagus tips or pieces
3 tablespoons flour
1 cup hot chicken stock or broth
$\frac{1}{2}$ cup dry white wine
$\frac{1}{2}$ cup heavy cream
$\frac{1}{2}$ cup diced cooked lean ham, or cut
   into thin strips
$\frac{1}{2}$ cup diced cooked veal or chicken
salt and white pepper
grated nutmeg
2 tomatoes, peeled, seeded and cut in
   thin strips, to garnish

Cook the mushrooms gently in half
the butter until the liquid has
evaporated. Set aside. Heat the
asparagus in its own liquid but do
not boil; set aside.
   Heat the rest of the butter in a
saucepan, stir in the flour to make a
roux and cook for 1 minute. Whisk
in the hot stock till combined, bring
to a boil, stirring all the time, then
reduce heat and simmer for 5
minutes till thick. Stir in the wine
and cream and heat through without
boiling.
   Remove from the heat and cool
slightly. Stir in the drained
mushrooms, asparagus and ham and
veal or chicken and season with salt,
pepper and nutmeg to taste. Spoon
a little of the filling into hot patty
shells and place on a heated serving
dish. Garnish with strips of tomato
and serve at once.

Appetizers

Pickled trout

Serves 4

2 trout, each weighing about ¾ lb,
  drawn, washed and dried
1 teaspoon white peppercorns
1 teaspoon sugar
1 teaspoon salt

Garnish
few lettuce leaves, washed and dried
chopped dill or parsley

Cut the tails and back fins off the
trout, then cut off the heads and
discard. Using kitchen scissors or a
sharp filleting knife, cut the trout
open along the abdomen to the tail.
Open out and place, opened side
facing downwards, on your work
surface.

With the palm of your hand, press
down gently on the backs of the
trout to free the backbone, then
turn over each one and ease the
bone out with the point of a knife.
Carefully fillet the fish and set aside
in a cool place.

Crush together the peppercorns,
sugar and salt; set aside.

Cover a flat dish with a piece of
waxed paper double its size. Place
two trout fillets on it. Place the
remaining fillets on your work
surface. Sprinkle all four equally
with the pepper mixture. Sandwich
the fillets together in pairs, place
them all on the paper, then fold it
over to enclose them completely,
tucking in well. Weight the package
with a small flat board or tray, with
cans on top, and refrigerate for
about 12 hours.

To serve, line a flat dish with the
lettuce leaves. Open up the package
and lay the sandwiched fillets on a
board. With a very sharp knife, cut
off paper-thin slices with slanting
strokes. Arrange the slices on the
lettuce, garnish with dill or parsley
and serve at once. Serve with
horseradish cream or mustard sauce.

Horseradish cream

1–2 tablespoons freshly grated, or
  2–3 tablespoons prepared
  horseradish
1 teaspoon sugar
2 tablespoons lemon juice
pinch of salt
1 cup whipping cream, stiffly
  whipped

Fold the horseradish and seasonings
into the cream. Spoon into a serving
bowl and chill till needed.
Makes about 1¼ cups

Mustard sauce

2 egg yolks
1 tablespoon prepared English
  mustard
1 cup corn oil
1 teaspoon sugar
2 tablespoons vinegar
½ bunch of dill, finely chopped

Whisk the egg yolks with the
mustard. Then beat in the oil, a
drop at a time, until completely
absorbed to give a mayonnaise-like
consistency. Beat in sugar and
vinegar to taste, then the dill. Pour
into a sauce boat and serve.
Makes about 1¼ cups

Vegetable mousses

Serves 4

1 (10-oz) package frozen spinach
1 cup strong chicken stock or broth
1 envelope unflavored gelatine
salt and pepper
pinch of grated nutmeg
¾ cup sour cream

Simmer the spinach in the stock
until tender — a few minutes after
the block has thawed. Purée the
mixture by processing it in a blender
or food processor.
   Dissolve the gelatine in 3
tablespoons of boiling water in a
bowl. Stir into the warm vegetable
purée and season to taste with salt,
pepper and nutmeg. Allow to cool.
When the mixture is on the point of
setting fold in the sour cream.
Adjust the seasoning then pour into
four ¾ cup molds and chill until firm.
   Before serving dip the molds into
hot water for a moment and unmold
the mousses onto four plates.
Garnish with slices of cucumber and
radish roses.

Variations
Carrot mousse Use 2½ cups peeled
and chopped carrots instead of the
spinach and cook for 15–20 minutes
until really tender before reducing to
a purée. Season with salt, pepper
and ginger instead of the nutmeg.
Garnish with watercress.

Watercress mousse Use 2 large or 3
medium-sized bunches of watercress
instead of the spinach. Wash well,
trim off the roots and chop roughly
before simmering for a few minutes
in the stock. Season as for spinach
mousse. This mousse may be
garnished with slices of lemon and
jumbo shrimp.

Avocado mousse Mash 3 ripe
avocados with the juice of ½ lemon
and purée with the stock, before
adding the gelatine. Garnish the
mousse with watercress and a twist
of lemon.

Appetizers

Broiled peaches with cheese

Serves 4

about ¼ cup butter, softened
4 slices of white bread
1 (8-oz) package cream cheese
½ cup finely chopped lean cooked
* ham*
⅓ cup finely chopped blanched
* almonds*
¼ cup brandy
salt and freshly ground black pepper
4 canned peach halves, drained and
* thinly sliced*

Butter the bread slices on both sides
and fry until golden brown on both
sides. Drain on paper towels.

In a bowl mix the cheese with the
ham, almonds and brandy. Season
with salt and pepper to taste.

Spread half the cheese mixture on
one side of the slices of fried bread.
Lay the peach slices on top, then
cover with the remaining cheese
mixture. Place under a hot broiler
and cook for 5–7 minutes or until
golden. Serve at once.

Shrimp and avocado toasts

Serves 4

about ¼ cup butter, softened
4 slices of white bread
1 ripe avocado, halved lengthwise,
* seeded and thinly sliced*
1 tablespoon lemon juice
½ lb peeled shrimp, thawed if frozen
freshly ground black pepper
1 cup grated Swiss cheese
¼ cup sour cream
pinch of paprika

Butter the bread on both sides then
fry the bread on one side only until
golden. Drain on paper towels.

Cover the unfried side of the
bread with avocado slices and
sprinkle them with lemon juice to
stop them discoloring. Strew the
shrimp over and season to taste with
pepper.

Beat together the grated cheese,
sour cream and paprika, then spoon
over the shrimp.

Cook under a hot broiler for a
few minutes till browned on top.

Fried cheese sandwiches

Serves 2–4

2 eggs
¼ cup sour cream
salt and pepper
8 large slices of bread
¾ lb mozzarella cheese, sliced
¼ cup olive or corn oil
2 tablespoons butter

Beat the eggs to a light froth with
the cream and salt and pepper to
taste. Soak the slices of bread in this
mixture.

Divide the cheese between four of
the slices of bread, cover with the
remaining slices and press to seal.

Heat the oil and butter together in
a skillet till hot. Fry the sandwiches,
two at a time, until golden brown on
both sides. Serve at once.

Marinated mushrooms

Serves 4

½ *cup white wine vinegar*
½ *cup dry white wine*
½ *cup sunflower or*
  salad oil
2 *cloves of garlic, peeled and lightly*
  crushed with a knife
1 *bay leaf*
½ *teaspoon salt*
6 *peppercorns*
3 *juniper berries*
1 *lb button mushrooms, wiped*

Heat the vinegar, wine and oil in a
large saucepan until simmering. Add
the garlic, bay leaf, salt,
peppercorns, juniper berries and
mushrooms and bring rapidly to a
boil. Reduce the heat and gently
cook the mushrooms for 10 minutes.
Remove from the heat and leave the
mushrooms to cool in the liquid
after removing the garlic.
    When cold, turn into a non-
metallic bowl or container, cover
and marinate in the refrigerator for
about 24 hours. To serve, drain the
mushrooms and serve with hot garlic
bread (see page 26).

Variations
Pearl onions or green beans can be
prepared in the same way; beans
should be cooked for 10–15 minutes.

Marinated onions

Serves 4–6

1 *lb shallots or pearl onions, peeled*
¼ *cup olive oil*
2 *tablespoons butter*
2 *teaspoons sugar*
salt
freshly ground black pepper
½ *cup red wine*

Garnish
½ *cup sour cream*
1 *tablespoon finely chopped parsley*

Fry the shallots or onions in the hot
oil and butter until golden brown.
    Sprinkle them with the sugar and
cook till they caramelize, stirring
often so they don't stick to the pan.
Season with salt and pepper to taste.
    Add the red wine to the pan,
cover and simmer the onions for 20
minutes. Pour into a serving dish
and leave to get cold, then chill.
    To serve, spoon the sour cream

over the middle and sprinkle with
parsley.

Variations
Other vegetables can be cooked in
the same way. For leeks, trim, wash
and cut across in rings; dry well,
then cook as above for 10 minutes.
For zucchini, wash and cut in thick
slices: dry well and cook as above
for about 10 minutes, adding a little
finely chopped garlic for extra
flavor.

Tip If the onions are very strongly
flavored, soak them in cold water
for 2 hours after peeling.

Appetizers

Spicy shrimp cocktail

Serves 4–6

¾ lb peeled shrimp
3 tablespoons lemon juice
2 cups wiped and thinly sliced
  mushrooms
2 oranges, peeled, white pith and
  seeds removed and thinly sliced,
  crosswise
1 egg yolk
½ teaspoon dry mustard
salt
½ cup olive oil
¼ cup orange juice
grated rind of ½ lemon
½ cup heavy cream, stiffly whipped
2 tablespoons green peppercorns in
  brine, mashed (optional)
4 small sprigs of mint to garnish

Sprinkle the shrimp with half of the lemon juice and marinate in the refrigerator. If using frozen shrimp, sprinkle them with lemon juice and leave to thaw, covered, in a cool place.

Sprinkle the mushrooms with the rest of the lemon juice and set aside. Halve the orange slices and reserve.

Mix the shrimp, mushrooms and their juices with the orange pieces and spoon into four large chilled glasses.

Beat the egg yolk with the mustard and a pinch of salt, then beat in the oil, drop by drop, until thick and creamy. Stir in the orange juice and lemon rind and check the seasoning. Fold in the cream together with the peppercorns, and chill.

Spoon the dressing over the shrimp just before serving, and garnish each cocktail with a sprig of mint.

Fish salad

Serves 4

½ lb haddock or cod fillet, bones and
  any skin removed
¼ cup lemon juice
salt
½ cup water
½ cup dry white wine
1 bay leaf
½ onion, peeled
4 sprigs of parsley
3 peppercorns
4 anchovy fillets, drained and soaked
  in ¼ cup milk
½ lb tomatoes, peeled
1 bunch scallions, trimmed, washed
  and sliced into rings
2–3 celery stalks, trimmed, washed
  and thinly sliced
1 small head of lettuce, washed and
  dried, to serve

Dressing

1 egg yolk
1 teaspoon dry mustard
¼ cup heavy cream
pinch of cayenne

Rinse the fish fillets and drain on paper towels. Then sprinkle with lemon juice and a little salt and leave for 10 minutes. Cut into bite-sized pieces.

Meanwhile bring the water and wine to a boil with the bay leaf, onion, parsley and peppercorns. Season with a little salt, add the fish with its juices, cover, reduce the heat so the liquid is simmering gently and cook the fish for 10 minutes. Do not let it boil.

Take out the pieces of fish with a slotted spoon and leave to cool. Reduce the cooking liquid to half the quantity by fast boiling, then set aside to cool.

Drain and halve the anchovies lengthwise. Cut the tomatoes into eighths, discarding the seeds. Mix together the tomatoes, scallions, and celery, then stir in the fish.

To make the dressing, beat the egg yolk with the mustard, then gradually beat in the strained, cooled fish stock. Add the cream and season with cayenne to taste, adding a little more salt if necessary.

Pour the dressing over the fish salad and mix carefully. Let chill in the refrigerator for 15 minutes.

Arrange the lettuce leaves in a serving dish or on four individual plates. Spoon on the fish salad and garnish with anchovies. Serve with warm French or wholewheat bread.

Cook's Tip

This basic recipe can be varied in many ways. Deseeded green and red peppers, cut into narrow strips, go well with it, as do apples, finely chopped and sprinkled with lemon juice.

Oranges, lemons and grapefruit, peeled, seeds removed and cut into segments are refreshing alternatives as well. Thinly sliced green or ripe olives also complement the flavor of the fish.

For a really creamy sauce, beat in a little extra heavy cream or plain yogurt. Use iceberg or bibb lettuce, or, if you like, substitute chicory or escarole for the lettuce.

Soups
Hot and Cold

Soups

Mussel soup

Serves 4

1 quart fresh mussels in the shell
1 onion, peeled and chopped
2 cloves of garlic, peeled and
    chopped
3 tablespoons butter
1 (8-oz) package frozen mixed
    vegetables
1¼ cups dry white wine
1 bay leaf
6 peppercorns
4 juniper berries
2½ cups chicken stock or broth
salt
freshly ground black pepper
4 celery stalks, trimmed, leaves
    reserved, and thinly sliced
2 small leeks, trimmed, well washed
    and thinly sliced
½ lb tomatoes, peeled, deseeded and
    diced
1 teaspoon Pernod

Garnish
1 tablespoon finely chopped parsley
1 tablespoon finely chopped dill

Scrub each mussel under running
cold water. Throw away any open
ones which do not close when
touched and any which have broken
shells. Pull or scrape off with a small
sharp knife the dark 'beards'
attached to the shells.

Fry the onion and the garlic in the
butter till golden in a very large
saucepan. Add the mixed
vegetables, still frozen, and cook
2 minutes. Add the wine, bay leaf,
peppercorns and juniper berries.
Bring to a boil, add the mussels,
cover and boil until the mussels
open — about 10 minutes. Any
mussels which have not opened after
this cooking must be discarded.
Strain the mussels into a colander,
returning the liquid to a clean pan.
Shell the mussels and set aside.

Add enough stock to the reserved
mussel broth to make 1 quart.
Season to taste with salt and pepper.
Add the celery, leeks and tomatoes,
cover and simmer 10 minutes. Add
the mussels to the pan, cover and
reheat but do not boil. Add the
Pernod to taste and check the
seasoning.

Pour into a warm tureen and
sprinkle over the herbs. Serve with
hot garlic bread.

Note If needs be, this soup can also
be made with mussels preserved in
brine. Use about ¾ lb mussel meat
packed without flavoring and, if
possible, use some fish stock or clam
juice, so that it tastes of the sea!

Crème d'escargots

Serves 4

4 slices of bacon, diced
2 tablespoons butter
1 small onion, peeled and finely
    chopped
2 cloves of garlic, peeled and crushed
24 canned snails, drained and
    roughly chopped
3½ cups white stock or broth
½ cup dry white wine
1 cup coarsely chopped parsley
6 dill stalks (optional)
1 egg yolk
1 cup whipping cream
1 tablespoon brandy
salt and freshly ground black pepper

In a large saucepan, fry the bacon
till the fat runs. Add the butter,
onion and the garlic and sauté till
golden brown. Add the snails and
cook for 2 minutes, stirring
constantly. Pour on the stock and
wine, cover and simmer gently for
30 minutes.

Meanwhile, set aside about 4
teaspoons of parsley and finely chop
the rest together with the dill if
using.

Whisk the egg yolk with a little of
the hot soup, then stir it back into
the pan of hot soup and reheat; do
not let it boil or the soup will
curdle.

Lightly whip the cream and fold
two-thirds of it into the soup. Add
the brandy and season well with salt
and pepper.

Preheat the oven to 450°. To
serve, pour into four ovenproof
bowls and top with the rest of the
cream. Heat in the hot oven for 3
minutes, then take out and sprinkle
with the remaining parsley. Serve at
once with puff pastry fingers or
toasted French bread.

Alternatively the cream topping
can quickly be finished under a very
hot, preheated broiler, if the soup
bowls are flameproof.

Garlic bread

Preheat the oven to 350°.

Cut deep into, but not completely
through, a loaf of French bread at
intervals of about ½ inch. Cream
softened butter with crushed garlic,
salt and a little lemon juice and
spread thickly into the incisions.
Press the bread back into shape,
wrap in foil, place on a cookie sheet
and bake for 15–20 minutes until all
the butter has soaked in and the
bread is crisp.

Soups

Pea soup with smoked salmon

Serves 4

2 lb fresh peas, shelled or
  1 lb frozen peas
2¼ cups chicken or veal stock or
  broth
5 tablespoons dry white wine
salt and pepper
pinch of sugar
1 cup light cream
2 tablespoons chopped parsley
2 oz smoked salmon, cut into very
  thin strips (optional)

Cook the peas in the boiling stock
for 15 minutes, lifting out about ½
cup of peas after 5 minutes. Purée
the remaining peas and stock in a
blender or food processor. Return
the purée to the pan, add the wine
and bring to a boil. Season to taste,
add the sugar and stir in the cream.
Add the reserved peas and heat
through gently. Serve garnished with
chopped parsley and the salmon, if
using.

Cream of cauliflower soup

Serves 4–6

1 cauliflower, broken into florets
2 large potatoes, peeled and diced
2½ cups hot chicken stock or broth
1¼ cups hot milk
¾ cup light cream
salt
grated nutmeg
1 tablespoon butter
2 tablespoons chopped parsley to
  garnish

Simmer the cauliflower and potatoes
in the boiling stock for 20–30
minutes, lifting out a few florets
after 10 minutes. Process the
mixture in a blender or food
processor. Return the purée to the
pan, add the milk, cream and
reserved florets and season lightly
with salt and nutmeg. Reheat gently
but do not boil.
  Pour the soup into a warmed
tureen and serve dotted with butter
and sprinkled with chopped parsley.

Cream of tomato soup

Serves 4

2 onions, peeled and finely chopped
1 clove of garlic, peeled and crushed
2 tablespoons oil
2 (12-oz) cans tomato purée
2½ cups hot chicken stock or broth
¾ cup red wine
salt and freshly ground black pepper
pinch each of sugar, dried thyme and
  dried oregano
¾ cup sour cream
4 slices of bacon, diced
few sprigs fresh basil (optional)

Gently fry half the onion and garlic
in the oil until transparent. Add the
tomato purée, stock, wine,
seasoning to taste, sugar and dried
herbs and cook for 20 minutes.
Process the mixture in a blender or
food processor. Stir in the cream
and heat through. Fry the bacon
until the fat runs, add the reserved
onion and garlic and cook till
golden. Serve the soup sprinkled
with the bacon mixture and garnish
with basil.

Hot chicken consommé

Serves 4

1 (4-lb) stewing chicken, dressed
2½ quarts cold water
salt
1 large onion, unpeeled and halved
1 bay leaf
2–3 cloves
2 carrots, peeled and sliced
2 stalks celery, washed and chopped
3–5 peppercorns
2 egg whites, beaten

Take out the giblets and rinse the chicken inside and out. Put in the water in a 3½ quart capacity pan, cover and bring slowly to a boil, skimming frequently. Add the salt when the water boils but not before. Turn down the heat and simmer gently for 1 hour.

Brown the cut surfaces of the onion in a skillet (this helps to color the soup). Add it to the pan with the bay leaf, cloves, vegetables and peppercorns. Simmer for a further 1 hour.

Lift out the chicken. Strain the broth, cool and skim.

To clarify the broth, stir in the beaten egg whites and bring slowly to a boil while whisking continuously until a thick froth starts to form. Stop whisking at once, reduce the heat and simmer gently, undisturbed and uncovered, for 20 minutes. If the broth bubbles too rapidly, the froth will break and turn the consommé cloudy.

Line a large fine strainer with scalded cheesecloth or a dish towel. Pour the broth through, holding back the froth at first, then letting it fall onto the cloth. Repeat the straining process to clarify the broth completely.

Reheat, adding strips of the chicken meat if liked, and check the seasoning; only add salt because anything else may turn it cloudy.

Variations
Consommé Jardinière Cook ½ cauliflower broken into florets, in boiling salted water until tender; heat 1 (8-oz) can of asparagus tips or pieces in their own liquid. Heat 1 quart chicken consommé (made as recipe above) and add to it the drained vegetables, together with 1 tablespoon cooked rice and the diced or sliced chicken breast meat. Serve sprinkled with finely chopped parsley. Serves 4.

Consommé Far-Eastern style Soak 2 heaping tablespoons dried Chinese mushrooms and 1 handful of thin egg noodles separately in cold water for about 30 minutes. Put 1 small leek, trimmed and cut into rings, 1 celery stalk, trimmed and thinly sliced, and 1 small onion, peeled and cut into rings, or 4 small scallions, trimmed, into a large saucepan with 1 quart chicken consommé (made as recipe above). Bring slowly to a boil, covered, and cook for 3 minutes. Add the drained mushrooms and noodles.

As soon as the broth returns to a boil, add 1 (8-oz) can of drained bamboo shoots, cut into narrow strips, and 1½ cups washed bean sprouts. Cook for a further 2 minutes. Season to taste with soy sauce, then stir in 2–3 tablespoons rice wine or dry sherry. Serve sprinkled with chopped parsley.

Soups

Cream of asparagus soup

Serves 4

¼ cup butter
1 small onion, finely chopped
3 tablespoons flour
¾ cup hot milk
2 cups hot chicken stock or broth
1 (8-oz) can asparagus tips or pieces,
drained and chopped and liquid
reserved
salt and pepper
¼ cup light cream

Heat the butter in a large saucepan, add the onion and cook gently until soft but not browned. Stir in the flour, then add the hot milk, stock and the liquid from the can of asparagus, stirring constantly. Bring to a boil, add the asparagus, cover and simmer for 20 minutes. Purée the soup by processing in a blender or food processor.

Return the soup to the rinsed-out pan, season to taste with salt and pepper. Bring to a boil, remove from the heat and stir in the cream. Pour into a warmed tureen or individual bowls and serve at once. Garnish with fresh herbs if liked.

Cream of spinach soup

Serves 4

2 lb fresh spinach, well washed and
drained
1 onion, peeled and finely chopped
1–2 cloves of garlic, peeled and
finely chopped
¼ cup olive oil
1¼ cups hot chicken stock or broth
salt
freshly ground black pepper
grated nutmeg
1¼ cups whipping cream

Garnish
¼ cup pine nuts
lemon slices (optional)

Blanch the spinach in a large pan of boiling salted water for 3 minutes. Drain, refresh under cold water, then drain again and press well to dry the leaves completely. Chop them finely or purée in a blender or food processor.

Soften the onion and the garlic in 3 tablespoons of the oil till the onion is transparent but not browned. Add the spinach, let it cook for about 5 minutes, then pour on the stock. If

necessary reduce rapidly over high heat to a thick creamy consistency. Season to taste with salt, pepper and nutmeg.

Meanwhile, fry the pine nuts in the rest of the oil till golden brown. Drain on paper towels and set aside.

To serve, remove the pan of soup from the heat. Stir in half of the cream; stiffly whip the rest. Pour the soup into a warmed tureen or individual bowls. Spoon on top the whipped cream and sprinkle with pine nuts. Serve at once with a lemon slice placed on the edge of each bowl, if liked.

Tip If you are pressed for time use frozen instead of fresh spinach.

French onion soup

Serves 4–6

2 large onions, peeled and chopped
¼ cup butter
2 tablespoons flour
1 quart clear beef stock or broth
1 cup dry white wine
salt and freshly ground black pepper

To finish
¼ cup butter
8 thin slices cut from a loaf of
  French bread
1 tablespoon brandy
1 cup grated Swiss or Cheddar cheese

Lightly brown the onions in the butter in a large saucepan. Sprinkle in the flour and cook about 2 minutes till light brown.

Pour on the stock, stir well, cover, bring to a boil, then reduce the heat and simmer gently for 20 minutes. Add the wine and season with salt and plenty of pepper to taste.

To finish: heat the butter in a large skillet. Put in the bread, in two batches if necessary, and fry until golden brown on both sides.

Warm the brandy a little, set light to it in a ladle and pour it, while still flaming, over the bread. Let it burn out. Preheat the broiler.

Pour the soup into four flameproof bowls, put 2 slices of bread on top of each one and sprinkle with grated cheese. Broil for 5 minutes or until the cheese is bubbling and golden, then serve immediately.

Variations

1 Use 3 instead of 2 slices of bread per person and 1¼ cups grated cheese in all. Lay the slices of fried bread, sprinkled with the cheese, one on top of another in the soup bowls, and fill up with the hot soup.

2 Substitute milk for half of the stock, and heavy or sour cream for the wine. Do not use bread or cheese in the cooking but serve toast with the soup and, if liked, add a little cayenne to the seasoning.

3 Thicken the soup with 2 egg yolks beaten with 1 tablespoon brandy and ¾ cup heavy cream. Add this at the end of the cooking time and do not boil after adding, otherwise the soup will curdle. Add fried croûtons and sprinkle with chopped parsley.

4 Cut the onions into thin rings instead of chopping them. Do not add flour, but simmer with 3 tablespoons pearl barley for 2–2½ hours. Sprinkle with grated Swiss or Parmesan cheese before serving.

5 Fry the onion rings in the butter, dust with a little flour and pour on the hot stock. Season with salt and pepper to taste and then add white wine and ¾ cup light cream. Finally, mix 1 egg yolk with a little hot soup, then return it to the pan and reheat gently until the soup is hot but not boiling. Pour into a warmed tureen or individual bowls and serve sprinkled with fried croûtons and plenty of chopped chives and parsley.

6 Soften 1–2 finely chopped or crushed cloves of garlic with the onions in the butter. Or, if you prefer it less pungent, use garlic salt to taste instead.

Soups

Mushroom and potato soup

Serves 4

*1¼ cups wiped and thinly sliced
  mushrooms*
1 teaspoon lemon juice
¼ lb bacon, finely chopped
*1 large onion, peeled and finely
  chopped*
1 clove garlic, peeled and crushed
3 cups peeled and diced potatoes
3 cups chicken stock or broth
salt
freshly ground black pepper
2 tablespoons chopped parsley
*1 small leek, trimmed, well washed
  and thinly sliced into rings*
2 egg yolks
1 cup sour cream

Reserve some of the mushrooms for
the garnish. Sprinkle these with the
lemon juice or leave them to soak in
water to cover, mixed with the
lemon juice, to prevent them going
brown.

Fry the bacon in a large saucepan
until the fat starts to run. Reserve 1
tablespoon of the fried bacon for the
garnish. Add the onion and cook
gently until soft but not colored.
Add the mushrooms and the garlic
and continue to cook over a low
heat for 5 minutes.

Add the potatoes to the pan,
together with the stock. Bring to a
boil, cover and simmer gently for 20
minutes. Purée in a food processor
or blender, then season to taste with
salt and pepper.

Stir half the chopped parsley into
the soup with the leek and simmer
for a further 10 minutes. Beat the
egg yolks and cream together, mix
with a little of the hot soup, then
stir back into the pan and reheat but
do not allow to boil.

Pour the soup into a warmed
tureen or individual bowls, sprinkle
with the rest of the parsley and
garnish with the reserved drained
mushrooms and fried bacon. Serve
immediately, with crusty French
bread if liked.

Note This soup is particularly tasty if
made with edible wild mushrooms
instead of cultivated mushrooms.

Hearty beef and potato soup

Serves 6

1 lb veal or beef bones, chopped
2 quarts water
salt
1 lb piece good quality lean beef
4½ cups peeled and diced potatoes
2 cups peeled and sliced carrots
2 cups peeled and diced celeriac
*2 leeks, trimmed, well washed and
  cut into thin rings*
*2 celery stalks, trimmed and roughly
  chopped or cut into thin strips*
freshly ground black pepper
pinch of grated nutmeg

To finish
¼ lb bacon, finely chopped
2 onions, peeled and chopped

Wash the bones well to remove any
splinters. Put them in a large
saucepan, cover with the cold water
and bring slowly to a boil, skimming
off any scum that forms on the
surface.

Add a pinch of salt and the beef,
cover the pan, reduce the heat and
simmer for 1 hour, skimming once
or twice. Then add all the vegetables
to the pan and simmer 30 minutes
more.

Remove all the bones. Take out
the meat, dice or slice and return to
the broth. Season to taste with extra
salt, pepper and nutmeg.

Fry the bacon till the fat starts to
run in a skillet; add the onions and
fry until the bacon and onions are
golden brown and crispy.

Pour the soup into a warmed
tureen or individual bowls. Sprinkle
over the bacon and onion mixture.
Serve immediately, with wholewheat
bread if liked.

Cheesy potato soup

Serves 6

3 cups peeled and diced potatoes
*1 (8-oz) package frozen mixed
  vegetables*
2 onions, peeled and chopped
2 cloves of garlic, peeled and crushed
1 quart chicken stock or broth
1 cup milk
1 cup light cream
*1 cup grated Swiss or mature Gouda
  cheese*
salt and freshly ground black pepper
grated nutmeg
1 egg yolk
1 tablespoon chopped chives
1 tablespoon chopped parsley

Put all the vegetables and the garlic
in a large saucepan, add the stock
and bring to a boil. Cover and cook
for 30 minutes.

Cool the soup for a few minutes,
then process in a blender or food
processor.

Heat the milk and cream but do
not boil. Remove from the heat and
stir in the cheese until melted. Add
the cheese mixture to the potato
purée in the rinsed-out pan, and
season to taste with salt, pepper and
nutmeg. Reheat but do not boil.

Blend the egg yolk with a little of
the hot soup, then return this to the
pan and heat gently, stirring
continuously. Pour into a warmed
tureen or individual bowls and
sprinkle over the chopped herbs.
Serve at once, with wholewheat
bread if liked.

Soups

Gazpacho

Serves 6

6 slices of stale white bread
$\frac{3}{4}$ cup water
2 lb ripe tomatoes, peeled, cored and
   cut into eighths
1 green pepper, deseeded and cut
   into strips or small chunks
1 small onion, peeled and chopped
2 cloves of garlic, peeled and crushed
2 tablespoons tomato paste
5 tablespoons olive oil
3 tablespoons red wine vinegar
1 cup chicken stock or broth
$\frac{1}{2}$ teaspoon salt

Accompaniments
4 slices of white bread, cut in small
   dice, for croûtons
3 tablespoons butter
$\frac{1}{2}$ cucumber, unpeeled and diced
6 shallots, peeled and finely chopped
$\frac{1}{2}$ lb tomatoes, peeled, deseeded and
   finely chopped
1 green pepper, deseeded and finely
   chopped
2 hard-cooked eggs, chopped
20 stuffed green olives, drained and
   thinly sliced crosswise
ice cubes

Soak the bread in the water for 10 minutes, then squeeze it dry. Put half of the bread, tomatoes, pepper, onion, garlic and tomato paste into a blender or food processor together with half of the oil, vinegar and stock. Process until completely smooth. Tip into a tureen. Repeat this process with the remaining ingredients. Add salt to taste and chill for at least 4 hours.

Prepare the accompaniments. Fry the croûtons in the butter until golden brown. Take out, drain on paper towels. Put all the accompaniments, except the ice cubes, separately into dishes.

Just before serving, stir the soup well and put in some ice cubes. Arrange the dishes of accompaniments around the soup so that everyone can help themselves.

Note For a more tangy version, cook the croûtons with garlic. First fry them in the butter as above, then sprinkle finely chopped or crushed garlic over them. The quantity of garlic can vary from 1 clove to 1 teaspoon, according to taste. Continue to heat for a few seconds only or the garlic will turn bitter.

Cook's Tip

To peel tomatoes, cut a small cross in the base of each one then place in a bowl. Pour over boiling water and allow to stand for a few seconds before plunging the tomatoes into cold water. The skin can then be quickly peeled back from the cross.

Alternatively, spear each tomato firmly on a fork and hold over a naked gas flame, rotating slowly until the skin starts to blister. It will then peel easily.

Cold chicken consommé

Serves 4

1 (4-lb) stewing chicken, dressed
2½ quarts cold water
salt
1 large onion, unpeeled and halved
1 bay leaf
2–3 cloves
2 carrots, peeled and sliced
2 stalks celery, with leaves, trimmed
    and chopped
3–5 peppercorns

To clarify
2 egg whites, beaten
1 egg shell, crushed
1 carrot, peeled and finely diced
1 small onion, peeled and finely
    diced
1 stalk celery, washed and finely
    diced

Remove the giblets and rinse the chicken inside and out. Put in a large saucepan and cover with the water. Bring to a boil, skimming from time to time. Add salt, turn down the heat and simmer gently for 1 hour.

Brown the cut surfaces of the onion in a skillet. Add it to the pan together with the bay leaf, cloves, vegetables and peppercorns. Simmer for a further 1 hour.

Lift out the chicken; strain the broth, allow to cool and skim well.

To clarify the broth, stir in the egg whites and shell and the finely diced vegetables. Bring slowly to a boil, whisking continuously until a thick froth starts to form. Stop whisking, reduce the heat and simmer very gently for about 20 minutes. It is important not to allow the consommé to bubble too rapidly as this will break up the foam and turn it cloudy.

Strain twice through a large strainer lined with scalded cheesecloth or a clean dish towel. Pour into individual bowls and cool. Chill for about 1 hour before serving.

Variation
Consommé with pepper and peas
Warm 1 quart chicken consommé (made as recipe above) until just pourable. Set aside. Blanch 1 red pepper, deseeded and diced, for 2 minutes in boiling salted water,

refresh with cold water and drain. Cook 1 cup shelled fresh or frozen peas in boiling salted water for 8 minutes or till tender, then refresh and drain. Stir the diced pepper, peas and 2 tablespoons finely chopped parsley into the consommé, pour into individual bowls and chill till firm.

To add a little piquancy to this consommé, a few drops of Worcestershire sauce or lemon juice may be added with the vegetables. Other herbs such as freshly chopped tarragon, lemon balm or mint, may also be added instead of parsley, but use sparingly so that the flavoring herbs do not mask the subtle flavor of the consommé.

Soups

Cold Avocado Soup

Serves 4

3 medium-sized ripe avocados
juice of 1 lemon
¼ cup dry white wine
5 tablespoons sour cream
1 cup cold chicken stock or broth
1–2 tablespoons olive oil
salt and pepper
dash of Worcestershire sauce
¼ teaspoon grated lemon rind
1 cup whipping cream, stiffly
  whipped
sprigs of lemon balm or mint to
  garnish

Halve and seed the avocados. Scoop the flesh out of five halves only and brush the sixth with lemon juice immediately to prevent discoloration; set it aside for the garnish.

Mash the scooped-out flesh until very smooth, then beat into the purée the remaining lemon juice, wine and sour cream. Alternatively purée these ingredients in a blender or food processor.

Continue to beat or blend while adding the chicken stock and the oil, drop by drop. When thoroughly combined, season with salt, pepper, Worcestershire sauce and lemon rind, cover and chill for 30 minutes. Then stir again, check the seasoning and lightly fold in the whipped cream.

Pour into individual bowls. Peel and slice the remaining ½ avocado and arrange 2 slices per bowl on top of the soup, together with the sprigs of herbs. Serve immediately.

Vichysoisse

Serves 4–6

2 large leeks, trimmed, well washed
  and cut into thin rings
2 onions, peeled and finely chopped
¼ cup butter
1½ cups peeled and finely diced
  potatoes
2 cups hot chicken stock or broth
1 cup milk
1½ cups whipping cream
salt and pepper
dash of hot pepper sauce
1 bunch of chives, finely chopped

Gently cook the leeks and onions in the butter in a large saucepan, stirring frequently, until soft but not brown — about 8 minutes. Add the potatoes together with the stock. Bring to a boil, cover, reduce the heat and simmer gently for about 30 minutes.

Cool the mixture slightly, then process in a blender or food processor.

Gently reheat the purée in the rinsed-out pan with the milk and 1 cup of the cream, whisking it in gently. Do not allow to boil. Remove the pan from the heat, season to taste with salt and pepper and hot pepper sauce and leave to cool. When cold, chill.

Just before serving pour the soup into individual bowls. Stiffly whip the rest of the cream and spoon it over the soup, sprinkle with chopped chives and serve, with triangles of toasted brown bread, hot if liked, spread with butter, or bread sticks, or potato chips.

Variation
If you like garlic, then cook 1–2 cloves of garlic, peeled and finely chopped or crushed, with the onions and leeks. Or season to taste at the end with a little garlic salt or the juice extracted from crushed garlic.

For a slightly sharp flavor, add a little dry white wine or a few drops of lemon juice, or substitute plain yogurt for some of the cream.

You can also put very small pieces of peeled tomato or cooked green beans and/or chopped hard-cooked egg yolk on each serving, to give color and flavor.

Fried onions or white bread croûtons fried in garlic-flavored oil, also go well with this soup but should only be sprinkled on at the last moment.

Cook's Tip

If short of time for cooling the soup, pour it out of the hot pan into a glass or metal bowl and dunk in several changes of cold water. For extra speed, put a quantity of ice cubes into a plastic bag, seal well and hang it in the soup. Don't forget to remove it before serving!

Gourmet Fish Dishes

Fish

Haddock with mussel and shrimp sauce

Serves 4

1 quart mussels
1¼ cups dry white wine
2 cups peeled and sliced carrots
2 onions, peeled and coarsely chopped
2–3 tablespoons roughly chopped parsley
1 bay leaf
½ teaspoon white peppercorns
generous pinch of salt
1 quart water
2-lb piece haddock (preferably center cut)
1 egg yolk
¾ cup sour cream
¾ cup peeled shrimps
salt and pepper
1 tablespoon chopped fresh dill or 2 teaspoons dried dill
sprigs of dill to garnish (optional)

Scrub and rinse the mussels thoroughly to remove any grit. Scrape the shells with a knife and scrape or pull away the beards. Discard any mussels which are open or damaged. Place the cleaned mussels in a large pan and pour over the wine. Bring to a boil and cover the pan. Cook over high heat, shaking the pan occasionally, for about 10 minutes until all the shells have opened — throw away any that remain closed. Drain and reserve the cooking liquid and remove the mussels from their shells.

Place the carrot, onion, parsley, bay leaf, peppercorns and salt in a fish kettle or large saucepan, pour over the water and bring to a boil. Wash and scrape the haddock to remove any scales. Add the reserved cooking liquid from the mussels to the pan, bring the liquid back to a boil and place the fish in the pan. Cover and cook gently for 15–20 minutes, then carefully remove the fish to a serving dish and keep it hot.

Strain the fish stock through a fine strainer, preferably lined with cheesecloth or a double thickness of paper towels. Pour the strained stock into a pan, bring to a boil and cook rapidly, uncovered, until reduced to half its original quantity. Whisk about 4 tablespoons of this into the egg yolk, then return it to the pan together with the sour cream, shrimp and mussels and heat through, stirring continuously, without boiling. Season to taste, stir in the dill and pour a little of the sauce over the fish. Garnish the dish with a few sprigs of fresh dill, if available. Serve the remaining sauce separately.

Variations
Mussel and celery sauce Omit the shrimp. Thinly slice 1 stalk of celery, sauté it in 2 tablespoons butter until soft and add it to the sauce just before serving.

Mussel and apple sauce Omit the shrimp. Peel, core and coarsely grate a small tart apple, toss in a dash of lemon juice and stir it into the sauce before adding the egg yolk. The fish may then be garnished with thinly pared lemon rind cut into fine shreds and blanched in boiling water for a few minutes. A tablespoon of brandy or sherry may also be added to the sauce before the egg yolk.

Note This dish also tastes good when served cold. Prepare the sauce and fish as above, omitting the egg yolk and sour cream and allow fish and sauce to cool. Before serving stir ⅔ cup whipped cream or plain yogurt into the sauce.

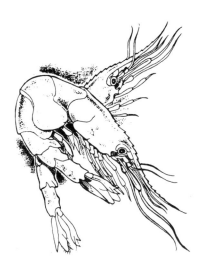

Fish

Flounder steamed in sherry

Serves 4

8 medium-sized flounder fillets
juice of ½ lemon
pinch of salt
2 tablespoons butter
1 small onion, peeled and thinly
　sliced
1 carrot, peeled and cut in thin strips
2 tomatoes, peeled and roughly
　chopped
1 sprig of tarragon
1 cup dry sherry
tarragon or parsley sprigs to garnish

Sprinkle the fish with the lemon juice and salt, cover and leave to marinate for 30 minutes.

Melt the butter in a skillet, add the onion and carrot and cook for a few minutes until just beginning to soften. Arrange over the bottom of a deep heatproof plate together with the tomatoes and tarragon. Alternatively use the steamer plate of a fish kettle or a thoroughly cleaned deep-fat fryer basket. Lay the fish fillets neatly on top of the vegetables and sprinkle 2–3 tablespoons of the sherry over them. Pour the remaining sherry into a saucepan and bring to a boil. Cover the plate closely with foil and place it over the saucepan. Reduce the heat and steam the fish for about 10–15 minutes until cooked. Uncover the plate and carefully drain any juices into the sherry in the saucepan. Keep the fish and vegetables hot.

Bring the sherry to a boil and continue to boil rapidly until it is reduced to half its original quantity, then pour over the fish and vegetables and serve at once. The fish may be garnished with sprigs of tarragon or parsley.

Fresh white bread or biscuits are the best accompaniment to this dish and dry sherry should be served rather than dry white wine.

Note Hot butter sauce (see page 110) goes very well with this dish. Alternatively, for a richer sauce, add ¾ cup of light cream to the reduced sherry liquid and reheat gently, without boiling.

Variation
Fillets of sole may also be cooked in sherry steam. For a stronger flavor, omit the carrots and tomatoes and replace the tarragon with 2 tablespoons chopped chives.

Sole with mushroom and shrimp sauce

Serves 4

8 medium-sized sole fillets
juice of 1 lemon
1 cup dry white wine
pinch of salt
1 bay leaf
4 peppercorns
1 small onion, peeled and sliced
½ cup butter
¾ cup peeled shrimp
¼ lb button mushrooms, wiped and
　stalks removed
1 teaspoon tomato paste
1 egg yolk
pinch of cayenne

Sprinkle the fish with a little lemon juice, roll up the fillets and secure them with wooden toothpicks. Heat the wine with the salt, bay leaf, peppercorns and onion, then cover and simmer for 10 minutes. Place the fish rolls in the pan and poach them gently for 10 minutes. Lift onto a warmed serving dish, standing each roll up on end, and keep hot. Remove the toothpicks. Strain the cooking liquid, return it to the pan and boil rapidly until reduced to half its original quantity.

Melt half the butter in a saucepan, add the shrimp and sauté lightly for a few minutes. Lift the shrimp out of the butter and place them on top of the fish rolls. Add the mushrooms

to the butter in the pan and cook them gently for a few minutes. Add these to the fish in the serving dish and keep hot.

Add the reduced cooking liquid to the buttery pan juices and stir in the tomato paste. Heat this mixture to just below boiling point. Lightly whisk the egg yolk with any remaining lemon juice in the top of a double boiler.

Gradually whisk in the hot cooking liquid and the remaining butter, in small pieces, until the sauce is slightly thickened and very creamy. Season lightly with a little cayenne and pour the sauce over the fish. Serve immediately with hot biscuits or freshly made toast.

Cook's Tip

Thawed frozen fish may be used successfully in both the above recipes but fresh fish, if you can get it, is even more delicious. When buying fish it is important to check that it is absolutely fresh. Look for bright eyes, firm flesh and a good sheen to the skin. Avoid fish with an unpleasant smell. Any markings such as the red spots on flounder should be clear and bright.

Fish

Fish au gratin

Serves 4

⅔ cup long-grain rice
salt
⅔ cup frozen peas, thawed
1 lb white fish fillets such as cod or
*   haddock*
¼ cup dry white wine
½ teaspoon peppercorns
1 shallot, peeled and chopped
1 small carrot, peeled and chopped
½ cup milk
½ cup light cream
1 cup grated Swiss or sharp Cheddar
*   cheese*
2 tablespoons soft white breadcrumbs
2 tablespoons butter

Cook the rice in 2½ cups boiling
salted water for about 20 minutes or
until tender. Drain thoroughly and
rinse with a little fresh boiling water,
then mix with the peas.

Cut the fish into bite-sized pieces.
Heat the wine with the peppercorns,
shallot and carrot until it reaches
boiling point. Cook for a minute
then strain and pour the liquid over
the fish in a saucepan. Poach gently
for about 5 minutes until cooked.

Add the rice and peas to the pan
and continue cooking over a low
heat until heated through. Spoon the
mixture into a gratin or other
shallow flameproof dish.

Gently heat the milk and cream
together, stir in all but 2 tablespoons
of the cheese, season to taste and
pour this mixture over the fish. Top
with the breadcrumbs and remaining
cheese and dot with butter. Cook
under a hot broiler until crisp and
golden.

Baked fish with vegetables

Serves 4

1 lb cod or haddock steaks
salt
juice of 1 lemon
3 tablespoons flour
2 cups wiped and thinly sliced
*   mushrooms*
1 leek, trimmed, washed and cut in
*   thin strips*
1 large carrot, peeled and cut in thin
*   strips*
¼ small celeriac, peeled and cut in
*   thin strips (optional)*

¼ cup butter
1 onion, peeled and finely chopped
1–2 cloves of garlic, finely chopped
3 ripe tomatoes, sliced
8 stuffed green olives, sliced
freshly ground black pepper
pinch of cayenne
2 tablespoons dry sherry
3 tablespoons sour cream
1 tablespoon chopped parsley to
*   garnish*

Preheat the oven to 400°.

Cut the fish into bite-sized cubes,
season it with a little salt and
sprinkle over half the lemon juice.
Coat lightly in the flour. Sprinkle
the remaining lemon juice over the
mushrooms and mix them with the
leek, carrot and celeriac, if used.

Melt the butter in a large skillet,
add the onion and garlic and cook
until transparent but not browned
then stir in all the prepared
vegetables except the tomatoes and
cook gently for 5 minutes. Spoon
about two-thirds of the vegetables
into a lightly greased baking dish
and arrange the fish on top. Spoon
over the remaining vegetables and
top with the tomatoes and olives.
Season with a little pepper and a

pinch of cayenne then pour over the sherry and cover the dish. Cook in the heated oven for 15 minutes. Uncover the dish, pour in the sour cream and cook for a further 5–10 minutes. Sprinkle the parsley over and serve immediately with boiled and buttered rice or potatoes.

Herrings with scrambled egg

Serves 4

4 medium-sized herrings, drawn
½ cup butter
6 eggs
¼ cup light cream
salt and pepper
pinch of paprika
2 tablespoons chopped parsley

Cut the heads and tails off the herrings. Open them out and place skin side up on a board or flat surface. Press along the back of the fish with your thumb to release the backbone. Turn the fish over and remove any loose bones then fold over to re-form the shape.

Melt ¼ cup butter in a large skillet and use to fry the herrings for about

15 minutes, turning once. Remove carefully and arrange on a warmed serving plate. Keep hot.

Whisk together the eggs and cream and season to taste with salt, pepper, and paprika. Melt the remaining butter in a saucepan and add the egg mixture. Stir over a medium heat until the eggs are just set. Arrange the scrambled egg around the herrings on the plate, sprinkle with chopped parsley and serve at once.

Marinated smoked fish

Serves 4

½ cup wine vinegar
¼ cup water
½ cup red wine
3 tablespoons olive oil
¼ cup sugar
8 black peppercorns, crushed
2 dried red chili peppers
pinch of salt
3 cloves of garlic, peeled and chopped
1 red pepper, deseeded and cut in strips
1 green pepper, deseeded and cut in strips

1 lb smoked eel, cut in 2-in lengths
2 tablespoons capers
2 tablespoons chopped parsley
2 tomatoes, halved and cut in wedges
12 stuffed green olives, halved

Mix the vinegar, water, wine, olive oil, sugar, peppercorns and chili peppers. Season with salt and bring to a boil. Skim the mixture, allow it to cool then remove the chili peppers. Add the garlic, peppers and smoked eel, cover and refrigerate for 24 hours.

Add the capers, parsley, tomatoes and olives and arrange the mixture in a serving dish. Serve with fresh, warm French or rye bread. Alternatively serve with sautéed potatoes or buttered new potatoes.

Note If you cannot obtain smoked eel then try using 4 medium-sized smoked mackerel or smoked haddock (finnan haddie) fillets — they will taste just as good. Place the fillets in a dish, prepare the marinade and proceed as above.

Fish

Spanish herrings

Serves 6

1 lb salted herrings, filleted
1 teaspoon sugar
1 cup dry sherry
2 tablespoons wine vinegar
1 teaspoon black peppercorns,
*   crushed*
3 tablespoons olive oil
1 onion, peeled and sliced
2–3 cloves of garlic, peeled and
*   chopped*
12 stuffed green olives, halved
2 sprigs of fresh thyme
1 small dried red chili pepper

Soak the herrings overnight and
rinse them before use. Cut the fish
into thin strips. Mix the sugar with
the sherry, vinegar, peppercorns,
oil, onion and garlic. Layer the
herrings and olives in a large jar or
dish and top with the thyme and
chili pepper. Pour over the sherry
mixture and cover closely. Leave to
marinate in the refrigerator for 1–3
days.
    Serve with warm French bread
and a glass of dry sherry or light
white wine.

Cook's Tip

Oily fish such as herrings or
mackerel are delicious when pickled
in a vinegar or brine solution which
stabilizes the protein in the flesh in
the same way that cooking does.
Salted herrings are usually sold
whole and need to be soaked
overnight before being trimmed and
filleted.

Herrings in yogurt

Serves 6

1 lb salted herrings, filleted
2 onions, peeled and chopped
1 large tart apple, peeled, cored and
*   chopped*
2 gherkins, chopped
2 pickled beets, sliced
1 teaspoon capers
¾ cup heavy cream
3 tablespoons plain yogurt
1 teaspoon prepared horseradish
pinch of sugar
pinch of freshly ground white pepper
1 tablespoon tarragon vinegar
1 tablespoon red wine vinegar
2 tablespoons chopped mixed fresh
*   herbs*
1 tablespoon chopped chives

Salted herrings should be soaked
overnight and rinsed before use. Cut
the fish into bite-sized pieces. Mix
the onion, apple, gherkin and
beets together with the fish and
capers. Stir in the cream and yogurt
together with the horseradish, sugar,
pepper and vinegars. Add the mixed
herbs and stir well. Cover and leave
to marinate in the refrigerator for
1–2 days. Serve sprinkled with
chives.
    Fresh bread or baked potatoes go
well with this dish.

Herrings in red wine

Serves 6

1 lb salted herrings, filleted
1 leek, sliced and thoroughly washed
1 onion, peeled and sliced
2 tablespoons green peppercorns
pinch of sugar
2 cloves
2 juniper berries
1 bay leaf
1 carrot, peeled and sliced
1 small red pepper, deseeded and
*   finely chopped*
grated rind of 1 orange
1 cup red wine
¼ cup red wine vinegar
2 tablespoons olive oil (optional)

Soak the salted herrings in water
overnight. Cut the fish into strips.
Place all the ingredients except the
wine, vinegar and oil in an
earthenware terrine or covered dish
and stir lightly. Mix together the
wine, vinegar and oil, if using, and
pour over the mixture in the terrine.
Cover well and leave to marinate in
the refrigerator for 24 hours. Serve
with baked potatoes.

Swedish style herrings

Serves 6

6 herrings, filleted
1¼ cups white wine vinegar
1¼ cups water
¾ cup sugar
1 tablespoon whole allspice
1 tablespoon black peppercorns
1 teaspoon mustard seed
2–3 small bay leaves
2 shallots, peeled and sliced
1 carrot, peeled and chopped
1½-in piece fresh horseradish, peeled
*   and finely sliced (optional)*
½-in piece fresh ginger root, peeled
*   and finely sliced*
sprig of dill or parsley to garnish

Cut the fish into strips. Put the wine
vinegar and water with the sugar,
spices and bay leaves in a saucepan,
bring to a boil and simmer for 5
minutes. Add the fish, bring back to
a boil and remove from the heat.
Allow to cool.
    Layer the fish with the vegetables,
horseradish, if using, and ginger in a
large jar or covered dish and pour
over the cooled marinade. Cover
and marinate in the refrigerator for
2 days. Garnish with a sprig of dill
or parsley before serving with plenty
of fresh bread and butter.

Fish

Mackerel with avocado stuffing

Serves 4

4 medium-sized mackerel, drawn
juice of 2 lemons
salt and freshly ground black pepper
1 ripe avocado
¼ lb Canadian bacon
2 tablespoons flour
½ cup butter
1 small leek, trimmed, washed and
   thinly sliced
2 carrots, peeled and cut in julienne
   strips
½ cup dry white wine
3 tablespoons dry vermouth
¾ cup sour cream

Garnish
1 lemon, cut in wedges
sprigs of dill or parsley

Preheat the oven to 350°. Dry the
fish on paper towels and trim off the
fins. Sprinkle the inside of the fish
with about half the lemon juice and
seasoning. Halve the avocado,
remove the seed and peel and
sprinkle the flesh with lemon juice.
Mash the avocado with the
remaining lemon juice. Chop the
bacon finely and stir it into the
avocado then season the stuffing
generously.

   Divide the mixture between the
mackerel and sew up the opening.
Alternatively use wooden toothpicks
to secure the opening. Dust the fish
with the flour and melt half the
butter in a skillet. Brown the fish
quickly in the butter, turning
carefully, then remove to a baking
dish. Toss the leek and carrots
quickly in the butter and arrange
them around the fish. Pour over the
wine and dot the top of the fish with
a little of the remaining butter.
Cook in the heated oven for 30
minutes.

   Arrange the fish on a warmed
serving platter on four individual
plates together with the vegetables.
Pour the cooking liquid into a pan,
stir in the vermouth and boil rapidly
until reduced by half. Stir in the
cream and heat gently without
boiling. Finally beat in the
remaining butter in small pieces.
Pour the sauce over the fish and
garnish with lemon wedges and
sprigs of dill and parsley. Serve with
boiled rice and a green salad.

Mushroom-stuffed fish steaks

Serves 4

4 large cod steaks
¼ cup oil
¼ cup lemon juice
½ cup dry white wine
salt and freshly ground black pepper
2 cups wiped and thinly sliced
   mushrooms
1 teaspoon chopped parsley
1 small onion, peeled and finely
   chopped
¼ cup butter
2 egg yolks
1 teaspoon wine or tarragon vinegar

Preheat the oven to 350°. Rinse the
fish steaks and dry them on paper
towels. Remove the central bone
then arrange them in a shallow dish.
Mix the oil, lemon juice and wine
together and season generously.
Pour this marinade over the fish and
leave to stand for 15–30 minutes.

   Mix the mushrooms with the
parsley and onion and season lightly.
Arrange the fish in a baking dish,
spoon the stuffing into the middle of
the steaks and arrange any
remaining stuffing over the top. Dot
the top with the butter and pour
over the marinade. Cover the dish
and bake in the heated oven for 20–
30 minutes. Carefully lift the fish
onto a warmed serving platter and
keep hot.

   Place the egg yolks and vinegar in
a double boiler and whisk until
foamy. Gradually whisk in the
cooking liquid from the fish until
pale and creamy. Season lightly.
Pour a little of the sauce over the
fish and serve the remainder
separately. Boiled and buttered new
potatoes and a fresh green salad are
the ideal accompaniments for this
dish. Alternatively use a melon
baller to cut out pieces of raw
potato and simmer them gently in
lightly salted water for about 10
minutes or until cooked. Toss in
butter before serving with the fish.

Note Other firm white fish steaks
such as haddock, hake or pollack
may be substituted for cod.

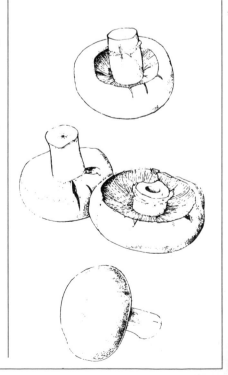

Fish

Gravad lax

Serves 6–8 as an appetizer

2 lb center cut fresh salmon
small bunch of dill, tarragon or
parsley
1 tablespoon white peppercorns,
crushed
¼ cup coarse (kosher) salt
3 tablespoons sugar
sprigs of dill to garnish (optional)

Rinse the salmon and dry it on paper towels. Using a sharp knife, make a horizontal cut along the back of the fish. Continue cutting lengthwise along either side of the backbone, keeping the knife as close to the bones as possible until the uppermost fillet is free. Slip the tip of the knife under the backbone and, keeping the knife horizontal, cut the bone free from the remaining fillet. Remove any small bones from the fillets with a small knife or tweezers.

Rinse and dry the herbs. Mix the peppercorns with the salt and sugar. Place one piece of fish, skin side down, in a deep dish and spread half the salt mixture evenly over it. Arrange the herbs on top, reserving a few sprigs for garnish, and sprinkle over the remaining salt mixture. Lay the second piece of salmon, skin side uppermost, on top and press down well. Cover with a double thickness of waxed paper and a plate or small chopping board, then weight down well and leave in the refrigerator for 2 days. Turn the salmon over twice during this time.

Pat the prepared salmon dry on paper towels and, using a sharp knife, cut it diagonally across the grain into very thin slices. Arrange these on a platter and serve with a little mustard sauce poured over. Garnish with sprigs of dill, if available. Thinly sliced bread and butter or boiled new potatoes should be served as accompaniments.

Mustard sauce

2 egg yolks
4 teaspoons prepared English
mustard
6 tablespoons oil
sugar to taste
3 tablespoons chopped dill, tarragon
or parsley
¼ cup juices from the Gravad lax or 2
tablespoons lemon juice
salt and pepper

Whisk the egg yolks with the mustard then gradually add the oil drop by drop, whisking continuously to produce a mayonnaise. Stir in a little sugar, the chopped dill, tarragon or parsley and the juices from the Gravad lax or lemon juice. Taste the sauce and adjust the sweetness and seasoning if necessary.

Poached salmon in watercress sauce

Serves 4

4 (8-oz) salmon steaks
salt and freshly ground white pepper
juice of ½ lemon
¼ cup butter
1 small onion, peeled and finely
chopped
1 bunch of watercress, washed,
trimmed and chopped
½ cup fish stock or water
½ cup dry white wine
½ cup light cream

Season the salmon steaks lightly with a little salt and pepper. Sprinkle over half the lemon juice and leave to marinate for 10 minutes. Melt the butter, add the onion and cook, stirring occasionally, until softened but not browned. Stir in remaining lemon juice and half the watercress, season lightly then add the stock and wine. Heat gently to simmering point, add the salmon steaks and simmer for about 5–7 minutes until just cooked.

Remove the fish to a warmed serving platter and keep hot. Stir the remaining watercress and cream into the sauce and heat through gently without boiling. Pour over the salmon and serve immediately with boiled potatoes and a cucumber salad or buttered asparagas.

Variations

Sorrel sauce Fresh sorrel is delicious with salmon. Substitute ½ lb sorrel for the watercress, wash, dry and chop it finely then cook as above.

Tarragon or chive sauce Both of these well-flavored herbs may be substituted for the watercress in the above recipe. They should be used sparingly, about 1–2 tablespoons is enough, and should be added to the sauce with the cream.

Lemon sauce Thinly pare the rind from 1 lemon and cut it into needle-fine shreds. Cook it with the salmon steaks, omitting the watercress from the recipe, and serve as above.

Broiled salmon Alternatively the sauce can be prepared as above and the salmon cooked separately under a hot broiler. Dot the fish steaks with butter and broil them for about 3 minutes on each side. Pour the sauce over them before serving.

Cook's Tip

Gravad lax is a traditional Swedish delicacy and, as it can be made some time in advance, is excellent as an appetizer for a dinner party or as part of a cold buffet meal. Maintain the Scandinavian mood by serving it on a wooden board garnished with lemon wedges and dill and accompanied by thinly sliced rye bread or crispbread.

Fish

Trout au bleu

Serves 4

4 freshly caught trout, drawn
½ cup vinegar
1 small onion, peeled and sliced
1 carrot, peeled and sliced
1 bay leaf
few sprigs of parsley
generous pinch of salt
2¼ quarts water
1 lemon, cut in wedges to garnish

Handle the trout with care so as not to remove the natural coating on the skin. Mix the vinegar, onion, carrot, bay leaf, half the parsley, salt and water in a large saucepan or fish kettle and bring it to a boil. Add the fish, curving them slightly in the pan and bring back to a gentle simmer. Cook for 7–10 minutes then carefully lift the trout out of the pan and arrange them on warmed serving plates. Garnish with lemon wedges and the remaining parsley.

Serve with plenty of melted butter, boiled potatoes and a fresh green salad. Creamed horseradish goes well with fresh trout.

Tip If you cannot obtain freshly caught trout bring the vinegar to a boil separately from the other ingredients and pour this over the fish before cooking it.

Variation
Trout au bleu may also be served cold. Allow the fish to cool in the cooking liquid then carefully remove the skin, leaving the head and tail in place. Arrange them on a large serving platter, lightly coat with aspic and garnish with boiled or steamed mixed vegetables, lemon wedges and sprigs of parsley or dill.

Trout meunière

Serves 4

4 medium-sized trout, drawn
salt and freshly ground white pepper
juice of 2 lemons
4–6 tablespoons seasoned flour
6 tablespoons butter
1 tablespoon oil
2 tablespoons chopped parsley

Rinse the trout under running water and dry on paper towels. Season the cavities lightly and sprinkle with half the lemon juice. Coat with seasoned flour.

Melt about half the butter and the oil in a large skillet and cook the trout over medium heat for about 8–10 minutes, turning once. Remove them to a warmed serving platter and keep hot.

Add the remaining butter to the pan juices and cook for a few minutes then stir in the remaining lemon juice and parsley. Heat through for a few seconds before pouring over the fish. Serve immediately with boiled new potatoes and a fresh green salad.

Tip When cooking trout, take care not to overcook the outside before the middle is cooked. Medium heat is necessary for this and to avoid breaking up the flesh.

Variation
A few sprigs of fresh parsley, dill or lemon balm may be placed in the body cavity of the fish before cooking or try cooking orange or lemon wedges in the pan with the fish to provide extra juices and a lovely flavor. A little ground aniseed may also be added to the flour before coating the fish — unorthodox, but delicious!

Fish

Trout en papillote

Serves 4

4 medium-sized trout, drawn
juice of ½ lemon
salt and pepper
¼ cup butter
small bunch of parsley, washed and
    dried
4 sprigs of tarragon, washed and
    dried (optional)
4 sprigs of dill, washed and dried
    (optional)
3 large tomatoes, peeled, deseeded
    and chopped
2 onions, peeled and finely chopped
2 tablespoons chopped parsley
sprigs of parsley to garnish

Preheat the oven to 350°. Rinse the
trout well, both inside and out, and
pat dry on paper towels. Sprinkle
the inside of each with a little lemon
juice and season generously. Divide
the butter into four and place in the
cavity of each fish, along with the
herbs, if using. Soak eight pieces of
parchment paper in cold water and
use to wrap each trout up in a
double thickness. Lay the fish in a
roasting pan, making sure that the

ends of the packages are tucked in
well and bake in the heated oven for
10 minutes. Carefully turn the fish
over, again ensuring that the
packages are secure, and cook for a
further 10 minutes.

Carefully open the paper,
removing the skin of the fish with it
and lift the uppermost fillet onto a
warmed serving platter. Remove and
discard the bone and cooked herbs
and carefully lift the lower fillet off
the skin, arranging it on the serving
platter with the first piece of fish.

Mix the tomatoes with the onions
and parsley. Season to taste and
serve this mixture with the fish.
Garnish with sprigs of parsley. A
green salad with a tangy lemon
dressing would be the ideal
accompaniment to this dish.

Note Mackerel or herrings can also
be prepared very successfully in this
way. Alternatively the fish can be
wrapped in foil and cooked over a
barbecue.

Tip A few dried dill or fennel seeds
may be sprinkled on the fish during
cooking to add extra flavor.

Cook's Tip

Cooking trout in paper is a
traditional method of cooking fish
which has very practical reasons
behind it. Whilst the paper keeps in
all the natural flavour and juices it
also adheres to the skin of the fish
making it easy to remove. For
successful results make sure that the
paper is moistened and that the
'parcels' are neat and well folded.

Moules marinière

Serves 4

2½ *quarts mussels*
¼ *cup butter or 6 tablespoons olive
  oil*
3 scallions, chopped
1 large carrot, peeled and finely diced
freshly ground black pepper
2 cups dry white wine

Scrub and wash the mussels
thoroughly. Scrape the shells to
ensure that they are clean and
scrape or pull away the beards.
Discard any mussels that remain
open as they are inedible. Melt the
butter or heat the oil in a large
saucepan with a close fitting lid.
Add the prepared vegetables and
cook until soft but not browned —
about 15 minutes. Season generously
with black pepper and pour over the
wine. Bring to a boil, add the
mussels and cover the pan. Cook
over fairly high heat, shaking the
pan frequently, for about 10 minutes
until all the mussels have opened.
  Discard any mussels which have
not opened and arrange the rest in
four serving bowls. Pour the cooking
liquid over the mussels taking care
not to transfer any grit which may
have settled in the bottom of the
pan. Alternatively the liquid may be
strained through a strainer lined
with cheesecloth or a double
thickness of paper towels.
  Serve with home-baked
wholewheat bread, French bread or
pumpernickel.

Tip The mussels can be flavored with
a chopped clove of garlic, added to
the vegetables, a peeled, deseeded
and diced tomato or a bay leaf, sprig
of rosemary or chopped parsley
which may be added to the cooking
liquid. The sauce may be enriched
by the addition of 2–4 tablespoons
of heavy cream which should be
gently heated in the sauce just
before serving.

Note Mussels should not be cooked
for longer than is required to open
the shells as continued cooking
toughens and wrinkles the mussel
meat, destroying its delicate flavor.

Variation
Broiled mussels Place the cooked
mussels in a large flat flameproof
dish. Top with a mixture of 1 cup
soft breadcrumbs, 1 finely chopped
clove of garlic, 1 tablespoon
chopped parsley, mint or grated
lemon rind and 2 tablespoons finely
grated cheese. Sprinkle generously
with olive oil and cook under a hot
broiler until lightly browned and
crisp. Serve with warm French
bread.

Fish

Boiled lobster

Serves 2

1 live lobster, about 1½ lb in weight
1 tablespoon salt
2 quarts water
1 lemon or lime
¼ cup butter, melted
sprigs of dill or parsley to garnish

Rinse the lobster under cold running water leaving any rubber bands which secure the claws. Place the salt in a large deep saucepan with a lid. Add the water and bring it to a boil then plunge in the lobster, head downwards. Place the lid on the pan and, holding it down firmly, bring the water back to a boil. Reduce the heat and simmer for 15 minutes. The lobster turns the characteristic red color during cooking.

Lift out the lobster with tongs or a large spatula and fork and split it down the back. Using a large sharp knife and starting at the point where the head and tail meet, cut firmly down through the tail then up through the head. Use a small hammer or meat mallet to tap the knife through the shell if necessary. Remove the white gills which are found in both halves of the head and the black intestine which runs down the length of the body. Remove and reserve any roe and the bright red roe or coral that is found in a female lobster. Place the lobster on a warmed serving platter and serve with wedges of lemon or lime and a little melted butter. The lobster may be garnished with sprigs of dill or parsley.

Note When buying live lobsters it is important to ensure that they are really fresh. Hold the lobster by the back and lift it up — if it is strong and fresh it should strike out with its tail. Lobsters with only sluggish movements should be avoided as these are not at the peak of freshness.

Lobster thermidor

Serves 4

2 (1½-lb) lobsters, cooked
6 tablespoons butter
2 shallots, peeled and chopped
salt and pepper
pinch of dry mustard
2 tablespoons flour
¾ cup dry white wine
¾ cup milk
2 tablespoons grated Parmesan or
    Swiss cheese
1 egg yolk
2 tablespoons light cream
1 cup soft white breadcrumbs
sprigs of dill or parsley to garnish

Remove the claws and legs from the lobster, crack the claws with lobster crackers or nutcrackers and remove all the meat making sure that bits of shell do not get into it. Remove all the meat from the shell and flake slightly.

Melt 2 tablespoons of the butter in a small saucepan, add the shallots and cook until soft but not browned. Stir in a little seasonong and the mustard, then add the flour and stir in the wine. Bring to a boil, stirring continuously, then gradually stir in the milk and heat through thoroughly. Remove the sauce from the heat and stir in the cheese until well blended. Mix the egg yolk with the cream and beat this into the sauce. Reheat without boiling to prevent the egg curdling.

Stir the lobster meat into the sauce and replace it in the halved shells. Sprinkle the breadcrumbs over the top then dot with the remaining butter and brown under a hot broiler. Garnish with sprigs of dill or parsley before serving.

Tip When finishing the lobster under the broiler take care not to cook for too long as this will cause the delicate lobster meat to dry up and become stringy. Some gourmets insist that lobster should be served lukewarm to bring out the characteristic delicate flavor but this is entirely a matter of personal preference.

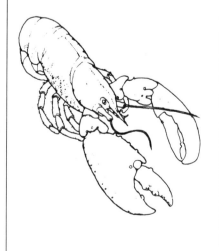

Fish

Scallops in mushroom sauce

Serves 4

1 lb scallops, shucked
1 cup water
½ cup dry white wine
2 shallots, peeled and sliced
sprig of thyme
1 bay leaf
6 peppercorns
1 clove
salt and freshly ground black pepper
½ cup butter
1 cup wiped and sliced mushrooms
2 teaspoons flour
2 tablespoons sour cream
1 egg yolk
1 tablespoon chopped parsley

If there is any red coral cut it away from the scallops and halve the white flesh. Place the water, wine, shallots, herbs and spices in a saucepan and boil rapidly for 10–15 minutes until reduced to about half its original volume. Add the white scallop flesh, season lightly and cook gently for 5 minutes. Add the corals (if available) and cook for a further 3–4 minutes. Lift the flesh out of

the stock and slice if the scallops are large.

Strain the stock and reserve. Melt 2 tablespoons of the butter in a saucepan and use to cook the mushrooms until all the liquid is evaporated. Melt another 2 tablespoons of butter in another pan and stir in the flour. Cook until golden then gradually whisk in the reserved cooking stock. Add the sour cream and simmer gently for 2 minutes, stirring all the time. Whisk the egg yolk with a little of the sauce and blend this mixture back into the rest. Heat through without boiling.

Whisk in the remaining ¼ cup butter, a piece at a time, then add the scallops and mushrooms. Season to taste. Serve in clean scallop shells or individual dishes, sprinkled with parsley.

Serve with thinly sliced bread and butter and a finely shredded green salad or with plain boiled rice.

Variations

Scallops au gratin Top the scallops with ½ cup soft breadcrumbs mixed with 1 tablespoon grated Parmesan cheese and brown under a hot broiler.

Saffron scallops Prepare the scallops as above, adding ¼ teaspoon saffron strands to the cooking liquid. Stir 1 teaspoon each of brandy and vermouth into the sauce and add 2 peeled, deseeded and chopped tomatoes before serving.

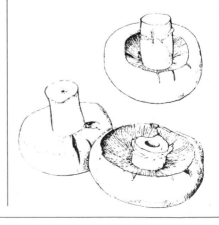

Japanese shellfish fritters

Serves 4

Most fish and seafood with firm flesh can be coated with batter and deep fried. The batter protects the fish from the hot oil and should be crisp, light and tasty.

1 lb bite-sized pieces of prepared fish and shellfish (see below)

Batter
3 egg whites
3 tablespoons sherry
3 tablespoons rice flour
2 tablespoons all-purpose flour
oil for deep frying

Garnish
1 lemon, cut in wedges
few sprigs of parsley

Prepare the fish and shellfish following the instructions below.
　Beat the egg whites until stiff then lightly stir in the sherry, rice flour and all-purpose flour. Heat the oil to 350°. Dip bite-sized pieces of the prepared seafoods in the batter and fry them in the hot oil for the suggested length of time. Drain on paper towels and serve immediately garnished with wedges of lemon and parsley. The fritters go well with a crunchy mixed salad and freshly cut bread and butter.

Note Do not make the batter in advance. It only forms a thin delicate crust if used at once.

Cod, flounder and whiting
Remove any skin and bones from the fillets. Season lightly and sprinkle with lemon juice. Cut into bite-sized pieces, coat in the batter as above and deep fry for 7–10 minutes.

Smoked halibut and haddock (finnan haddie)
Remove any skin and bones from the fillets. Cut the flesh into strips, coat in the batter and cook for about 5 minutes.

Shrimp and scallops
Peeled shrimp should be coated in batter and fried for 5 minutes. Scallops should be shucked, rinsed and cut in half then coated in batter and cooked for 7–10 minutes.

Squid
Remove the heads, tentacles and intestines from the squid, carefully pulling out the transparent cartilage. Pull off the skin and rinse and dry the flesh. Cut it into rings and coat in the prepared batter. Cook the pieces of squid for 10 minutes.

Pacific prawns (jumbo shrimp)
Cooked and peeled prawns can be dipped in batter and deep fried for 7–10 minutes.

Roasted and Broiled Meat

Roasted and Broiled Meat

Roast beef in a salt crust

Serves 6

*1 (2½-lb) beef tenderloin or rib eye
roast
4 egg whites
1⅓ cups coarse sea salt*

Preheat the oven to 450°.

Dry the meat with paper towels.
Carefully score any fat several times,
without cutting into the meat.
Lightly beat the egg whites and salt
together to a dry paste.

Line a roasting pan with a double
thickness of foil. Spread over it a
layer of the salt paste as long and as
wide as the meat. Lay the meat, fat
side up, on the salt paste and cover
it completely with the rest of the
paste. Wrap the foil carefully over
the top to enclose the meat
completely and cook in the heated
oven for 55 minutes to 1 hour for
rare meat; cook 10 minutes longer
for medium done meat. Place the
foil-wrapped meat on a large board;
fold down or tear off the foil.

To serve, carefully break open the
salt crust with a hammer or meat
mallet. Lift the meat off its bed of
salt onto a warmed serving platter,
brushing off any salt adhering to it,
then let it rest for a few minutes
before carving.

Serve with Cumberland or Spiced
cranberry sauce (see recipes, page
115) passed around separately,
together with croquette potatoes,
green beans or fried mushrooms.

Note This roast appears to do the
impossible. In general salt attracts
moisture and draws it out of food,
thereby drying out anything it comes
into contact with — on this occasion
a beef roast. But here the beef
remains very juicy and succulent
because there is a trick to it. The
salt is mixed with a liquid (the egg
whites) which it soaks up like a
sponge. The salt paste then bakes
into a hard shell which, while it
imparts a flavor to the meat, ensures
it doesn't dry out or overcook.

To make the salt and egg white
bind more easily, add about ⅓ cup

flour with the salt: it has no
noticeable effect on the taste. For
the best results choose unrefined sea
salt or kosher salt which imparts a
delicious aroma to the meat.
Moreover, the crust does not have
to be thrown away once opened:
pounded in a mortar or worked in a
blender or food processor it can be
used as a seasoning for other meats
as it will have taken on the
unmistakeable flavor of a roast. For
a stronger flavor, push a few slivers
of garlic in between the fat and the
meat, or mix some dried herbs with
the salt.

Shoulder of lamb provençale

Serves 6

*1 (5-lb) lamb shoulder square cut, or
leg of lamb
3 cloves of garlic, peeled
2 teaspoons salt
4 juniper berries
6 peppercorns
3 allspice berries
1 teaspoon fresh rosemary leaves or
½ teaspoon dried rosemary
¼ cup olive oil
2 cups peeled, deseeded and finely
chopped tomatoes
½ cup stock or broth
½ cup red wine*

Wipe the lamb with a damp cloth
and cut off excess fat. Crush the
garlic with the salt, juniper berries,
peppercorns, allspice berries and
rosemary in a mortar. A little of the
olive oil may be added to make it
smooth. Rub this mixture over the
lamb.

Preheat the oven to 425°. Heat
the oil in a roasting pan, together
with the fat trimmings from the
lamb. Put in the lamb and cook for
10 minutes. Reduce the heat to 375°,
put the tomatoes around the meat,
mix the stock with the wine and
pour half over the lamb. Put the
lamb back in the oven and cook for
1¼–1½ hours, basting from time to
time with the juices in the pan.
Replenish the stock and wine from
time to time.

At the end of the cooking time
turn the oven off and let the lamb
rest for 5 minutes.

Strain the roasting juices, skim off
the fat and serve as gravy, together
with ratatouille and French bread,
or noodles and green or snow peas.

Tip Sauce lovers may add more wine
to the gravy if liked, then boil to
reduce it a little and thicken with a
little kneaded butter or cornstarch.

Cook's Tip

A square cut shoulder is a prime
large cut and therefore excellent for
a party or celebration meal. For a
family meal, leg of lamb makes a
good alternative.

Roasted and Broiled Meat

Roast chicken with cream cheese and herb stuffing

Serves 4–6

1 (3½–4 lb) dressed roaster chicken,
  thawed if frozen
2 cloves of garlic, peeled and crushed
salt and freshly ground black pepper
¼ cup butter

Stuffing
1 (8-oz) package cream cheese
2 tablespoons sour cream
1 egg yolk
1 cup soft breadcrumbs
1 shallot or small onion, peeled and
  finely chopped
3 tablespoons chopped parsley
½–1 tablespoon chopped chives or
  rosemary
salt and pepper

To finish
½ cup sour cream
2 tablespoons tomato paste
1 teaspoon lemon juice
1 tablespoon brandy

First make the stuffing: beat the cream cheese, sour cream and egg yolk into the breadcrumbs. Stir in the shallot or onion and the herbs. Season to taste with salt and pepper and set aside.

Preheat the oven to 400°.

Using a sharp knife, cut into the skin of the chicken along the backbone. Carefully cut the meat from the bones without detaching it from the skin. Put in the stuffing through this opening, and push it down under the breast meat. Pull the skin together and sew it up. Alternatively use the mixture to stuff the body cavity of the chicken. Mix the garlic to a paste with salt and pepper, then spread over the chicken.

Grease a large piece of foil with some of the butter, put the chicken on it, breast side up, then dot with the rest of the butter, cut into flakes. Draw the foil up and over the chicken loosely and pinch the edges together to seal. Place in a roasting pan and roast for 1¼–1½ hours in the heated oven, then open up the foil for 5–10 minutes more to let the chicken brown.

Remove from the oven and place the chicken on a warmed serving platter. Pour off some of the fat from the roasting pan and transfer the juices to a saucepan. Whisk in the cream and reduce the mixture by about one-third over gentle heat. Flavor to taste with tomato paste, lemon juice and brandy. Carve the bird and serve the gravy separately.

Variation
This stuffing is also excellent with chicken legs. Either remove the leg bones from the chicken yourself or ask the butcher to do it for you. Fill the cavities with the stuffing and cook in foil as above, reducing the overall cooking time to 30 minutes.

Roast stuffed turkey

Serves 6–8

A whole turkey should in principle be cooked with a stuffing, whether or not both are to be eaten at the same time. The stuffing imparts a special flavor to the meat, and helps to keep it moist during long cooking.

1 (10-lb) dressed turkey, thawed if
   frozen
½ lemon
salt and pepper
¼ lb slices of bacon
¼ cup butter, melted

Stuffing
⅔ cup golden raisins
⅔ cup port wine or sherry
1 lb pork sausagemeat
butter for frying
turkey liver from giblets, finely
   chopped
1 egg
salt and pepper
dried thyme

First make the stuffing. Steep the raisins in the port or sherry for 1 hour, then drain, reserving any juices for the gravy. Fry the sausagemeat in a little butter, then stir in the raisins and liver, and cook 1–2 minutes longer. Remove from the heat, cool and stir in the beaten egg. Season to taste with salt, pepper and thyme. Set aside in a cool place.

Preheat the oven to 375°.

Rub the lemon around the body cavity of the turkey, then season inside and out with salt and pepper. Fill the body cavity with the stuffing.

Wrap the bacon slices over the breast and legs, then truss the bird. Place in a large roasting pan. Pour over the melted butter and roast in the heated oven for about 4 hours, basting from time to time with the juices in the pan and occasionally sprinkling with a little water.

Ten minutes before the end of cooking time, remove the bacon, spoon over some of the juices from the pan and leave to brown the breast. Test with a skewer — the bird is done if the thigh juices run out clear (a meat thermometer should register 185°). Remove from the oven and pour off the cooking juices. Cover the turkey with foil and if possible leave in a warm place for 10 minutes before carving, to allow the meat and juices to settle.

Strain the pan juices into a saucepan and skim off any fat. Add strained giblet stock (see note below) and if you like, thicken the gravy by whisking in a little kneaded butter and add 1–2 tablespoons of red wine or sherry or the port left over from making the stuffing. Bring to a boil, check the seasoning and pour into a gravy boat to serve.

Note To make giblet stock: wash the gizzard and heart and simmer in about 1 quart water seasoned with salt, pepper and bouquet garni for 1 hour. Strain well before using.

Roasted and Broiled Meat

Roast stuffed goose

Serves 8

1 (9-lb) dressed goose, thawed if
*   frozen*
salt and pepper
2 tablespoons butter
1 cup boiling water

Stuffing
1 lb tart apples, peeled, cored and
*   diced*
1 onion, peeled and finely chopped
2 cups soft breadcrumbs
⅔ cup golden raisins

Rub inside the goose with salt and
pepper. Preheat the oven to 400°.

For the stuffing, mix together the
apples, onion, breadcrumbs and
raisins. Stuff the breast of the goose
with this mixture and sew up with
fine string or secure with skewers.
Rub all over the bird with salt and
pepper and prick it with a fork in
several places so that the fat can run
out during roasting. Remember to
prick under the breast and under the
legs. Spread the butter over the
breast.

Pour the boiling water into the
roasting pan. Put in the goose on a
rack, breast side uppermost. Cook
in the heated oven for about
2½ hours, basting from time to time
with the cooking juices. Then turn
the bird over and brown the back
for about 20 minutes. Turn it over
again, brush well with salted water
and let it brown until crisp, about
10 minutes. Take out, cover with
foil and let it rest for 10 minutes in a
warm place before carving.

Serve with croquette potatoes,
glazed chestnuts, Brussels sprouts
and chopped, fried mushrooms. The
goose itself may be garnished with
fried apple rings and parsley sprigs.

Sage gravy

Pour 1 cup boiling water into the
roasting pan to dissolve the meat
juices. Skim off as much fat as
possible. Pour the liquid into a
saucepan and add 2 tablespoons
chopped fresh or 2 teaspoons dried
sage. Reduce over high heat for a
few minutes. Strain, and season to
taste with salt and pepper. Stir in a
little cream if liked, and serve
separately in a gravy boat.

Brussels sprouts

Serves 8

2 lb Brussels sprouts
2 tablespoons butter
grated nutmeg
freshly ground black pepper

Clean the sprouts and make shallow
crossed cuts in the stalk ends.
Plunge them into boiling salted
water, cover and cook for about 10
minutes until just tender. Drain
well. Melt the butter in the same
saucepan, put in the sprouts, season
with nutmeg and pepper to taste and
toss them well. Serve hot.

Glazed chestnuts

Serves 6–8

1½ lb fresh chestnuts or ¾ lb dried
*   chestnuts, soaked in cold water*
6 tablespoons stock or broth
¼ cup butter
1 tablespoon sugar

Slit open the chestnut skins
crosswise, if using fresh ones, cook
in boiling water to cover for 5
minutes or until the skins curl
outwards. Drain and peel them,
removing the furry inside skin as
well. Or drain the dried chestnuts.

In another pan, bring the stock to
a boil, put in the chestnuts, butter
and sugar, cover and cook for 15–20
minutes. Remove the lid and cook
for a further 5 minutes until the
chestnuts are soft and lightly
caramelized. Serve hot.

Variations

Potato stuffing Cook 1 lb peeled
potatoes in boiling salted water for
10 minutes. Drain and dice them.
Mix with 1 chopped onion and
2 tablespoons chopped parsley, then
season to taste with dried marjoram
and sage. Use to stuff the goose as
above.

Orange stuffing Peel 4 large oranges
and divide into segments. Mix with
2 large tart apples, peeled, cored
and diced, 2 cups soft breadcrumbs
and 1 egg to bind. Use to stuff the
goose as above. ⅓ cup each golden
raisins and chopped, blanched
almonds may also be added, if liked.

Alternative accompaniments Try red
cabbage braised with apples, and
flavored with cinnamon and ginger.
Or canned sauerkraut, drained and
heated with a little dry white wine
and mixed with pineapple chunks or
slices of orange.

Note The same stuffings and
accompaniments can be used for
roast duck.

Cook's Tip

Goose is a delicious meat,
traditionally eaten at Christmas, but
is avoided by some because it has a
reputation for being somewhat fatty.
However if cooked using the method
above the fat will run out of the bird
and collect in the roasting tin. The
skimmed fat can be used for making
well-flavored roast or sautéed
potatoes and in many cooked dishes.

Roasted and Broiled Meat

Roast pheasant with mushroom cream

Serves 2

$\frac{1}{4}$ *lb button mushrooms, wiped, or*
$\frac{3}{4}$ *oz dried morels, soaked in*
  lukewarm water
1 dressed hen pheasant (about 1$\frac{1}{2}$ lb),
  thawed if frozen
salt and pepper
2 large slices bacon
$\frac{1}{2}$ *cup butter*
2 shallots, peeled and finely chopped
1 tablespoon brandy
$\frac{3}{4}$ *cup heavy cream*
$\frac{1}{2}$ *teaspoon lemon juice*
1 tablespoon chopped parsley

Preheat the oven to 425°.

If using fresh mushrooms, halve or quarter them if large. If using morels, drain and rinse well under running cold water to wash out any grit trapped inside their crinkly caps; halve, quarter or coarsely chop if large.

Rub inside the pheasant with salt and pepper. Wrap the bacon around the breast meat. Tie with fine string and season all over the outside. Lay the pheasant on its side on a rack in a roasting pan and pour over 6 tablespoons of the butter, melted.

Place the roasting pan with the bird in the heated oven and roast for 35–50 minutes, according to size, basting frequently with cooking juices, and turning the bird halfway through so it cooks evenly. About 5 minutes from the end of the cooking time, remove the bacon so the breast can brown lightly, and baste again.

Lift out the pheasant, wrap it in foil and replace in the turned-off oven or with the door ajar for 10 minutes so the meat juices can settle.

Put the roasting pan on the stove and reheat the cooking juices. Add the shallots and cook till softened, then add the mushrooms or morels, cook briefly and add the brandy. Skim off any fat, stir in the cream and cook gently for 6–8 minutes. Add the lemon juice and parsley to the sauce, remove the pan from the heat and stir in the rest of the butter in small pieces.

Cut the legs off the pheasant, then the wings, and lastly carve the breast. Put all the pieces on a warm serving platter and pour the mushroom cream around them. Serve with potato pancakes or croquette potatoes.

Note Leeks, cut into 3-in pieces, then blanched, softened in butter and seasoned with salt and pepper, go extremely well with this dish as do baby sprouts. White cabbage cut into wide strips and cooked in the same way as the leeks, but seasoned with grated nutmeg as well, is also very good with the pheasant.

Tip A hen pheasant generally serves 2 people whereas a cock pheasant which is much larger will serve 3 or sometimes 4 people.

Tenderloin of beef in bacon

Serves 6

1 (3-lb) beef tenderloin roast
1 clove of garlic, peeled and crushed
1 teaspoon salt
1 teaspoon freshly ground black
*   pepper or roughly crushed black*
*   peppercorns*
1 teaspoon paprika
¼ lb pork fat or slab bacon, cut into
*   paper-thin slices*

Wipe the beef with paper towels. Mix the garlic to a thick paste with the salt, pepper and paprika. Rub this paste all over the beef, working it in well. Preheat the oven to 450°.

Wrap the pork fat or bacon around the beef and tie with thin string. Put the beef on a rack in the roasting pan and roast in the heated oven for 30–35 minutes, depending on the thickness of the cut: the beef should still be pink inside. For well done meat, cook 5–10 minutes longer.

When cooked, let the meat rest for 5 minutes before carving. Serve with croquette potatoes and gooseberry chutney.

Gooseberry chutney

1 lb green gooseberries, trimmed
1 lb ripe apples, peeled, cored and
*   thinly sliced*
3 onions, peeled and finely chopped
½ cup white wine vinegar
1 cup sugar
½ teaspoon powdered cinnamon
½ teaspoon powdered ginger
pinch of ground coriander
grated rind of ½ lemon
3 tablespoons white rum

Thoroughly wash and drain the gooseberries. Mix with the apples, onions, wine vinegar, sugar and spices and put in a large saucepan. Cover and leave to stand for 2 hours. Slowly bring to a boil, stirring continuously, until the fruits are quite soft but the gooseberries are still whole.

Remove the pan of chutney from the heat and stir in the lemon rind and rum. Pour into hot, clean jars, seal, label and keep in a cool, dry place or the refrigerator for at least 14 days. For longer storage, process in a boiling-water-bath. Once opened, keep for about a week only and store in the refrigerator.

Serve with the roast beef, or with individual steaks or chops.

Variations
Apple chutney Replace the gooseberries and apples with 2 lb apples and add 4 oz chopped raisins.

Peach chutney Use 2 lb peaches, peeled and chopped, instead of the apples and gooseberries. Omit the cinnamon and replace the grated lemon rind with the grated rind of 1 orange.

Roasted and Broiled Meat

Roast leg of pork

Serves 6

1 (3-lb) leg of pork (fresh ham)
salt and freshly ground black pepper
2 tablespoons lard or butter
1 cup boiling water
1 onion, peeled and quartered
1 bay leaf
2 cloves
4 juniper berries
6 tablespoons dark beer
stock or broth
1 tablespoon cornstarch, dissolved in
*   a little cold water*

Preheat the oven to 400°.

Rub the pork very thoroughly with salt and pepper. Heat the lard in a roasting pan and fry the pork in it for 15 minutes or until browned all over. Pour on half of the boiling water. Add the onion, bay leaf and spices and roast in the heated oven for 2 hours, basting it at intervals with a little of the beer. Transfer to a warm serving platter and keep warm.

Dissolve the meat juices in the roasting pan with the rest of the water and beer, bring to a boil and then strain. Skim off any fat. Make the liquid up to 2 cups with stock, and stir in the cornstarch mixture. Bring back to a boil, taste for seasoning and pour into a gravy boat.

Serve the roast pork with mashed potatoes and braised cabbage with caraway seeds.

Variation
Roast pork with apple The sharp taste of apple complements the flavor of pork well. Add two cooking apples, peeled, cored and halved, to the onion when roasting the meat and use hard cider instead of dark beer.

Baked pork

Serves 4–6

1 large carrot, peeled and chopped
2 stalks celery, washed and chopped
1 onion, peeled and stuck with
*   4 cloves*
1 bay leaf
5 juniper berries
10 peppercorns
2 tablespoons vinegar
1 (2-lb) boneless pork roast
6 tablespoons butter, melted
½ cup dry white wine
1 teaspoon cornstarch, dissolved in a
*   little cold water*
1 tablespoon tomato paste
2 tablespoons light cream
salt and freshly ground white pepper
1 teaspoon sugar

Put the vegetables, bay leaf, spices and vinegar in a large pan with the meat. Cover with water and bring to a boil. Cook over moderate heat for 20 minutes. Then lift out the meat, drain it well and cool for a few minutes. Strain and reserve the stock. Meanwhile, preheat the oven to 400°.

Heat half the butter in a roasting pan, put in the pork and brush with a little of the melted butter. Roast in the heated oven for 60–70 minutes, basting it frequently.

When done, remove from the oven, cover with foil and let rest in a warm place for 10 minutes. Place on a warmed serving dish and pour the remaining butter over it.

Dissolve the juices in the roasting pan with 1½ cups of the reserved, stock then pour into a saucepan, add the wine and boil rapidly until reduced by about one-third. Stir in the cornstarch mixture, bring back to a boil, stirring, then add the tomato paste and cream and season to taste with salt, pepper and sugar. Simmer for 5 minutes, then pour into a gravy boat.

Serve with green vegetables or salad if you prefer, together with mashed potatoes or ribbon noodles. Try also a light potato salad, with plenty of herbs, mixed with thinly sliced cucumber and chopped dill.

German style roast pork

Serves 4

1 (2¼-lb) leg of pork (fresh ham),
*   with the fat scored in a diamond*
*   pattern*
salt and freshly ground black pepper
6 cloves (optional)
2 onions, peeled and halved
1 clove of garlic, peeled
2 carrots, peeled and chopped
1 turnip, peeled and chopped
¼ cup beer or hard cider
2 teaspoons cornstarch, dissolved in
*   a little cold water*

Preheat the oven to 400°.

Rub the meat with salt and pepper, push the cloves, if using, into the fat where the incisions cross.

Bring a little water to a boil in a roasting pan, put in the pork, fat side downwards and roast in the heated oven for 30 minutes. Remove from the oven. Place the pork on a rack with the fat uppermost, put back in the roasting pan and continue cooking for 30 minutes longer. Then add to the roasting pan the onions, garlic, carrot and turnip and cook 30 minutes more. If necessary add more water from time to time. Ten minutes before the end of the cooking time, brush the fat with the beer or cider to help it crisp. Remove the pork from the oven to a warmed serving platter, cover with foil and let rest in a warm place for at least 10 minutes.

To make the gravy, dissolve the juices in the roasting pan with 2 cups boiling water or stock or broth, then strain into a saucepan. Bring to a boil and stir in the cornstarch mixture. Bring back to a boil, stirring, and pour into a gravy boat.

Serve the pork with croquette potatoes and braised red cabbage with apple.

Roasted and Broiled Meat

Veal Olives

Serves 4

4 thin veal cutlets (each about 6 oz)
1 teaspoon anchovy paste
4 very thin slices of Canadian bacon
4 hard-cooked eggs, shelled
2 tablespoons butter
1 onion, peeled and finely chopped
1 cup stock or broth
¾ cup dry white wine
2 tablespoons tomato paste
¼ cup sour cream
salt and pepper
parsley sprigs to garnish

Pound the cutlets as for Beef olives. Spread each one thinly with the anchovy paste, then cover with a bacon slice. Place a whole egg on each one, then roll up the cutlets to enclose the eggs completely and fasten with wooden toothpicks or fine string.

Heat the butter in a large heavy pan. Put in the 'olives' and brown them all over for 5 minutes, then add the chopped onion and cook for a further 5 minutes. Pour on the stock and wine, cover and simmer for 20 minutes. Lift the 'olives' out

of the pan, remove the toothpicks or string and place on a warmed serving plate. Keep warm.

Reduce the sauce by about one-third over high heat, stir in the tomato paste and cream and season to taste.

Halve the 'olives' crosswise, pour some of the sauce around them and serve the rest separately. Garnish with parsley.

Beef olives

Serves 4

4 thin slices of beef top round steak (each about 6 oz)
1 teaspoon prepared English mustard
salt and freshly ground black pepper
4 slices of bacon, cut into thin strips
2 gherkins, finely chopped
1 onion, peeled and finely chopped
2 tablespoons lard, butter or oil
2 cups stock or broth
1 bay leaf
3 juniper berries
½ cup sour cream

Lay the slices of meat between two sheets of dampened wax paper and pound each one with a meat mallet or rolling pin as thinly as possible. Remove from the paper, then spread each one thinly with mustard and sprinkle with salt and pepper.

Mix together the bacon, gherkins and onion, then cover about two-thirds of each slice of meat with the mixture. Roll up the meat and secure with wooden toothpicks or tie with fine string.

Heat the fat in a large heavy pan. Put in the 'olives' and brown them well on all sides for 10 minutes. Pour on the stock, add the bay leaf and juniper berries, cover and simmer gently for 1¼ hours. Take out the meat, put on a heated serving plate, remove the toothpicks or string and keep the meat warm. Reduce the liquid in the pan over high heat by about half, strain, then stir in the sour cream and reheat slowly; do not let it boil. Season to taste with salt and pepper and pour into a sauce boat.

Serve the 'olives' with macaroni or noodles and a green salad, or boiled potatoes and a green vegetable.

Steak tartare

Serves 1

¼ lb beef round steak, very finely
    ground
salt and freshly ground black pepper
1 tablespoon vodka
1 egg yolk
6 anchovy fillets, soaked, drained
    and finely chopped
1 tablespoon chopped parsley
1 tablespoon chopped ripe olives
1 tablespoon chopped dill pickle
1 tablespoon chopped cooked beet
1 tablespoon chopped onion
1 tablespoon chopped red pepper

Season the steak well and mix with
the vodka. Shape into a mound in
the center of a large serving plate
and place the egg yolk in the center
as for Steak tartare with herbs (see
below). Arrange the chopped
ingredients in little piles around the
meat. Serve with wholewheat or
pumpernickel bread and mix the
meat with any of the
accompaniments to taste.

Steak tartare with herbs

Serves 1

¼ lb beef round steak, very finely
    ground
salt and freshly ground black pepper
pinch of paprika
1 tablespoon grated onion
1 teaspoon chopped capers
1 teaspoon chopped mixed herbs
1 teaspoon oil
dash of Worcestershire sauce
1 egg yolk

Season the steak well with salt,
pepper and paprika. Add the onion,
capers, herbs, oil and
Worcestershire sauce and mix well.
Shape into a mound on a serving
plate. Make a shallow depression in
the center of the mound with a
whole egg or the back of a spoon
and carefully slip the egg yolk into
this.
    Serve with thinly sliced, buttered
rye or wholewheat bread.

Chicken liver tartare

Serves 3–4

¼ cup butter
½ lb chicken livers, finely ground or
    chopped
2 teaspoons grated onion
1 apple, peeled, cored and finely
    diced
1 tablespoon Calvados or brandy
salt
pinch of dried thyme
pinch of dried marjoram

Melt the butter in a skillet. Add the
chopped liver and the onion and fry
gently for about 2 minutes, stirring
constantly until just cooked. Allow
to cool.
    Mix the apple into the liver
mixture, together with the Calvados
or brandy. Season to taste with salt
and the herbs.
    Spoon into individual dishes and
chill; serve with hot toast.

Note For a milder onion flavor, cook
it in the butter by itself for a while
before adding the liver to the pan.

Roasted and Broiled Meat

Chateaubriand

Serves 2

1 (1-lb) beef tenderloin,
  chateaubriand
2 tablespoons oil
freshly ground black pepper
2 tablespoons butter

Rub the beef well with the oil.
Cover and let it stand for 1 hour at
room temperature. Then rub over it
with pepper. Brown it quickly to
seal the meat in a skillet for 5
seconds, without adding any fat.
Remove and set the meat aside.

Heat the butter in the skillet, put
back the meat and fry for 4–5
minutes on each side. The outside
should be brown and crisp, the
inside remaining bright pink and
tender. Do not season the meat
after frying it but let it rest in a
warm place for 5 minutes before
serving. Slice diagonally and arrange
on a warmed serving plate.

The classic accompaniment is
Béarnaise sauce (page 122).

Chateaubriand bordelaise

Serves 2

2 tablespoons butter
2 shallots, peeled and chopped
½ clove of garlic, peeled and crushed
5 peppercorns, crushed
½ bay leaf, crumbled
½ teaspoon dried thyme
1 cup red wine
salt
2 oz fresh beef marrow, wiped
  (optional)
1 (1-lb) beef tenderloin,
  chateaubriand
freshly ground black pepper
¼ cup oil

Heat the butter in a skillet, add the
shallots and garlic and fry till golden
brown. Add the peppercorns, bay
leaf, thyme and wine, and bring
to a boil. Cook rapidly until reduced
by about two-thirds. Season to taste
with salt.

Meanwhile cut the beef marrow, if
using, into six slices and blanch
them in boiling water. Drain well,
then finely chop two of the slices.

Strain the sauce from the pan and
mix in the sliced marrow. Set aside

in a warm place.

Gently press out the beef with the
ball of your hand; score the fat with
a knife and rub well with pepper.
Sear it in a hot heavy skillet,
without adding any fat, for 3
seconds on each side, then remove
from the skillet.

Heat the oil in the same skillet
and use to fry the meat quickly for 2
minutes on each side to brown and
crisp the outside but still leaving the
inside a rosy pink. Season with salt,
leave for 3 minutes, then slice
diagonally and arrange on a warmed
serving plate. Heat the marrow
slices in the sauce and arrange them
on top of the meat; serve the rest of
the sauce separately.

Stuffed filet mignon

Serves 4

8 (3–4 oz) filets mignon
2 oz (about ¼ cup) smooth liver
  sausage
1 tablespoon brandy
1 tablespoon green peppercorns,
  drained and chopped
2 fresh sage leaves, finely chopped or
  pinch of dried sage
4 thin slices of bacon
3 tablespoons oil
2 tablespoons butter
salt and freshly ground black pepper

Pound the steaks until thin. Cream
the liver sausage with the brandy
and stir in the peppercorns and sage.
Spread this mixture over four of the
steaks, lay each of the remaining
four on top and press gently
together. Wrap a bacon slice around
each steak "sandwich" then tie with
fine string.

Heat the oil and butter in a
skillet, put in the steaks and brown
for 1 minute on each side over high
heat. Lower the heat and cook them
for 2–3 minutes on each side,
according to how well done you like

your meat. Season with salt and
pepper and serve at once.

Suitable accompaniments are
lamb's lettuce (corn salad) tossed in
vinaigrette, or green beans or
broccoli plus little potato pancakes
or croquette potatoes.

Filet mignon with tomatoes and shallot sauce

Serves 4

4 (4–6 oz) filets mignon
3 shallots, peeled and finely chopped
¼ cup butter
1 tablespoon red wine or sherry
  vinegar
½ cup dry white wine
¼ cup sour cream
salt and pepper
2 cloves of garlic, peeled and finely
  chopped or crushed
2 cups peeled, deseeded and finely
  chopped ripe tomatoes
1 tablespoon chopped fresh or
  1 teaspoon dried basil
3 tablespoons oil
freshly ground black pepper
sprigs of fresh basil to garnish
  (optional)

Wipe the steaks and press into shape
with the ball of the hand. Cook the
shallots till transparent but not
browned in half the butter. Add the
vinegar and wine, stir in the cream
and reduce the sauce over high heat
to a creamy consistency. Season to
taste with salt and pepper.

Cook the garlic and tomatoes in
1 tablespoon of the remaining butter
for 2–3 minutes, then add the basil
and salt and pepper to taste and
keep warm.

In a skillet heat the oil with the
rest of the butter. Put in the steaks
and brown them 2–3 minutes on
either side. Season them with salt
and black pepper and serve with the
tomatoes and the shallot sauce.
Garnish with sprigs of fresh basil, if
available.

Variation
Instead of the tomatoes and shallot
sauce serve the filets with a white
wine sauce and garnish with a slice
of truffle.

Roasted and Broiled Meat

Broiled steaks

Broiled steaks should be served as soon as they are cooked so prepare any sauces or accompaniments ahead so that they are ready at the same time as the meat. Season the meat with a little salt just before serving.

Marinating steaks before they are cooked helps to tenderize them and give them a special flavor. The marinade liquid can then be turned into a sauce to serve with the steak, or reserved for adding to gravy, soups or stews. As long as the basis of a marinade comprises oil with vinegar, lemon juice or wine you can experiment to produce endless combinations of delicious flavors.

Types of steak

T-bone steak Taken from the center of the short loin. It comes with a bone, shaped like a 'T', hence its name, and includes a piece of tenderloin. It may be cut to serve 2 or as a large individual steak.

Porterhouse steak This steak is cut from the larger end of the short loin, giving a large succulent piece that can weigh 3 lb.

Filet mignon is a small and tender cut from the tenderloin.

Chateaubriand steak This is cut from the center of the tenderloin. It is usually large enough to serve 2.

Sirloin steaks are named according to the shape of the bone they contain: wedge bone, round bone, flat bone, pin bone and shell. They weigh 3–4½ lb, and will serve 4–5. Boneless sirloin is cut from nearest the rump of the round.

Top round steak, if of good quality, can be broiled. It usually weighs 1½–2½ lb.

Rib steaks, with or without bone, are cut 1-inch thick, the best being from near the short loin. Rib eye or Delmonico steaks are cut across the grain from the center of the rib roast.

Top loin, or club, steaks have no tenderloin and weigh 8–12 oz, serving 1–2.

Tips for cooking steaks

Steaks taste better if left to rest for a few minutes in a warm place before serving as this allows the juices to permeate the meat. Cooking times are always calculated in minutes. The broiler must be heated long enough to have reached its maximum heat when the meat is put on. The thinner the steak, the nearer it should be to the heat source. Meat broiled on a charcoal fire tastes the best, and the wood from fruit trees or vines gives the best aroma. But this type of grilling is not available for most of us, so ordinary charcoal or briquettes have to suffice. An equally irresistible aroma can be achieved by sprinkling sprigs of herbs like rosemary, bay or juniper over the fire, or even spoonfuls of mixed dried herbs.

Broiling times for steaks

The length of cooking time is dependent on the thickness of the steak, rather than the type, and the degree to which you like your meat cooked: rare, medium rare or well done, are the usual terms, although even these are somewhat arbitrary. The table below will give a rough guide. All the times are given in minutes.

Thickness	Rare	Medium Rare	Well Done
¾ in	5	9–10	12–15
1 in	7	12	15–18
1½ in	10	15	18–20

The times given are total cooking times. It is best to broil the meat close to the heat on either side for 1–2 minutes according to thickness and to finish further away. It must be stressed that the times can only be approximate because the quality and thickness of the meat, personal taste and the strength of the broiler all play a part. It is best, therefore, to begin testing the meat a couple of minutes before the estimated cooking time is up.

Accompaniments for broiled steaks

Béarnaise sauce (page 122) or a pat of Maître d'hôtel (parsley) butter put on top are traditional accompaniments. Other delicious accompaniments are matchstick or French fried potatoes, broiled tomatoes and mushrooms, or green or mixed salad.

Marinades for steaks

Basic marinade Mix equal parts of wine or vermouth and olive oil and flavor as required with lemon juice and crushed garlic. Put the meat in the marinade, cover and place in the refrigerator for 6–24 hours, turning the meat from time to time. Drain the meat well, and dry with paper towels before broiling. Use for all small steaks.

Wine marinade Mix 2½ cups red wine with 6 tablespoons lemon juice or vinegar, 6 tablespoons olive oil, 2 peeled, chopped onions, 2 peeled, diced carrots, a few peppercorns, 1 crumbled bay leaf, 2 tablespoons chopped parsley and a sprig of thyme. Particularly good for large steaks. Marinate and drain as above.

Spicy marinade Mix together 6 tablespoons tomato juice, 6 tablespoons red wine and 6 tablespoons olive oil. Add 3 peeled, chopped cloves of garlic, 2 deseeded, chopped fresh chili peppers, 1 teaspoon sugar and 2 tablespoons soy sauce. Thin steaks need 30–60 minutes only in this marinade; large ones should be left for up to 6 hours in the refrigerator. Drain as above.

Roasted and Broiled Meat

Austrian boiled beef

Serves 4

1½ quarts salted water
1 (2-lb) piece corned beef brisket
1 onion, peeled and halved
1 bay leaf
1 teaspoon white peppercorns
1 large carrot, peeled and chopped
2 stalks celery, washed and chopped

Bring the water to a boil in a deep pan. Put in the beef and let it come back to a boil before putting in the onion, bay leaf and peppercorns. Cover and simmer for 30 minutes; add the carrot and celery and cook 1½ hours or until the meat is tender.

Remove the meat and let it rest for a few minutes in a warm place before carving and arranging on a hot serving platter. Serve with boiled potatoes, tossed in parsley, as well as apple and horseradish sauce and chive sauce (recipes below).

Note Extra vegetables can be added to the pan towards the end of cooking and served with the meat. Diced potatoes may also be cooked in the meat broth.

Chive sauce

Serves 4

3 slices of bread, crusts removed
½ cup hot milk
2 hard-cooked eggs, shelled
2 teaspoons prepared English
    mustard
6 tablespoons oil
salt
sugar
about 2 tablespoons lemon juice or
    vinegar
3 tablespoons finely chopped chives

Soak the bread in the hot milk for 10 minutes. Squeeze it dry then sieve, blend or process with the hard-cooked eggs. Stir in the mustard, then beat in the oil, drop by drop, to make a thick mayonnaise-like sauce. Season with salt, sugar and lemon juice or vinegar to taste, then stir in the chives.

Apple and horseradish sauce

Serves 4

3 tablespoons prepared horseradish
2 tablespoons broth, reserved from
    cooking the beef
3 tablespoons corn oil
1 teaspoon sugar
salt
1 small tart apple, cored and grated

Add the horseradish to the hot broth and reheat but do not let it boil. Remove from the heat and cool, then whisk in the oil, drop by drop, to make a thick sauce. Season to taste with the sugar and salt. Add the freshly grated apple just before serving. Pass separately with the boiled beef. If a smooth sauce is preferred, purée in a blender or food processor before serving.

Vitello tonnato

Serves 4

1 (2-lb) boneless veal leg sirloin or
    rump roast, rolled and tied
2 cups dry white wine
2 cups water
1 onion, peeled and chopped
1 carrot, peeled and chopped
1 stalk celery, with leaves, chopped
1 bay leaf
sprig of tarragon (optional)
5 peppercorns
2 cloves
salt

Sauce
1 (7-oz) can tuna in oil, drained
4 anchovies, drained
¼ cup olive oil
1 egg yolk
1 tablespoon lemon juice
1 tablespoon capers, drained
salt and pepper

Put the veal into a deep pan with the wine and water. The meat must be completely covered by the liquid, so add more wine and water in equal quantities if necessary. Bring slowly to a boil, skim and then add the vegetables, herbs and spices. Season with salt, cover, reduce the heat and simmer for about 1½ hours or until the meat is tender.

Make the tuna sauce. Mash the tuna and anchovies together with 1 tablespoon oil. Beat in the egg yolk, then rub through a sieve. Stir in 1 teaspoon of the lemon juice, then add the rest of the oil, drop by drop, beating well after each addition. Alternatively put the fish, egg yolk, and 1 tablespoon of oil in a blender or food processor and work until smooth, then add the lemon juice and oil as above. When thick, like mayonnaise, stir in about 2 tablespoons of the cooled veal broth to give a pouring consistency. Add the capers, seasoning and lemon juice to taste.

Drain the meat, allow to cool and carve into slices. Arrange on a serving platter. Pour over the sauce, cover with foil and chill at least 30 minutes before serving with a green salad.

Roasted and Broiled Meat

Chicken liver kabobs

Serves 4–6

1 lb chicken livers
¼ lb thin slices of bacon
16 button mushrooms, wiped
8 shallots, peeled and halved
freshly ground black pepper
¼ cup butter
1 tablespoon flour
¾ cup hot water, stock or broth
3 tablespoons sherry
½ cup heavy cream
2 tablespoons tomato paste
dash of Worcestershire sauce
salt

Rinse the livers under cold running water, then dry them with paper towels. Cut them into bite-sized pieces, if necessary, and wrap them in the bacon. Thread these packages and the mushrooms and shallots alternately onto small skewers and season well with pepper. Melt the butter in a large skillet and fry the kabobs all over for 8 minutes, then take them out of the pan and keep warm.

Add the flour to the juices in the skillet and stir well. Add the hot water or stock, sherry and cream and bring to a boil, stirring constantly. Add the tomato paste and Worcestershire sauce and season to taste. Pour into a sauceboat and serve immediately.

Plain boiled rice or ribbon noodles and a green salad go well with these kabobs.

Beef olive kabobs

Serves 4

4 thin slices of beef top round steak
2 teaspoons strong prepared mustard
8 thin slices of bacon
12 small onions, peeled and halved
3 green or red peppers, deseeded and cut in large chunks
2 tablespoons oil
1 teaspoon celery salt
1 teaspoon paprika
pinch cayenne

Lay the slices of beef on your work surface. Spread them with mustard and then cover each one with two slices of bacon. Roll up the beef, then cut each roll into six equal pieces. Preheat the broiler

Thread 8 small skewers with three pieces of beef roll each, alternating the meat with the onions and peppers. Mix the oil, celery salt, paprika and cayenne together, lay the skewers across the broiler rack and brush them all over with the oil mixture. Place the rack with the kabobs in the broiler pan and cook for about 15 minutes or until browned all over.

As soon as they are cooked, serve with noodles in tomato sauce and a mixed salad, or a sauce made by dissolving the meat juices in the pan over the heat in equal quantities of stock and wine, then thickening it with a little cream.

Tip Soak wooden kabob skewers for at least 45 minutes in cold water before use to stop charring.

Roasted and Broiled Meat

Liver Berlin-style

Serves 4

½ cup butter
*2 tart apples, peeled, cored and cut
    into ¼-in thick rings*
*4 medium-size onions, peeled and cut
    into rings*
1 lb lamb liver, thinly sliced
2 tablespoons flour
salt and freshly ground black pepper

Heat 2 tablespoons of the butter in a
skillet, put in the apple rings and
cook until golden brown on both
sides — about 2–3 minutes. Remove
them from the pan and keep warm.

Add another 2 tablespoons butter
to the skillet, put in the onions and
cook till a crisp brown, turning them
frequently, then take out and keep
warm.

Meanwhile lightly dust the liver
with the flour. Heat the rest of the
butter in another skillet. Quickly fry
the liver on both sides (about 2–4
minutes each side). It should still be
light pink inside. Season with salt
and pepper to taste and serve at
once, topped with the hot apple and
onion rings. Pour over any pan
juices and serve with mashed
potatoes and a green salad with a
herby dressing.

Turkey breast
with fruity curry sauce

Serves 4

*4 (6-oz) slices of turkey breast,
    thawed if frozen*
6 tablespoons butter
salt and white pepper
*1 (16-oz) can fruit cocktail, drained
    and syrup reserved*
juice of ½ lemon
1 teaspoon honey
1–2 tablespoons curry powder
sprigs of parsley to garnish

Dry the turkey slices thoroughly
with paper towels. Heat the butter
in a skillet, put in the turkey slices
and cook for about 2 minutes on
each side until just cooked through.
Remove them from the skillet,
season with salt and pepper to taste
and keep warm.

Add the fruit cocktail to the juices
in the skillet and cook them quickly
over high heat for about a minute to
warm through. Stir in the lemon
juice, honey and curry powder,
moisten with some of the reserved
syrup, then simmer for 2 minutes.

Check the seasoning, then pour
over the turkey slices and garnish
with parsley. Serve with boiled rice
and a salad.

Tip A few drops of wine vinegar and
a liberal amount of finely chopped
dill added at the end impart a
subtle, sweet-sour flavor to the
sauce.

Roasted and Broiled Meat

Chops with cheese sauce

Serves 4

4 pork or veal chops
salt and pepper
1 tablespoon paprika
2 tablespoons olive oil
2 tablespoons butter
½ cup dry white wine
1 tablespoon brandy
*1 (3-oz) package cream cheese with
    herbs, cut into pieces*
¾ cup sour cream
*2 tablespoons chopped fresh mixed
    herbs*

Season the chops with salt and
pepper then dust lightly with
paprika; rub this in well.

Heat the oil and butter together in
a skillet till hot, put in the chops,
two at a time if necessary, and cook
gently for about 8 minutes on each
side until cooked through. Remove
from the pan to a hot plate and
keep warm.

Dissolve the juices in the pan over
a moderate heat in the wine and boil
rapidly until reduced by half. Add
the brandy, cheese and cream and
stir until the cheese has melted; do
not let it boil. Pour over the chops,
then sprinkle with the herbs.

Serve with tender young
vegetables or with a vegetable purée
for a change.

Cheesy stuffed meatballs

Serves 4

1 lb ground beef
1 onion, peeled and finely chopped
*1 clove of garlic, peeled and finely
    chopped*
1 teaspoon chopped dill
2 tablespoons chopped parsley
2 tablespoons chopped mint
3 cups soft breadcrumbs
1 egg plus 1 egg yolk
salt and freshly ground black pepper
pinch of cayenne
*2 (3-oz) packages cream cheese, cut
    into ¾-in cubes*
oil for deep frying

In a large bowl or a food processor,
combine the beef, onion, garlic,
herbs, half the breadcrumbs, the egg
and yolk till smooth. Season to taste
with salt, pepper and cayenne.

Shape the meat mixture into 2-in
balls. Press into the center of each
one a cube of cheese, making sure it
is completely enclosed. Roll the
balls in the remaining breadcrumbs,
pressing them on lightly with a
palette knife.

Heat the oil till hot (375°) and fry
the meatballs, a few at a time, for 5
minutes till crisp and brown. Lift out
and drain on paper towels. Serve
them hot or cold, with a mixed or
potato salad.

Cook's Tip

When making meatballs or burgers
wet your hands under the tap before
handling the meat. This will prevent
the meat sticking to your hands and
make it easier to shape.

Roasted and Broiled Meat

Spit-roasted stuffed pork

Serves 6

1 (3-lb) piece fresh pork side
salt and freshly ground black pepper
2 tablespoons oil
1 tablespoon paprika
1 teaspoon dried rosemary
pinch of garlic salt

Stuffing

2 onions, peeled and finely chopped
1 clove of garlic, peeled and finely
  chopped
1 green pepper, deseeded and finely
  chopped
¾ cup finely diced cooked ham
2 tablespoons chopped parsley
1 bay leaf, crushed

Trim any surplus fat from the meat.
Flatten it out a little with a rolling
pin or meat mallet. Rub over with
salt and pepper. Preheat the
rotisserie.

Mix all the stuffing ingredients
together. Spread this evenly over the
meat, leaving a 2-inch border at the
end nearest you. Roll up the meat
starting at the far end and secure
with wooden toothpicks or skewers,
then tie with fine string.

Mix together the oil, remaining
flavorings and a little salt to a thick
paste and rub this into the outside of
the meat roll. Thread it onto the
rotisserie spit and place under the
heat. Cook for 1 hour 20 minutes till
a crisp brown all over and cooked
through, brushing it from time to
time with the juices in the pan
underneath. Alternatively cook in a
preheated 400° oven for 1 hour then
reduce the temperature to 350° and
cook for a further hour. Baste as
above. Remove the meat from the
spit or the oven, let it rest in a warm
place for a few minutes, then slice it
thickly. Serve with potato salad
made with plenty of fresh herbs, and
radishes.

Variations
Use any of the following to replace
the ham and pepper stuffing:

Blue cheese creamed with freshly
chopped herbs.

Small cubes of white bread, soaked
in seasoned beaten egg, with
chopped cooked ham and plenty of
chopped parsley.

Plenty of freshly chopped herbs
mixed with crushed green
peppercorns, grated apple and sifted
or finely chopped hard-cooked egg
yolk.

Finely chopped garlic mixed with
chopped sage and finely chopped
scallions.

Tip Other suitable cuts for cooking
by the rotisserie method are pork
tenderloin, boneless veal leg sirloin
(cooking time about 35 minutes),
boneless rack of lamb (30 minutes),
or beef tenderloin (this is best when
rubbed with oil and left to marinate
for about 5 hours before cooking
with a very moist stuffing). Any of
the above stuffings may be used with
the meat of your choice.

Roasted and Broiled Meat

Broiled veal or pork chops

Serves 4

4 veal or pork chops
3 tablespoons butter, melted
paprika
salt and freshly ground black pepper
extra butter or oil for greasing
4 sprigs of rosemary
4 sprigs of thyme

Preheat the broiler. Flatten the chops a little with a rolling pin or meat mallet. Brush the melted butter thinly over the chops, then sprinkle them with the seasonings.

Grease the broiler rack with a little butter or oil and arrange the herbs on it. Lay the chops on top and cook under the broiler, brushing frequently with melted butter. After about 6 minutes, turn the chops over and brush again with more melted butter. Cook for a further 5 minutes or until cooked through.

Tip If you want to barbecue the chops, remember that the barbecue temperature cannot be controlled as precisely as a conventional broiler. Brush over the bars of the rack as well as the meat with oil as this doesn't burn as readily as butter. The chops can also be basted with butter during the last few minutes cooking to give them a special buttery flavor. Before you start cooking on the barbecue, make sure it has reached the right heat: there should be no red flames and the briquettes should be covered with a layer of white ash.

Spicy lamb chops

Serves 4

12 small lamb chops, trimmed
2 tablespoons olive oil
3 tablespoons tomato paste
1 teaspoon dried marjoram
pinch of powdered cinnamon
pinch of ground cloves
salt

Marinade
1 cup red wine
¼ cup olive oil
4 cloves of garlic, peeled and finely crushed
8 peppercorns, crushed
1 bay leaf, crumbled
1 teaspoon dried rosemary

Put all the marinade ingredients in a large non-metallic bowl and mix together. Put in the chops, cover and marinate in the refrigerator overnight. If the chops are not covered completely by the liquid, turn them occasionally.

Preheat the broiler. Drain the chops and dry them carefully on paper towels. Mix the remaining oil with the tomato paste, marjoram, spices and salt and brush over the chops on both sides. Lay them on an oiled broiler rack and cook under the heated broiler for 4–5 minutes on each side. Season with salt just before serving with hot garlic bread, and a tomato, cucumber and pepper salad in a yogurt or lemon dressing.

Note These chops can also be barbecued. If you like the flavor and smell of rosemary, marjoram or sage, then sprinkle more of these herbs into the barbecue fire: the rising smoke gives off a wonderful aroma that pervades the chops.

Spit-roast garlic chicken

Serves 4

½ cup olive oil
¼ cup lemon juice
1 teaspoon salt
10 cloves of garlic, peeled and crushed
1½ cups chopped parsley
2 (2-lb) dressed broiler-fryers, thawed if frozen
6 tablespoons butter, well chilled

Mix together the oil, lemon juice, salt and garlic; finely chop half of the parsley and add to the garlic mixture.

Put each chicken on a piece of foil large enough to enclose it, then rub with the garlic oil. Wrap them up in the foil and leave to marinate for 10 minutes.

Preheat the rotisserie. Open up the packages, and carefully wipe off the oil with paper towels. Push half of the butter, cut up in little pieces, under the skin of each chicken breast without breaking the skin; divide up the rest of the parsley and put a little inside each chicken.

Thread the birds onto the spit, fastening the wings and legs with wooden toothpicks or skewers and the fold of the skin at the neck. Cook for 40–45 minutes under the heated rotisserie, turning and basting them from time to time with the juices in the pan underneath.

When cooked, remove the birds from the spit, cut in half and remove the parsley. Serve with boiled rice, mixed with chopped dill or parsley, plus sautéed onions and a salad.

Tip Blisters sometimes form on the poultry skin during cooking, especially if the birds are too near the heat. Don't make the mistake of pricking these blisters as this will cause the juices to run out; instead brush them with a little melted fat.

Heartwarming
Casseroles

Casseroles

Pork and orange stew

Serves 6

2 tablespoons butter
2 lb lean boneless pork, cut into bite-
    sized pieces
½ lb shallots or pearl onions, peeled
    and finely chopped
grated rind of 1 orange
¾ cup fresh orange juice
¼ cup dry sherry
salt and pepper
small pinch of sugar
1 bay leaf
1 teaspoon cornstarch, dissolved in a
    little cold water (optional)
¾ cup light cream
1 orange, peeled, white pith removed
    and cut into segments

Preheat the oven to 350°.

Heat the butter in a flameproof
casserole, put in the meat, a third at
a time, brown quickly and remove.
Add the shallots or onions to the
casserole and brown them all over,
then put back the meat and stir in
the orange rind and juice and
sherry. Season with plenty of salt,
pepper and the sugar. Add the bay
leaf, cover and cook in the heated
oven for 1½ hours or till tender.
Remove the bay leaf. If necessary,
thicken the liquid with the
cornstarch and adjust the seasoning.
Stir in the cream.

Put the orange segments into the
stew and heat through. Serve
immediately, with noodles lightly
fried in butter, or boiled rice mixed
with cooked peas.

Tip Blood oranges, although not
available all year around, do give a
very special flavor and appearance
to the sauce. If you like a strongly
flavored stew, add some green
peppercorns.

Yugoslavian meat medley

Serves 4

½ lb beef for stew
½ lb pork for stew
½ lb lamb for stew
6 tablespoons olive oil
2 onions, peeled and chopped
2 cloves of garlic, peeled and crushed
1 small red pepper, deseeded and
    diced
1 small green pepper, deseeded and
    diced
1 small eggplant, diced
1½ lb ripe tomatoes, peeled and
    chopped
salt and pepper
paprika
¼ lb green beans, trimmed and cut
    into 2-inch pieces
1 cup shelled peas, fresh or frozen
½ lb zucchini, trimmed and diced

Preheat the oven to 350°.

Cut the meats into bite-sized
pieces. Grease inside a large
casserole with half the oil and put in
the meats, onions, garlic, peppers,
eggplant and tomatoes. Season with
plenty of salt, pepper and paprika
and pour over the rest of the oil.
Cover, place in the heated oven and
cook for 1½ hours or till the meat is
tender, if necessary adding a little
water to prevent the meat sticking.
Add the green beans, peas and
zucchini for the last 20 minutes of
the cooking time. Serve immediately
with crusty bread.

Variations
To the above ingredients, add ½ cup
long-grain rice together with
6 tablespoons each stock or broth
and wine or equal quantities of wine
and tomato juice. Or make with
lamb only and include ½ lb okra.

Try making it with veal only, with
tomatoes and peas but omitting the
eggplant and zucchini, and adding
instead ½ lb seedless grapes.

Cook's Tip

Casseroles and stews may be cooked
on top of the stove as well as in the
oven. It is important to use a thick-
based flameproof casserole or
saucepan with a heavy close-fitting
lid. Enamelled cast iron is ideal as it
ensures even distribution of the heat
and can be used to seal the meat
before the liquid is added. When
casseroling on top of the stove make
sure that the heat is turned to the
lowest setting so that the liquid is
only just bubbling, otherwise the
meat may become toughened by too
rapid cooking.

Casseroles

Ratatouille

Serves 4

1 large eggplant, trimmed and thinly sliced
salt
¾ cup olive oil
1 large onion, peeled and sliced into rings
3 green peppers, deseeded and cut in strips
½ lb zucchini, sliced
1 (8-oz) can tomatoes, or 1 cup coarsely chopped, fresh tomatoes
3 large cloves of garlic, peeled and crushed
2 tablespoons Italian seasoning herbs

Place the eggplant slices in a colander, sprinkle with salt, place a plate on top and leave for 10 minutes. Rinse and pat dry with paper towels.

Heat 2 tablespoons of the oil in a large saucepan and add the vegetables in layers so there are two layers of each type. Season as you go with salt, garlic and herbs, sprinkling a little oil over each layer. Finish with a layer of eggplant and season only with salt; spoon over the rest of the oil. Bring to a boil, cover, reduce the heat and simmer for 45–60 minutes.

Ratatouille can be eaten by itself with crusty bread or served as an accompaniment to roast or broiled meats, fish or sausages.

Sausage goulash

Serves 4–6

½ lb knockwurst or frankfurters
½ lb bratwurst
¼ cup dry sherry
1 tablespoon Worcestershire sauce
1 tablespoon pickled green peppercorns, drained (optional)
¼ lb slab bacon, diced
1 large onion, peeled and chopped
1 clove of garlic, peeled and crushed
2 tablespoons paprika
1 (16-oz) can tomatoes
1 tablespoon tomato paste
salt
freshly ground black pepper
2 tablespoons chopped parsley
¾ cup sour cream (optional)

Cut each sausage in half. Put them in a bowl with the sherry, Worcestershire sauce and peppercorns, cover and marinate for 1 hour in the refrigerator.

Fry the bacon in a pan till the fat runs. Add the onion and garlic and fry rapidly till golden brown.

Drain the sausages and dry on paper towels. Add them to the onion in the pan with the paprika and cook for 1 minute. Stir in the tomatoes with their juice, tomato paste and seasoning to taste, cover and simmer for 15 minutes. Taste for seasoning, sprinkle with the parsley and serve with the cream spooned into the middle, if you like. Serve at once.

Variation
Curried sausages A few apple pieces can be added to the onion, and the goulash then flavored to taste with curry powder instead of the paprika, lemon juice, mango chutney and honey. For this version, substitute light cream for the sour cream.

Oxtail ragoût

Serves 4

$\frac{1}{4}$ lb slab bacon, diced
2 tablespoons butter
2$\frac{1}{2}$ lb oxtail sections
2 large onions, peeled and chopped
2–3 cloves of garlic, peeled and
  crushed
1 cup wiped and thinly sliced
  mushrooms
4 stalks of celery, trimmed and
  chopped
2 carrots, peeled and chopped
4 large tomatoes, peeled, deseeded
  and chopped
few sprigs of parsley, thyme or
  marjoram
salt and black pepper
1 teaspoon paprika
pinch of sugar
1 tablespoon brandy
1 cup dry white wine
2 cups hot stock or broth
$\frac{2}{3}$ cup light cream

Fry the bacon in a large flameproof
casserole. Add the butter to the
casserole, put in the oxtail pieces
and the onions and brown. Then
add the garlic, mushrooms, celery
and carrots and let them brown.
Add the tomatoes and the parsley,
thyme or marjoram, tied together.
Season to taste, add the paprika,
sugar, brandy, wine and stock.
Cover and simmer for about 2 hours
till the meat is just falling off the
bones.

   Remove the herbs. Reduce the
liquid by boiling over high heat till
thick and syrupy, stir in the cream
and serve immediately.

Heart ragoût

Serves 6

$\frac{1}{4}$ cup butter
2 lb lamb hearts, ducts and fat
  removed, and cut into bite-sized
  pieces
3 large onions, peeled and sliced into
  rings
1–2 cloves of garlic, peeled and
  crushed
1 small leek, trimmed, washed and
  cut into rings
2 carrots, peeled and cut into julienne
  strips
1–2 tablespoons flour
2 cups hot stock or broth
$\frac{1}{2}$ cup red wine
1 tablespoon tomato paste
1 cup peeled and chopped ripe
  tomatoes
salt and freshly ground black pepper
pinch of sugar
$\frac{1}{2}$ teaspoon dried thyme
$\frac{1}{2}$ teaspoon dried rosemary
2 gherkins, finely chopped
2 teaspoons capers, drained
$\frac{3}{4}$ cup light cream
1 tablespoon chopped chives to
  garnish

Heat the butter in a flameproof
casserole. Put in the pieces of heart
and sauté them quickly, then
remove and keep warm.

   Add all the vegetables, except the
tomatoes, and let them brown.
Return the meat to the pan, stir in
the flour and cook for about 1
minute till brown. Pour in the stock
and wine, stir in the tomato paste
and tomatoes, season to taste and
add the sugar and the herbs.

   Cover and simmer for about 50
minutes or until the heart is tender.
Stir in the gherkins, capers and
cream. Sprinkle with chives just
before serving accompanied by plain
boiled rice.

Casseroles

Cassoulet

Serves 6

1¾ cups dried navy beans, soaked
   overnight in cold water to cover
1 tablespoon Italian seasoning herbs
4 cloves of garlic, peeled and
   chopped
¼ cup lard or butter
½ lb slab bacon, cut into bite-sized
   pieces
1 lb boneless pork shoulder or fresh
   sides, cut into bite-sized pieces
2 onions, peeled and chopped
4 carrots, peeled and sliced
1 lb tomatoes, peeled and chopped
¼ cup chopped parsley
½ lb knockwurst, sliced
¾ cup red wine
salt and pepper

Drain the beans, then put in a pan
with fresh water to cover, add the
herbs and 2 chopped cloves of
garlic. Cover and simmer for 1 hour.
   Heat the lard or butter in a large
flameproof pan. Put in the meats
and brown them all over, then add
the onions and carrots with the
remaining garlic and fry for 5
minutes till browned. Stir in the
tomatoes and half the parsley and
cook gently for 30 minutes. Add the
sausage to the pan, together with
the wine and the bean mixture,
cover and simmer for 30 minutes.
Taste for seasoning.
   Chop the rest of the parsley and
sprinkle it over just before serving.

Chili con carne

Serves 4

1½ cups dried red kidney or pinto
   beans, soaked overnight in cold
   water to cover
¼ cup olive oil
1 lb lean ground beef
1 tablespoon paprika
½–1 teaspoon chili powder
4 onions, peeled and finely chopped
2 cloves of garlic, peeled and finely
   chopped
2 red or green chili peppers,
   deseeded and finely chopped,
   optional
2 carrots, peeled and diced
2 leeks, washed, trimmed and sliced
1½ lb tomatoes, peeled and chopped
   or 1 (16-oz) can tomatoes
1 beef bouillon cube
1 teaspoon dried thyme
3 bay leaves
salt

Drain the beans, cover with fresh
cold water, bring to a boil and cook
for at least 30 minutes. Set aside.
   Meanwhile, heat the oil in a deep
pan, put in the beef and cook till
lightly browned; sprinkle over the
paprika, with chili powder to taste.
Add the onion, garlic and chili
peppers if using and fry till golden
brown.
   Stir in the carrots, leeks, tomatoes
and beans with their cooking liquid;
crumble in the bouillon cube, add
the herbs, cover and simmer gently
for 35 minutes. Remove the bay
leaves and season to taste with salt.
   Serve immediately with crusty
French bread.

Country pork stew

Serves 4

1½ cups dried split peas, soaked
  overnight in cold water to cover
1 ham bone, rinsed (if available)
1 (¾-lb) piece fresh pork side
2 cloves of garlic, peeled and crushed
1 onion, peeled and chopped
1 cup red wine
1 large carrot, peeled and finely
  chopped
2 leeks, washed and finely sliced
salt and freshly ground black pepper

Drain the peas, cover with fresh
cold water and bring to a boil; cook
for 20 minutes then add the ham
bone, if using. Cook for 20 minutes
more.

Add the pork, garlic, onion and
wine, cover and cook gently for 20
minutes, then add the carrot and
leeks and cook for a further 20
minutes. Remove the ham bone.

Take out the pork and slice,
return the slices to the pot and
season with salt and pepper to taste.
Pour into a warmed casserole dish
and serve immediately.

Thick pea and pork hotpot

Serves 4

2 cups dried peas, soaked in cold
  water overnight
3 onions, peeled
4 cloves
1 bay leaf
2 tablespoons lard or butter
1 (1-lb) piece fresh pork side
2 carrots, peeled and diced
½ celeriac (celery root), peeled and
  diced
1 leek, trimmed, washed and sliced
salt
pinch of dried thyme
pinch of dried marjoram
2 tablespoons chopped parsley

Drain the peas, cover with fresh
cold water in a pan and bring to a
boil, together with 1 onion, stuck
with the cloves, and the bay leaf.
Cover, reduce the heat and simmer
for 30 minutes. Remove the onion
and bay leaf.

Meanwhile, heat the lard in a
large flameproof pan, put in the
pork and brown all over. Chop the
remaining onions, add to the pan
and fry till golden.

Add the peas with their cooking
liquid to the pan and cook for 15
minutes. Add the carrots and
celeriac and cook for 15 minutes,
then add the leek. Season to taste
with salt and the dried herbs and
cook for 15 minutes.

To serve: take out the pork and
carve into 4 slices. Sprinkle the
parsley over the pea and vegetable
mixture, put the pork slices on top
and serve immediately, with boiled
potatoes.

Casseroles

Veal and pepper stew

Serves 4

¼ cup lard or butter
1½ lb veal for stew, cut into
bite-sized pieces
3 large onions, peeled and sliced
1–2 cloves of garlic, peeled and
crushed
2 red peppers, deseeded and cut into
thick strips
2 cups peeled and coarsely chopped
ripe tomatoes
3 tablespoons paprika
1 tablespoon tomato paste
1 cup red wine
1 cup stock or broth
salt and freshly ground black pepper
pinch each of caraway seeds and
sugar
1½ cups peeled and diced potatoes
¾ cup sour cream to finish

Heat the lard in a flameproof
casserole, put in the meat and
brown all over. Remove and keep
warm. Add the onion, garlic and
peppers to the pan and fry till
browned. Put back the meat
together with the tomatoes, paprika
and tomato paste, and cook together

for a few seconds. Pour on the wine
and stock, season to taste, add the
caraway seeds and sugar and bring
to a boil.

Add the potatoes, cover, reduce
the heat to simmering point and
cook for 40–60 minutes till the meat
is tender. Spoon the sour cream
over the center just before serving.

Chicken curry

Serves 4–6

⅓ cup raisins
2 tablespoons sherry
1 (3-lb) dressed broiler-fryer
salt and freshly ground white pepper
1 teaspoon paprika
¼ cup butter
1 tablespoon oil
1 onion, peeled and chopped
1 apple, peeled, cored and diced
1–2 teaspoons honey
1–2 teaspoons curry powder to taste
2 cups chicken stock or broth
½ cup dry white wine
1 large banana, peeled and mashed
with 2 tablespoons lemon juice
¼ cup light cream
⅓ cup sliced blanched almonds,
toasted to garnish

Soak the raisins in the sherry for
about 30 minutes. Cut up the
chicken into 4 or 6 portions; sprinkle
all over with salt, pepper and
paprika.

Heat two-thirds of the butter with
the oil in a skillet and sauté the
chicken till golden brown.

Heat the remaining butter in the
skillet, add the onion and the apple
and cook gently till the onion is soft.
Stir in the honey and curry powder
to taste, then pour in the stock and
wine and the raisins in the sherry.
Add the chicken, cover and cook
gently for about 40 minutes till the
chicken is tender.

Remove the chicken portions.
Reduce the liquid in the skillet by
boiling hard for 10 minutes. Stir in
the banana mixture and cream.
Replace the chicken portions and
heat through gently. Serve with
boiled rice with a sprinkling of
almonds over the chicken.

Chicken fricassée

Serves 4

6 tablespoons butter
3 tablespoons flour
3 cups chicken stock or broth
¾ cup heavy cream
1 carrot, peeled and chopped
2 small parsnips, peeled and sliced
¼ lb shallots, peeled
¼ lb mushrooms, wiped
1 (3-lb) dressed broiler-fryer, cooked and boned
salt and pepper
grated rind of ½ lemon

Heat 2 tablespoons of the butter in a saucepan, stir in the flour to make a roux. Gradually add the stock, stirring continuously, then add the cream. Cook for 1 minute till thick. Reduce over high heat for 2 minutes.

Cook the carrot, parsnips and shallots in boiling salted water for 12 minutes, then drain and sauté them gently in half the remaining butter for 10 minutes.

In another pan, fry the mushrooms in the rest of the butter for 1–2 minutes.

Add the chicken meat and vegetables to the sauce. Season to taste and stir in the lemon rind. Serve immediately with boiled potatoes.

Veal fricassée

Serves 4

2 tablespoons butter
2 lb veal for stew, cut in bite-sized pieces
2 tablespoons flour
¾ cup dry white wine
2 cups white stock or broth
1 onion, peeled and stuck with 2 cloves
1 large carrot, peeled and chopped
1 stalk celery, wiped and sliced
1 bay leaf
1 sprig parsley
4 peppercorns

Dumplings
2 chicken breasts, boned and finely ground
2 tablespoons chopped parsley
1 egg yolk
2–3 tablespoons soft breadcrumbs
salt and pepper
grated nutmeg

To finish
¼ cup light cream
1 egg yolk
2 cups cooked peas
¼ lb cooked tongue, cut in strips

In a flameproof casserole heat the butter and sauté the veal until light golden. Sprinkle on the flour and stir, then stir in the wine and stock.

Add the onion, carrot, celery, bay leaf, parsley and peppercorns. Cover and cook for 50 minutes over a gentle heat.

For the dumplings, mix the ground chicken with the parsley, egg yolk, breadcrumbs and seasonings. Roll into walnut-sized pieces and simmer gently in salted water for 10 minutes. Drain well and set aside.

Remove the veal. Strain the sauce and reduce it by boiling hard. Mix together the cream and egg yolk, stir into the sauce and reheat until thickened, but do not boil. Season to taste. Return the meat, add the peas, tongue and dumplings and heat through. Serve with boiled rice.

Casseroles

Sliced bean hotpot

Serves 4–6

1 ($\frac{1}{2}$-lb) ham bone
2 quarts water
1 lb potatoes, peeled and roughly
* chopped*
1 lb green beans, trimmed and sliced
* diagonally*
salt
3 sprigs of savory or thyme
$\frac{1}{4}$ lb slab bacon, diced
1 large onion, peeled and chopped
freshly ground black pepper
$\frac{1}{2}$ teaspoon vinegar

Wash the ham bone, put it in a large pan with the water and bring to a boil. Reduce the heat, cover and simmer for 2 hours. Remove the bone.

Cook the potatoes in the broth till just soft. Cook the beans in boiling salted water for 5 minutes, then drain, rinse under cold running water and drain again.

Mash the cooked potatoes into the broth, then add the beans and the savory or thyme. Simmer for 15 minutes.

Meanwhile, fry the bacon till the fat runs, put in the onion and cook till golden brown. Season with salt and pepper to taste, and add the vinegar. Pour the potato and bean hotpot into a hot tureen, sprinkle over the bacon and onion mixture and serve at once.

Note A little light or sour cream may be stirred in just before serving.

Layered meat casserole

Serves 6

$\frac{1}{2}$ lb beef for stew
$\frac{1}{2}$ lb pork for stew
$\frac{1}{2}$ lb lamb for stew
$\frac{1}{2}$ lb veal for stew
1 medium-size celeriac (celery root),
* peeled and diced*
1 large onion, peeled and sliced
2 cups peeled and sliced carrots
1$\frac{1}{2}$ cups peeled and diced potatoes
3 cups shredded white cabbage
salt and pepper
grated nutmeg
dried marjoram
2 cups stock or broth
3 tablespoons chopped parsley to
* garnish*

Cut all the meats into bite-sized pieces and layer with vegetables in a large flameproof pan or casserole, seasoning each layer with salt, pepper, nutmeg and marjoram to taste.

Pour in the stock, cover and bring to a boil. Reduce the heat and simmer for about 1$\frac{1}{2}$ hours, or cook in a preheated 350° oven for about 2 hours.

Serve from the pan, sprinkled with chopped parsley.

Note If you like, flavor the casserole additionally with caraway seeds, bay leaf and/or lovage.

Spanish hotpot

Serves 6

¾ cup dried chickpeas (garbanzo
  beans), soaked overnight in cold
  water to cover
¼ cup olive oil
1 ham bone or beef marrowbone
3 cloves of garlic, peeled
1 small pig's foot (optional)
1 (¾-lb) piece boneless beef round
  steak
1 (½-lb) piece boneless lamb
1½ quarts water
2 carrots, peeled and cut into strips
2 leeks, trimmed, washed and cut
  into strips
1 onion, peeled and chopped
1 small celeriac (celery root), peeled
  and cut into strips
2 cups peeled and diced potatoes
2 large tomatoes, peeled and chopped
salt and pepper
1 bay leaf
¼ lb chorizo or knockwurst

To finish
2 tablespoons chopped parsley
1 small head of lettuce, shredded

Drain the chickpeas, rinse well, and
drain again. Heat the oil in a large
flameproof pan, add the ham bone
or marrowbone and garlic and
brown. Put in the pig's foot, if
using, with the meats and water and
bring to a boil slowly; cover, then
cook gently for 1 hour, skimming
from time to time.

Add the chickpeas to the pan and
cook for 30 minutes. Then add the
remaining vegetables and the
tomatoes, season with salt and
pepper to taste, add the bay leaf and
the sausage. Cook 25–30 minutes.

Take out all the meat, slice and
arrange on a warmed platter. Throw
away the bone and pig's foot. Boil
up the broth again, add the parsley
and lettuce and cook for 1 minute.
Check the seasoning. Serve the
broth separately in a hot tureen with
the platter of meats.

Cook's Tip

If you do not have time to soak the
chickpeas try substituting canned
chickpeas. These should be drained
and added to the hotpot towards the
end of the cooking time. Other
types of canned pulses, such as
cannellini beans, could be used
instead.

Casseroles

Casseroled duck with cabbage

Serves 4

2 tablespoons oil
4 duck portions, thawed if frozen
salt and black pepper
½ small white cabbage (about ¾ lb),
   finely sliced
1 small bulb of fennel, trimmed and
   finely sliced
2 onions, peeled and finely sliced
2–3 cloves of garlic, peeled and
   crushed
pinch of dried marjoram
pinch of dried thyme
¼ cup white wine vinegar
¼ cup finely chopped Canadian bacon
   to garnish

Heat the oil in a skillet, put in the
duck portions and brown them all
over. Take them out and drain well
on paper towels. Sprinkle with salt
and pepper.
   Preheat the oven to 350°.
   Layer the vegetables and garlic in
a large casserole. Sprinkle with the
herbs then arrange the duck portions
on top. Pour the vinegar over the
duck, cover and cook in the heated

oven for 50–60 minutes till the duck
is tender.
   Fry the bacon until crisp and
sprinkle over the casserole just
before serving.

Osso buco

Serves 4

2–3 cloves of garlic, peeled
salt
2 tablespoons butter
2 onions, peeled and finely chopped
2 carrots, peeled and finely chopped
5 stalks of celery, trimmed and finely
   diced
freshly ground black pepper
8 equal-sized pieces of veal shank
   (about 2 lb altogether)
2 tablespoons flour
3 tablespoons oil
¾ cup dry white wine
¾ cup strong stock or broth
¼ teaspoon dried basil
¼ teaspoon dried thyme
1 bay leaf
¼ cup chopped parsley
1 (8-oz) can tomatoes, drained and
   roughly chopped
grated rind of 1 lemon

Crush the garlic with a little salt and
set aside. Heat the butter in a large
flameproof casserole. Put in the
vegetables and brown lightly for
about 10 minutes, then remove from
the pan.
   Season the veal pieces with salt
and pepper and dip them in the
flour. Add the oil to the casserole,
put in the veal, a few pieces at a
time, and brown all over, adding a
little more oil if necessary. Remove
the veal and set aside.
   Dissolve the juices in the pan with
the wine, over high heat, then boil
hard to reduce the liquid by half.
Put back the veal, together with the
vegetables, stock, herbs, half of the
parsley and the tomatoes. Cover and
simmer for 1 hour till the veal is
tender.
   Mix the remaining parsley with
the lemon rind and sprinkle on top.
Serve immediately with risotto (page
163).

Veal or pork stroganoff

Serves 4–6

$\frac{1}{4}$ *cup butter*
2 tablespoons oil
1$\frac{1}{2}$ lb veal cutlets or pork tenderloin,
  cut into thin strips, about 1$\frac{1}{2}$-in
  long
2 shallots, peeled and finely chopped
$\frac{3}{4}$ *cup dry white wine*
$\frac{3}{4}$ *cup light or sour cream*
salt and pepper
1 tablespoon chopped parsley

Heat half the butter with 1
tablespoon oil in a large skillet. Put
in half of the meat and cook rapidly,
turning all the time, for 2 minutes.
Remove the meat and put in a
colander over a bowl to catch the
juices. Sauté the rest of the meat,
using the remaining butter and oil,
then drain as above.

Add the shallots to the skillet and
cook gently till soft but not
browned. Pour in the wine. Over
high heat, stir in the cream, with the
meat juices, and continue stirring
while reducing the liquid over a
moderate heat to about half its
original quantity.

Put the meat back in the skillet
and cook gently for about 3 minutes
to warm through. Season to taste
with salt and pepper and sprinkle
with parsley. Serve at once with
noodles or boiled rice.

Beef with wine and pepper sauce

Serves 4–6

$\frac{1}{4}$ *cup butter*
2 onions, peeled and sliced into rings
1 clove of garlic, peeled and crushed
1 red pepper, deseeded and cut into
  strips
1 green pepper, deseeded and cut
  into strips
2 large, ripe tomatoes, peeled,
  deseeded and sliced
salt and freshly ground black pepper
2 tablespoons oil
1 lb steak, cut into $\frac{1}{2}$-inch strips
$\frac{3}{4}$ *cup red wine*
3 tablespoons sour cream
2 sprigs of basil to garnish (optional)

Heat half the butter in a heavy stew
pan or flameproof casserole. Put in
the onion, garlic and peppers and
cook till the onion is soft and

transparent but not browned: Add
the tomatoes. Season with salt and
pepper, cover and cook gently for
10 minutes.

In a skillet, heat the oil with the
rest of the butter, put in the steak in
two batches, and sauté to seal for
1–2 minutes. Remove the meat and
place in a colander over a bowl to
catch any juices.

When all the meat has been
sautéed, dissolve the juices in the
skillet with the wine, then reduce
the liquid by boiling hard for
1 minute. Pour this over the
vegetables in the stew pan or
casserole, adding the juices from the
meat.

Bring the mixture to a boil, add
the meat and reheat gently but do
not boil. Remove from the heat,
check the seasoning, then stir in the
cream. Garnish with basil, if
available, and serve at once with
noodles or boiled rice.

Casseroles

Rabbit stew

Serves 4

3 tablespoons oil
2 cloves of garlic, peeled
2 tablespoons butter
4 large rabbit portions
¼ lb shallots or pearl onions, peeled
½ lb mushrooms, wiped
2 cups peeled and chopped ripe
    tomatoes
¾ cup dry white wine
1 chicken bouillon cube
1 teaspoon dried basil
1 tablespoon chopped parsley
salt
paprika

Heat the oil in a skillet and fry the garlic until golden, then remove and discard it.

Heat the butter in the oil, add the rabbit pieces and brown on all sides. Remove them and set aside.

Add the shallots or onions and mushrooms to the pan and cook for 2–3 minutes, then add the tomatoes, wine, crumbled bouillon cube and basil. Cook for 1–2 minutes.

Put the rabbit pieces into a large flameproof casserole, add the onion and mushroom mixture, cover and simmer for 25 minutes; add the parsley and cook for a further 15 minutes.

Remove the lid and reduce the liquid by boiling over high heat for about 5 minutes till it becomes syrupy. Season to taste with salt and paprika.

Serve immediately with paprika or saffron rice (page 150), or green noodles tossed with fried breadcrumbs and a seasonal salad with a sour cream or yogurt dressing.

Note The sauce can also have cream stirred into it to give it a creamy, glossy finish. Or a little sour cream can be spooned over the casserole just before serving.

Variations
Use two tablespoons dried mushrooms, soaked overnight, instead of fresh mushrooms to enrich the flavor. If the sauce needs thickening, stir in a little kneaded butter at the end. The white wine can be replaced by a full-bodied red wine to darken the stew and give it a more robust flavor.

Other additions to try Add thin rings of red or green pepper with the tomatoes, or stir in finely chopped gherkins and capers at the end. Or add frozen peas — put them in still frozen about 10 minutes before the end of the cooking time. Canned whole kernel corn is also tasty: just heat through in the stew for the last few minutes.

Jugged hare or rabbit

Serves 4

1 hare or rabbit, dressed, skinned
    and cut up
1 onion, peeled and sliced
2 cloves of garlic, peeled and crushed
1 carrot, scraped and diced
8 peppercorns
1 bay leaf
¾ cup red wine vinegar
2 cups red wine
¼ lb slices of bacon, diced
16 shallots or pearl onions, peeled
1 cup hot stock or broth
salt and freshly ground black pepper
2 sprigs of thyme
pinch of powdered cinnamon

Rinse the hare or rabbit pieces and place them in a large, non-metallic bowl. Cover them with the sliced onions, garlic, carrot, peppercorns and bay leaf. Mix together the vinegar and half the wine and pour this over the meat and vegetables. Cover and marinate for 12 hours in the refrigerator, turning the meat from time to time.

Fry the bacon in a flameproof casserole till the fat runs, then take it out and reserve. Drain the hare or rabbit portions and pat dry with paper towels. Put them in the pan and brown all over in the bacon fat. Then take out and add the shallots or pearl onions and brown them.

Return the meat to the pan, add the strained marinade, the stock and the rest of the wine, season with salt and pepper and add the thyme. Cover and simmer gently for 1 hour or till the meat is tender.

Remove the lid and reduce the liquid by about half by boiling hard. Return the bacon to the casserole and check the seasoning, then add the cinnamon. Serve at once with boiled potatoes.

Cook's Tip

For a thicker sauce, dust the hare or rabbit portions with flour after browning them so the flour soaks up some of the fat. Or, when the dish is done, add a little sour cream and reduce the sauce to a creamy consistency. You can also scatter over the pieces of cooked bacon after reheating them, or add chopped herbs at the end if you like.

Casseroles

Italian pork and cabbage casserole

Serves 6

6 large pork loin chops
2 tablespoons olive oil
½ cup dry white wine
1¼ cups hot stock or broth
1 lb carrots, peeled and sliced
3 stalks of celery, chopped
3 leeks, trimmed, washed and sliced
2 cloves of garlic, peeled and crushed
salt and freshly ground black pepper
1 lb garlic sausage
1 small white cabbage, shredded

Preheat the oven to 350°.

Trim any excess fat from the chops then rinse and pat dry with paper towels. Heat the oil in a large frying pan and fry the chops until browned on both sides. Do this in two batches, adding more oil if necessary.

Transfer the chops to a large ovenproof casserole and pour over the wine and stock. Add the carrots, celery, leeks and garlic and season to taste with a little salt and pepper. Cover the casserole with a tight fitting lid and cook in the moderate oven for 30–40 minutes.

Remove any skin from the garlic sausage and slice thickly. Add the garlic sausage with the shredded cabbage to the casserole and return it to the oven for a further 20 minutes or until the cabbage is tender but not unpleasantly soft. Alternatively put the whole garlic sausage in with the cabbage and remove and slice it just before serving.

Serve piping hot with crispy French bread or oven-baked potatoes.

Variations
A bay leaf and some chopped mixed herbs such as sage or thyme go very well with this casserole. Or for a more unusual subtle flavour add the grated rind of half an orange with the stock and wine.

Cook's Tip

When frying meat that is to be casseroled it is important to have the fat hot so that the outside of the meat browns quickly, sealing in the juices. This will help to keep the meat tender and moist and also give the gravy a good flavor and color. Pork chops can additionally be browned along the edge by holding each chop in turn on its side until the fat colors.

Irish stew

Serves 6

2 lb potatoes, peeled and sliced
4 large onions, peeled and sliced
12 lamb shoulder neck slices,
*   trimmed of fat*
salt and freshly ground black pepper
dried thyme
chopped parsley

Put alternate layers of potato, onion
and lamb slices in a deep saucepan,
seasoning as you go with salt,
pepper and thyme, and finishing
with a layer of onion and potatoes.
   Pour in enough water just to
cover the top layer of potatoes,
cover and simmer gently for 1½–2
hours. Add a few tablespoons of
boiling water from time to time to
prevent the stew from burning.
Sprinkle with chopped parsley just
before serving.

Polish hunter's hotpot

Serves 6

¼ lb slab bacon, chopped
1½ lb boneless pork shoulder, cut into
*   bite-sized pieces*
4 onions, peeled and finely chopped
4 cups shredded white cabbage
1 (16-oz) can sauerkraut, drained
*   and pulled apart with 2 forks*
1 cup peeled and chopped ripe
*   tomatoes*
2 cloves of garlic, peeled and crushed
*   with a little salt*
¾ oz dried mushrooms, soaked in
*   water for 2 hours, then drained*
salt
1 tablespoon paprika
1 teaspoon caraway seeds
1 teaspoon dried marjoram
4 bay leaves
1 cup stock or broth
½ lb kielbasa (Polish sausage), sliced

Preheat the oven to 350°.
   Fry the bacon in a large
flameproof casserole till the fat runs.
Add the pork with the onions and
brown all over.
   Add the cabbage, sauerkraut,
tomatoes, garlic and drained
mushrooms, stir well and season
with salt, paprika, caraway seeds
and herbs. Pour on the stock and lay
slices of sausage on top.
   Cover and cook for 1½ hours in
the heated oven, or till the meat is
tender. Remove the bay leaves
before serving.

Note This casserole makes a good
party dish. The dried mushrooms
can be replaced by ¼ lb fresh
mushrooms if liked. Serve with a
crisp salad to start with, and a light
dessert to follow.

Casseroles

Boeuf à la mode

Serves 8

1 (3-lb) boneless beef round rump
  roast, rolled and tied with string
¼ lb slices of bacon
1 lb shallots or pearl onions, peeled
salt and freshly ground black pepper
2 tablespoons brandy, warmed
  (optional)
1 bouquet garni
1 lb carrots, peeled and sliced

Marinade
2½ cups red wine
2 onions, peeled and chopped
2 carrots, peeled and sliced
2 cloves of garlic, peeled and crushed
2 bay leaves, crumbled
1 teaspoon dried thyme
¼ cup chopped parsley

Put the meat in a deep non-metallic
bowl, pour over the wine, then add
the rest of the marinade ingredients.
Cover and marinate for 12 hours in
the refrigerator, turning the meat
occasionally.

Set aside 2–3 bacon slices and
dice the rest. Fry the diced bacon in
a large heavy pan or flameproof
casserole until the fat runs. Remove
it and reserve (see *Tip*). Put in the
shallots or pearl onions and brown
them all over. Remove and put
them to one side.

Drain the meat, reserving the
marinade, and dry the meat
thoroughly with paper towels. Rub
over it with a little salt and pepper
then brown it in the remaining
bacon fat for about 15 minutes.
Take it out, pour off any fat
remaining, then line the botton of
the pot with the rest of the bacon
slices.

Put in the beef and heat till the
bacon slowly begins to cook. Flame
the brandy, if using, pour it over the
meat and let it burn itself out.

Add the strained marinade and
add enough water so that the liquid
three-quarters covers the beef. Add
the bouquet garni, cover with a lid
and simmer very gently for 2 hours.

Add the carrots and the browned
onions to the pan, cover, and
simmer gently for another hour.
Remove the pan or casserole from
the heat, take out the meat and let
it stand in a warm place for about 5
minutes. Then carve and arrange the
slices on a warm serving platter,
surrounded by the vegetables.

Strain the sauce, skimming off any
fat, bring to a boil and taste for
seasoning. Pour a little over the
meat and serve the rest separately.

Serve at once with boiled new
potatoes.

Tip Make this dish even more tasty
by warming up the reserved cooked
diced bacon at the end, browning it
with a little chopped garlic, then
scattering over the meat with
2 tablespoons chopped parsley.

Hungarian goulash

Serves 6

2 tablespoons lard or butter
1 large onion, peeled and finely
  chopped
2 lb beef for stew, cut into ¾-inch
  cubes
1 clove of garlic, peeled
1 teaspoon caraway seeds
salt
2 tablespoons paprika
2½ cups hot water
1 cup peeled and chopped tomatoes
2 green peppers, deseeded and cut
  into strips
2 cups peeled and diced potatoes

Heat the lard in a skillet, put in the
onion and cook till soft but not
colored. Put in the meat and brown
for 10 minutes, stirring all the time.

In a pestle and mortar or with a
rolling pin, pound the garlic with the
caraway seeds and a little salt. Mix
with the paprika and stir into the
meat mixture over medium heat
until well combined. Add the hot
water, bring to a boil and simmer
very gently for 1 hour.

Add the tomatoes, the strips of
pepper and the diced potato. Cook
for a further hour, then check the
seasoning.

Serve very hot with small pasta
shapes.

German mixed-meat hotpot

Serves 6

½ lb beef for stew
½ lb veal for stew
½ lb pork for stew
2 onions, peeled and chopped
2 tablespoons lard or butter
1 cup peeled and chopped tomatoes
1 green pepper, deseeded and diced
1 tablespoon paprika
salt
8 peppercorns, crushed
2 bay leaves
1 teaspoon caraway seeds
1 cup hot stock or broth
1 (16-oz) can sauerkraut, drained
1 cup sour cream to finish

Cut the meat into 1½- × ½-in strips.
Fry the onions in the lard or butter
till golden. Add the tomatoes and
pepper, cover and cook gently for 15
minutes.

Add the meat and paprika, and
increase the heat a little; stir until
the paprika has been absorbed.
Then season with salt, the crushed
peppercorns, bay leaves and caraway
seeds. Pour on the hot stock, cover
and simmer for 30 minutes. Stir in
the sauerkraut and cook gently for
40 minutes. Remove the bay leaves.

Serve immediately, with the sour
cream stirred in, together with
boiled potatoes or dumplings.

Sauces

the Finishing Touch

Sauces

Béchamel sauce

2 tablespoons butter
¼ cup finely chopped cooked ham
1 large onion, peeled and finely
 chopped
3 tablespoons flour
1 cup boiling milk
1 cup hot chicken stock or broth
salt and pepper
grated nutmeg

Heat the butter in a saucepan and gently cook the ham and onion till the onion is soft and transparent. Sprinkle in the flour and stir over low heat until it makes a soft paste. Whisk in the boiling milk, a little at a time, making sure each addition is mixed in before adding the next. When all the milk is incorporated, add the stock then simmer gently over very low heat for 15 minutes.

Season to taste with salt, pepper and nutmeg, strain through a fine strainer and serve at once.
Makes about 2 cups

Tip If serving with vegetables such as cabbage or potatoes, there's no need to strain the béchamel sauce.

Variations
Prepared according to this basic recipe, béchamel sauce can be served with a variety of dishes. It can also be used as a basis for many other sauces.

Mornay (cheese) sauce Mix the finished sauce with ¾–1 cup grated cheese, then thicken with an egg yolk mixed with 1–2 tablespoons heavy cream.

Herb sauce Stir chopped herbs such as parsley or chives into the finished sauce.

Brown sauce Cook the flour and butter mixture until it is well browned, stirring constantly. Replace the milk with a mixture of red wine, tomato paste and gravy or beef broth.

Mushroom sauce

4 slices of bacon, diced
2 tablespoons butter
2 onions, peeled and diced
1 clove of garlic, peeled and finely
 chopped or crushed
3 cups wiped and chopped
 mushrooms
2½ tablespoons flour
1½ cups hot stock or broth
½ cup red wine
salt and freshly ground black pepper
pinch of dried thyme
pinch of sugar
pinch of paprika
¼ cup sour cream
1 tablespoon chopped parsley

Fry the bacon in a saucepan until the fat runs. Remove the bacon and reserve for use in another dish or for adding to the sauce at the end.

Melt the butter in the bacon fat remaining in the pan. Add the onions, garlic and mushrooms and cook, stirring constantly, until the onions are lightly colored. Sprinkle in the flour and continue cooking over a moderate heat until it turns golden brown. Add the stock and wine, a little at a time, beating constantly. When all is incorporated smoothly, bring to a boil, then simmer gently over a low heat for 20 minutes.

Season with salt and pepper, thyme, sugar and paprika to taste and stir in the cream just before serving. Strain, if preferred, into a sauce boat, sprinkle with chopped parsley and serve.

Mushroom sauce is good served with most meats. The meat juices left in the pan after cooking can be stirred into the sauce. Serve also with boiled or steamed cauliflower, pasta or rice.
Makes about 2½ cups

Note For a more extravagant mushroom sauce, use dried mushrooms but soak and drain them first. Adding finely chopped or puréed cooked chestnuts also gives the sauce an unusual delicate flavor.

Mock béchamel
with wine and herbs

¼ lb bacon, diced
2 onions, peeled and finely chopped
1 clove of garlic, peeled and finely
 chopped or crushed
½ cup dry white wine
½ cup light cream
salt and pepper
pinch of sugar
pinch of grated nutmeg
¾ cup sour cream
1 tablespoon chopped chives
1 tablespoon chopped parsley

Fry the bacon in a saucepan, preferably non-stick, until the fat runs. Add the onions and garlic and cook until golden brown. Stir in the wine and cream and season with salt, plenty of pepper, sugar and nutmeg. Heat through over a gentle heat, stir in the sour cream and, if necessary, allow the sauce to reduce to a thick creamy consistency over a low heat.

Add the herbs and cook without boiling for a few minutes, then serve at once with hot potato salad, or vegetables like cauliflower, kohlrabi, or salsify.
Makes about 1¾ cups

Tip For a stronger vegetable flavor, stir in some very thin slices of cooked leek or some cooked puréed celery and heat thoroughly in the sauce.

Sauces

Hollandaise sauce

2 egg yolks
1 teaspoon cold water
1 teaspoon lemon juice
1 cup chilled butter, cut into small
  cubes
salt and pepper
cayenne (optional)

Whisk the egg yolks in a double
boiler or heatproof bowl with the
water and lemon juice. Place the
bowl in a roasting pan half-filled
with hot water and continue beating
till the yolks are pale and frothy.
Whisk in the pieces of butter, one at
a time, making sure each one is
completely absorbed before adding
the next.
    When all the butter is
incorporated, season to taste with
salt, pepper and cayenne if liked and
add a little more lemon juice if
necessary.
    Serve with boiled, poached or
steamed fish, or with delicate
vegetables such as asparagas,
broccoli, globe artichokes, or with
quick-fried meat dishes.
Makes about 1¼ cups

Variation
Mousseline sauce Make the basic
Hollandaise sauce as above. Allow
to cool a little, then fold in ½ cup
stiffly whipped cream.
Makes about 1¾ cups.

Tip Should a butter sauce get too
hot and start to separate, it can
usually be saved by removing the
pan or bowl from the heat
immediately and whisking in a little
cold water or an ice cube. If this
fails, whisk in an extra beaten egg
yolk.

Hot butter sauce

3 tablespoons dry white wine
3 tablespoons wine vinegar
2 shallots, peeled and finely chopped
salt and pepper
1 cup chilled butter, cut into small
  pieces

Place the wine and vinegar in a
small pan with the shallots and a
pinch of salt. Cook, uncovered, over
a medium heat until reduced to
about 1½ tablespoons. Season with
pepper to taste and, with the pan
over a low heat, beat in the butter a

piece at a time. When all is
incorporated, serve at once.
    This sauce is excellent served with
boiled, poached or steamed fish. It
is also good with shellfish and
delicate vegetables.
Makes about 1 cup

Noisette butter sauce

The French word noisette literally
means hazelnut, and describes the
color of the finished sauce; no nuts
of any kind are added to it.
    Allowing 2 tablespoons butter per
person, carefully heat a quantity of
butter in a skillet or saucepan until
it just turns a golden brown. Serve
at once poured over baked, poached
or broiled fish.

Horseradish sauce

3 stale biscuits
1¼ cups chicken stock or broth
salt and pepper
grated nutmeg
large pinch of sugar
juice of ½–1 lemon
1 teaspoon butter
⅔ cup freshly grated horseradish or 3
   tablespoons prepared horseradish
2 tablespoons heavy cream
1 egg yolk

Grate the biscuits to remove the crusts. Slice them thinly and soak in the stock for about 5 minutes, then work through a potato ricer into a small pan. Heat till hot but not boiling, then season to taste with salt, pepper and nutmeg, sugar and lemon juice.

   Stir in the butter in small pieces, then add the horseradish. Mix 2–3 tablespoons of the sauce with the cream and egg yolk, whisk together then stir back into the hot sauce. Reheat without boiling or it will curdle. Serve immediately with boiled or roast beef.
Makes about 2 cups

Note Several variations of this sauce are possible. It can be mixed with grated apple and/or chopped blanched or ground almonds, with crushed garlic, finely chopped herbs, prepared mustard or green peppercorns.

Mustard sauce

2 tablespoons butter or margarine
1 small onion, peeled and grated
3 tablespoons flour
3–4 tablespoons prepared mild
   mustard to taste
2 cups hot stock or broth
salt and pepper
large pinch of sugar
juice of ½ lemon
½ cup heavy cream

Melt the fat in a saucepan. Stir in the onion and flour and cook gently, stirring, until all the fat is absorbed and the mixture becomes foamy. Stir in the mustard and continue cooking for 2 minutes.

   Pour on the hot stock, a little at a time, stirring till smooth after each addition. Bring to a boil, then reduce the heat and cook gently for 5 minutes till thickened, stirring from time to time. Season well with salt, pepper, sugar and lemon juice, adding a little more mustard if necessary. Stir in the cream and heat without boiling until thick and smooth. Pour into a sauce boat and serve at once, with baked or broiled fish such as herrings or mackerel.
Makes about 2½ cups

Variation
To make a stronger flavored sauce, add green peppercorns and snipped chives to taste. Make it even stronger by substituting mustard powder mixed with vinegar and/or dry white wine for some of the prepared mustard.

Sauces

Mayonnaise

3 large egg yolks
large pinch of salt
1 tablespoon vinegar or lemon juice
1–2 teaspoons prepared English
*   mustard*
2 cups corn or sunflower oil
white pepper or cayenne (optional)

To make mayonnaise successfully, it is essential to have all the ingredients at room temperature to reduce the risks of the eggs curdling while the oil is being added.

Beat the yolks with the salt, a few drops of vinegar or lemon juice and the mustard to a creamy foam (use either an electric beater or blender as it is important to beat steadily and continuously).

Beat in the oil, drop by drop at first then in a steady stream, until thick and completely incorporated. Flavor with the remaining vinegar or lemon juice, and season to taste with a little pepper or cayenne and salt.
Makes about 2½ cups

Note Mayonnaise can also be made with olive, almond or walnut oil mixed with corn or sunflower oil. Each different oil gives the mayonnaise a subtly different flavor.

Cook's Tip

If mayonnaise should curdle while you are making it remove the curdled mixture to another bowl and beat up a further egg yolk with a little vinegar and seasoning. Add the curdled mixture a little at a time as for the oil to produce a smooth mayonnaise again.

Variations
Mayonnaise is used as the basis for many other sauces.

Tartare sauce Stir into the basic mayonnaise finely chopped gherkins, capers and herbs to taste. Very finely grated onion or chopped pickled cocktail onions can also be added.

Cream mayonnaise Make the basic mayonnaise with lemon juice instead of vinegar. Fold in ¼ cup stiffly whipped cream and adjust the seasoning, using cayenne, salt and lemon juice. Sour cream may also be used instead of ordinary cream.

Russian mayonnaise Make a cream mayonnaise (see above) using tarragon vinegar instead of lemon juice and sour cream; season to taste with freshly grated horseradish.

Ham mayonnaise Mix into the basic mayonnaise very finely chopped cooked ham and a few peppercorns to taste.

Fruit mayonnaise For every ⅔ cup basic mayonnaise, fold in a purée made with 1 tart apple, peeled and cored and cooked in 1 tablespoon water and 1 ripe peach, skinned and pitted. Season with curry powder and lemon juice to taste, and a pinch of sugar.

Olive mayonnaise Mix ⅔ cup basic mayonnaise with 3 tablespoons sour cream, 10 chopped green olives, ¼ cup chopped blanched almonds and freshly ground black pepper to taste. Season to taste with freshly ground black pepper, vinegar and a little sugar.

Caviar mayonnaise Make the basic mayonnaise with lemon juice only. Stir in one-third as much sour cream as the quantity of mayonnaise. Just before serving, fold in red or black caviar to taste.

Shrimp mayonnaise For every ⅔ cup basic mayonnaise, fold in ½ cup very finely chopped cooked shrimp and 1 tablespoon red salmon caviar. Season to taste with lemon juice, a little Worcestershire sauce and a pinch of sugar.

Swedish-style mayonnaise Beat grated apple, freshly grated horseradish to taste and a little white wine into the basic mayonnaise. Season to taste with salt and sugar.

Gribiche sauce

4 eggs
2 teaspoons strong prepared mustard
1 tablespoon white vinegar
salt
1 cup olive oil
1 teaspoon chopped chervil
1 teaspoon chopped tarragon
1 tablespoon chopped parsley
1 tablespoon snipped chives
1 teaspoon capers, drained
1 small pickled gherkin, drained and
*   finely chopped*
garden cress, washed and drained

Soft-cook the eggs for 4 minutes only. Cool under running water, remove the shells and sieve. Beat them to a smooth paste with the mustard, vinegar and salt to taste. Then beat in the oil, a drop at a time. Mix in the chopped herbs, the capers and the gherkin. Just before serving add some cress.
Makes about 1½ cups

Serving suggestions for mayonnaise based sauces All mayonnaise based sauces go excellently with cold cuts, steamed or poached fish, with hard-cooked eggs or with cold pickled or smoked fish. Gribiche sauce is especially good as a dip for all kinds of fresh vegetables or for serving with boiled potatoes.

Sauces

Aïoli

*1 large slice of white bread, crusts
  removed*
2 tablespoons milk
*4–5 cloves of garlic, peeled and
  finely chopped*
salt
2 egg yolks
1–1½ cups olive oil
1 tablespoon lemon juice
freshly ground white pepper

Soak the bread in the milk for about
2 minutes, then squeeze dry. Pound
the garlic with the bread and a little
salt in a mortar to a smooth paste.
Transfer to a small bowl, beat in the
egg yolks and 2 tablespoons of the
oil until well mixed together. Then
stir in the lemon juice, a drop at a
time, followed by the rest of the oil,
beating it in a drop at a time at first,
then in a thin steady stream till
thoroughly combined. Season to
taste with salt and pepper.
  Aïoli is especially good with
poached fish, broiled meat or baked
potatoes. It is also excellent as a dip
for pieces of fresh vegetables, or as
a fondue sauce for meat.
Makes about 2 cups

Note In the making of aïoli, as with
all other mayonnaise-based sauces,
all the ingredients must be at the
same temperature — ideally room
temperature — to help prevent the
sauce curdling.

Tip Aïoli needs first-class
ingredients. Use only the best olive
oil and the freshest possible garlic. If
you buy garlic towards the end of
the season, the green shoot in the
center of each clove should be
removed as it will taste bitter.
  The bread is soaked in milk to
stabilize this rather oily sauce and
help keep it from separating. You
can also mix a few tablespoons of
soft breadcrumbs with the chopped
garlic and work this into a smooth
paste in a mortar and then make the
sauce as above.

Rémoulade sauce

2 egg yolks
*1 tablespoon prepared English
  mustard*
1 tablespoon lemon juice
salt and pepper
1 cup corn oil
*3 small gherkins, drained and finely
  chopped*
*1 tablespoon capers, drained and
  chopped*
2 sprigs of tarragon, finely chopped
1 tablespoon chopped parsley
¼ teaspoon anchovy paste

Beat or blend the egg yolks with the
mustard, lemon juice, salt and
pepper to taste. Beat in the oil, a
drop at a time, with an electric
beater or work in a blender or food
processor to a creamy mayonnaise.
  Mix in the rest of the ingredients
seasoning it to taste with anchovy
paste. Chill until ready to serve.
Makes about 1¼ cups

Spiced cranberry sauce

1 (8-oz) can whole-berry cranberry
  sauce
pinch of ground ginger
½ teaspoon mustard powder
½ teaspoon turmeric
2 tablespoons orange juice
1 tablespoon lemon juice
1 tablespoon sweet sherry
1 tablespoon brandy

Mix the cranberries with the spices,
fruit juices, sherry and brandy.
Cover and chill till needed, and
adjust the seasoning before serving.
   Serve with hot or cold roast
poultry, especially turkey, roast
beef, tongue or ham.
Makes about 1 cup

Tip Cooked unsweetened cranberry
purée, made from fresh or frozen
cranberries can be used instead of
canned cranberry sauce.

Cumberland sauce

thinly pared rind and juice of
  ½ lemon
thinly pared rind and juice of
  ½ orange
1 shallot, peeled and finely chopped
3 tablespoons red wine
½ cup red currant jelly
1 teaspoon mustard powder
pinch of ground ginger
1 tablespoon port
cayenne

Cut the lemon and orange rinds into
very narrow shreds. Put them in a
pan with the shallot and the red
wine, bring to a boil, cover, reduce
the heat and simmer over a low heat
for 5 minutes. Add the lemon and
orange juice with the red currant
jelly, mustard powder and ginger
and stir over a gentle heat until
thoroughly combined. Leave to cool
before seasoning to taste with the
port and cayenne.
   Serve with roast game, roast beef,
or cold cuts.
Makes about 1½ cups

Gooseberry sauce

1 lb gooseberries, trimmed
¼ cup sugar
½ cup dry white wine
¼ cup butter
2 small onions, peeled and chopped
grated rind of ½ lemon
2 tablespoons orange marmalade
1 tablespoon Kirsch
salt
cayenne

Sprinkle the gooseberries with the
sugar in a large bowl and leave to
stand for 30 minutes.
   Bring the wine to a boil in a large
pan, add the gooseberries and cook
over a low heat for 15 minutes till
they are very soft.
   Meanwhile heat the butter, add
the onions and cook gently till soft.
Add to the gooseberries, together
with the lemon rind, marmalade,
Kirsch, salt and cayenne to taste.
   Serve with rich meats like roast
pork, liver or boiled or baked fish.
Makes about 2 cups

Sauces

Hot Mango chutney

*3 ripe but firm mangoes, peeled and
  pitted*
⅔ cup raisins
*2 red chili peppers, seeded and finely
  chopped*
*4 large cloves of garlic, peeled and
  finely chopped*
*1 piece of fresh ginger root, about
  2 in long, peeled and finely
  chopped*
1 cup dark brown sugar
1 cup wine vinegar
1 teaspoon salt
1 teaspoon turmeric

Cut the mango flesh into ½-in cubes.
Put the raisins in a large bowl
together with the pieces of mango,
chili peppers, garlic, ginger and
sugar, cover and stand overnight.

Next day, pour into a large
preserving kettle or saucepan, add
the vinegar and bring slowly to a
boil, stirring all the time. Reduce
the heat and simmer gently for 15
minutes. Add the salt and simmer
for 10 minutes more. Add the
turmeric and simmer for a further 5
minutes.

Pour into hot sterilized jars, seal,
process in a boiling-water bath and
label. Store in a cool, dry place for
up to 1 year.

Serve with curries or with cold
cuts, baked fish, broiled poultry or
pilaffs.
Makes about 1¼ lb

Variations
Peach chutney Substitute 4 large ripe
peaches, peeled and pitted, for the
mangoes and add 3 tablespoons very
finely chopped parsley.

Apricot chutney Use 2 lb apricots,
peeled and pitted; add 1 cup
pistachio nut kernels and substitute
mustard for the turmeric.

Tomato chutney Peel, seed and
finely chop 2¼ lb ripe tomatoes.
Make the chutney as above, adding
the tomatoes and a little ground
allspice instead of the turmeric.

Tomato catsup

*4½ lb ripe tomatoes, peeled, halved
  and stalks removed*
*2 large onions, peeled and roughly
  chopped*
6–8 cloves of garlic, peeled
¼ cup roughly chopped parsley
*3 tablespoons finely chopped dill
  (optional)*
*1 tablespoon dried basil or 2
  tablespoons chopped basil*
*1 tablespoon dried oregano or 2
  tablespoons chopped marjoram*
2 celery stalks, chopped
*4 chili peppers, seeded and finely
  chopped*
1¼ cups light brown sugar
1½ cups wine vinegar
6 tablespoons olive oil

Put the tomatoes, onions and garlic
in a blender or food processor and
work to a coarse pulp or chop by
hand. Put the pulp in a large
aluminum or enamel preserving
kettle or saucepan, add the herbs,
celery and chili peppers and bring
slowly to a boil, gradually stirring in
the sugar and vinegar.

Cook, uncovered, over a high
heat, stirring all the time, until
reduced and thick. Stir in the oil and
bring to a boil. Remove the pan
from the heat.

Pour into hot sterilized jars, seal,
process in a boiling-water bath and
label. Store in a cool, dry place for
up to 1 year.

Serve with sausages, cold cuts,
fried or scrambled eggs, steaks etc.
Makes about 2 quarts

Variation
To make a red pepper catsup, broil
4 lb red peppers until the skins
become charred and blistered. Rub
or peel them off, remove the seeds
and proceed as for the tomato
catsup, above. Makes about 5 cups.

Tomato and onion chili relish

*2-in long piece of fresh horseradish,
  peeled and grated or 2 tablespoons
  prepared horseradish*
salt
1¾ lb green tomatoes, finely chopped
4 red peppers, deseeded and chopped
*4 large onions, peeled and finely
  chopped*
6 cloves of garlic, peeled and crushed
1 cup red wine vinegar
1⅓ cups dark brown sugar
½ teaspoon ground coriander
½ teaspoon aniseed
*3 green or red chili peppers,
  deseeded and finely chopped*

If using fresh horseradish, pound or
blend with a little salt. Then mix the
fresh or prepared horseradish with
the tomatoes, peppers, onions and
garlic. Stir in the vinegar, sugar and
2 teaspoons salt, cover and leave to
marinate overnight.

Next day, heat the mixture in a
large pan and bring to a boil stirring
all the time. Then turn down the
heat to low, add all the spices and
cook gently for 30–40 minutes until
the mixture is very thick. Adjust the
seasoning. Pour into warm, sterilized
jars, seal, process in a boiling-water
bath and label. Store in a cool, dry
place for up to 1 year.

Serve this relish with all sorts of
cold cuts, sausages, steaks, fried
chicken or baked fish.
Makes about 3 lb

Variations
Onion relish Substitute equal
quantities of extra onions and red
peppers for the green tomatoes.
Add a few tablespoons of chopped
parsley and 2 crumbled bay leaves.
When packing in jars, spoon a little
vegetable oil on top.

Vegetable relish Use 1 lb each of
firm, red tomatoes, celery, green
peppers and onions with 1 cup sugar
only. Season additionally with some
yellow mustard seeds and roughly
crushed black peppercorns. A little
finely sliced leek, peeled and
chopped celeriac or diced apple may
also be added.

Sauces

Herb sauce

6 hard-cooked egg yolks, sieved
2 teaspoons prepared mustard
2 tablespoons white wine vinegar
salt and pepper
up to 1 cup olive oil
¼ cup chopped fresh mixed herbs (for example dill, chives, parsley, chervil, borage, burnet, tarragon, lovage, lemon balm)

Beat the egg yolks with the mustard, vinegar and salt to taste. Whisk in the oil, a drop at a time, until a mayonnaise-like sauce. Season with salt and pepper to taste, then add the herbs.
Makes about 1¼ cups

Cheese sauce with basil

4 cloves of garlic, peeled and roughly chopped
1 tablespoon chopped basil or ¼ teaspoon dried basil
salt
¼ cup pine nuts
½ cup crumbled mild goat's cheese
½ cup grated Parmesan cheese
½ cup olive oil

Work all the ingredients together in a blender or food processor to a smooth, thick sauce. If making by hand, pound the garlic and the basil leaves with salt in a mortar, then gradually add the pine nuts, cheese and oil, pounding all the time.
Makes about 1½ cups

Vinaigrette sauce

½ teaspoon prepared mustard
2 tablespoons herb vinegar
¾ cup vegetable oil
¼ cup chopped mixed fresh herbs (for example parsley, chervil, chives, dill, tarragon)
2 teaspoons capers, drained and chopped
salt and white pepper

Mix the mustard with the vinegar. Beat in the oil, drop by drop. Stir in the herbs and capers and season well with salt and pepper.
Makes about 1 cup

Note Substitute a little walnut or other nut oil for the vegetable oil to give your vinaigrette sauce extra flavor.

Cucumber cream dip

½ hothouse (English) cucumber,
   unpeeled and finely diced
salt
1 (8-oz) package cream cheese
2 egg yolks
2 cups sour cream
2 tablespoons lemon juice
1 tablespoon chopped watercress
1 tablespoon finely chopped mint
1 tablespoon chopped parsley
2 cloves of garlic, peeled and crushed
freshly ground black pepper .

Put the cucumber in a colander and
sprinkle with 1 teaspoon salt to draw
out the juices; leave for 10 minutes,
then rinse and pat dry with paper
towels.

   Beat the cheese, egg yolks, cream
and lemon juice until smooth, add
the watercress, mint, parsley, garlic
and cucumber, and season to taste
with salt and pepper. Chill before
serving.
Makes about 2½ cups

Parsley cream sauce

1 onion, peeled and finely chopped
1 clove of garlic, peeled and finely
   chopped
3 tablespoons butter
3 tablespoons chopped parsley
1 cup sour cream
2 egg yolks
pinch of salt
2 teaspoons lemon juice
white pepper
1 tablespoon snipped chives

Gently cook the onion and garlic in
the butter till soft and transparent.
Add 2 tablespoons of the chopped
parsley and cook gently for 2
minutes, stirring all the time. Stir in
the sour cream and heat until almost
boiling. Remove from the heat at
once.

   Put the egg yolks with the salt and
lemon juice in a double boiler over
hot but not boiling water and beat
till thick and creamy. Remove from
the heat and gradually stir in the
parsley cream a tablespoon at a
time. Season to taste with salt and
pepper and sprinkle with the
remaining parsley and the chives.
Makes about 2 cups

Egg and herb dip

2 hard-cooked eggs, sieved
1 teaspoon prepared English mustard
½ cup vegetable oil
2 tablespoons vinegar or
   3 tablespoons lemon juice
salt and freshly ground black pepper
1 tablespoon finely chopped parsley
1 tablespoon finely chopped chives
2 tablespoons finely chopped fresh
   mixed herbs

Mix the eggs with the mustard to
make a smooth paste. Whisk in the
oil, a drop at a time, to make a
mayonnaise-like cream. Season to
taste with the vinegar or lemon
juice, salt and pepper.

   Stir the herbs into the egg
mayonnaise. Serve at once to enjoy
the full flavor of the herbs.
Makes about ½ cup

Vegetable Accompaniments

Vegetables

Asparagus

For each person

4–6 spears of fresh asparagus,
  scraped and trimmed to even
  lengths
2 tablespoons butter
pinch each of salt and sugar
hot water (see method)

When preparing the asparagus, use a sharp knife and take care to remove any hard, woody parts from the spears. Arrange the trimmed spears in small bundles with the tips pointing in the same direction. Tie firmly in place with fine string just below the tips and about 1 in from the base of the spears.

Melt the butter in a large skillet, without allowing it to brown. Lay the bundles of asparagus carefully in the melted butter, season with salt and sugar and add enough hot water almost to cover.

Cover the pan, bring the water to a boil, then lower the heat and cook the asparagus for 15–20 minutes, or until tender (the younger the shoots, the less time they will take). Do not allow the asparagus to overcook or it will be unpleasantly soft.

Drain well and arrange on a heated plate for serving. The classic accompaniments are Vinaigrette dressing (p 118) or a butter-based sauce such as Hollandaise (p 110) or Maltese or Béarnaise sauce (below).

Variations

Serve cooked asparagus as an appetizer with ¼ lb smoked or Parma ham per person, cut into strips, or smoked chicken or smoked salmon or trout. New potatoes tossed in butter and parsley, and a butter sauce (see above) make perfect accompaniments if the asparagus is to be served with a main dish.

Flemish-style asparagus Serve each portion with 1–2 hard-cooked eggs mashed with a little softened butter.

German-style asparagus To each serving add ¼ lb smoked or Parma ham, cut into strips, a portion of Crêpe crisps (see below) and a helping of melted butter and a butter sauce.

Crêpe crisps

Serves 4

1¼ cups flour
pinch of salt
2 cups milk
4 eggs
butter for frying

Sift the flour and salt into a large mixing bowl. Make a well in the center.

Beat together the milk and eggs. Pour into the well in the flour and gradually beat in the flour to form a smooth, thin batter. Cover and leave to stand for 30 minutes.

Melt a pat of butter in a skillet, tilting it so the fat coats the sides. Pour off any surplus fat.

Pour enough of the batter to cover the bottom of the pan thinly. Swirl it around quickly, then cook for about 1 minute till golden-brown underneath. Flip over with a spatula or toss, take the pan off the heat, and cut or tear the crêpe into small, thin strips. Replace the pan and toss the strips, frying them until crisp, adding extra butter, if necessary.

Tip onto a hot plate, cover with another hot plate and keep warm in the oven. Repeat until all the batter is used up. Serve with cooked asparagus.

Béarnaise sauce

Serves 4

2 shallots, peeled and finely chopped
6 peppercorns
3 tablespoons tarragon vinegar
¼ teaspoon meat extract (optional)
3 egg yolks
1 tablespoon hot water
½ cup butter
1 teaspoon chopped fresh tarragon
1 tablespoon chopped fresh chervil
  or parsley
pinch of cayenne
pinch of salt

Put the shallots in a pan with the peppercorns, vinegar and meat extract (if used). Bring the liquid to a boil and continue boiling until it is reduced by half. Strain and allow to cool. In a bowl over a pan of hot, but not boiling, water (or in the top of a double boiler over hot water), whisk the egg yolks with the reduced vinegar mixture and hot water until thick and creamy.

Melt the butter, skim off any foam that rises to the surface, then add this to the egg yolks a teaspoon at a time, whisking between each addition. Stir in the chopped herbs and season the sauce to taste with cayenne and salt.

Variation

Choron sauce Add 1 tablespoon tomato paste to the finished Béarnaise sauce.

Maltese sauce

Serves 4

½ cup + 2 tablespoons butter
2 egg yolks
2 teaspoons hot water
1 tablespoon lemon juice
2 tablespoons fresh orange juice
pinch of salt
pinch of cayenne
1–2 teaspoons thinly grated orange
  rind

Melt the butter in a pan, without allowing it to brown. Remove the pan from the heat. Skim off any froth that rises to the surface. Whisk the egg yolks with the water and lemon and orange juice in a bowl set over a pan of hot, but not boiling, water or use the top of a double boiler. Remove the pan from the heat and whisk in the clarified butter, a teaspoon at a time. Season to taste with salt and cayenne and sprinkle with the grated orange rind for serving.

Vegetables

Cauliflower — basic recipe

Serves 4

1 medium-size cauliflower, trimmed
 and divided into florets
salt
2 tablespoons butter (optional)

Rinse the cauliflower well, and set aside. Bring a large pan of salted water to a boil, add the cauliflower florets, lower the heat and simmer, uncovered, for 10–15 minutes, or until the florets are tender but not too soft. Drain well and add a pat of butter before serving with roast beef, lamb or veal.

Cauliflower polanaise

Serves 4

¼ cup butter
2 tablespoons soft breadcrumbs
salt and freshly ground pepper
1 medium-size cauliflower, cooked as
 above without butter
1 hard-cooked egg, sieved
1–2 tablespoons chopped parsley

Melt the butter in a pan, skim off any foam and discard. Take care not to allow the butter to color. Add the breadcrumbs and fry until golden brown, then season and pour over the cauliflower florets.

Sprinkle the hard-cooked egg over the cauliflower with the parsley and serve at once.

Broccoli — basic recipe

Serves 4

1 lb broccoli, well-washed, stalks
 removed and heads cut into florets
salt
pinch of grated nutmeg
2 tablespoons butter

Cut the stalks into 1-in slices. Bring a pan of water to a boil, season with salt and nutmeg, then add the broccoli, lower the heat and allow it to simmer for 5–6 minutes, or until cooked but still slightly crisp. (If using frozen broccoli, cook according to the directions on the package in salted water flavored with nutmeg. Snip into florets and slice the stalks when cooked.) Drain thoroughly.

Melt the butter in a pan over low heat and toss the cooked broccoli for a minute or two, until coated with butter and glossy.

Serve with Hollandaise sauce (page 110) or Mornay sauce (page 108).

Variation
Broccoli omelette Soften 1 chopped onion and 1 crushed clove of garlic in 2 tablespoons each butter and oil. Add ½ cup chopped cooked ham and ½ lb broccoli, cooked as above. Season to taste. Beat 4 eggs with ¼ cup light cream, add 2 tablespoons chopped parsley and season with salt and paprika. Pour over the broccoli and cook until the eggs are set.

Lima beans in cream sauce

Serves 4

1 lb frozen or shelled fresh lima
  beans
2 tablespoons butter
1 small onion, peeled and finely
  chopped
1 clove garlic, crushed with a little
  salt
¾ cup cream
¼ cup cooking liquid from the beans
pinch of salt
pinch of grated nutmeg
pinch of sugar
2 tablespoons chopped parsley or
  chervil to garnish

Cook the beans in salted water to
cover. Drain, reserving ¼ cup of the
cooking liquid. Allow the beans to
cool slightly, then remove the gray-
green outer skins.

Melt the butter in a pan and cook
the onion and garlic over gentle heat
until transparent but not browned.
Stir in the cream and the reserved
bean cooking liquid and cook until
the sauce is thoroughly heated and

slightly thickened. Season to taste
with salt, nutmeg and sugar.

Add the beans and heat them
through in the sauce. Serve,
sprinkled with the chopped parsley
or chervil, with roast beaf, broiled
lamb or pork and poultry or game
dishes.

Glazed carrots

Serves 4

¼ cup butter
1 lb young carrots, wiped and
  scraped
1 tablespoon sugar
pinch of salt

Melt two-thirds of the butter in a
pan over gentle heat, add the carrots
and stir until coated with the butter.
Sprinkle in the sugar, and cook until
the carrots are lightly glazed. Pour
over just enough water to cover, add
the salt and bring to a boil.

Lower the heat, and cook the
carrots slowly until all the water has
evaporated. Add the rest of the
butter and toss the carrots so that
the butter blends into the glaze.

Serve with roast meat, especially
beef; poultry; broiled pork chops or
veal cutlets.

Note Young carrots are best for this
dish. If using older carrots, trim and
peel them, then quarter and cut
them into even lengths.

Variation
Put the prepared carrots into a pan
with enough cold water to cover.
Add 2 teaspoons sugar and ¼ cup
butter. Cook as above until all the
liquid has evaporated, then stir in a
little heavy cream or sour cream for
serving. Sprinkle with chopped
parsley, if liked.

Vegetables

Italian-style beans

Serves 4

1 onion, peeled and halved
1 clove garlic, chopped
2 sprigs savory or parsley
10 peppercorns
salt
1 lb green beans, trimmed
¼ cup grated Parmesan cheese
2 tablespoons butter

Put the onion, garlic, savory or parsley and peppercorns into a pan with 1 quart well-salted water. Bring rapidly to a boil, then add the beans and bring the water back to a boil. Lower the heat and cook gently for 10–15 minutes until the beans are tender but still crisp.

Drain the beans in a colander and rinse them quickly under cold running water. Remove the onion, herbs and peppercorns. Toss the beans in a clean pan over gentle heat for a minute or two until thoroughly dry and reheated. Arrange the beans lengthwise in a heated serving dish, sprinkle with Parmesan and keep hot. Heat the butter in a pan over gentle heat until very lightly browned (take care not to allow it to burn) and pour it over the beans and Parmesan just before serving.

Italian-style beans go with most roast meat or poultry dishes and are particularly good with broiled or poached fish.

Variations
Choose very young green beans; trim them and cook in fast-boiling salted water until tender but still crisp. Drain well in a colander and rinse briefly under cold running water. Drain again.

Meanwhile cook a chopped, medium-size onion with a crushed clove of garlic in a little olive oil until transparent, then add the beans with 1 cup peeled, deseeded and chopped tomatoes. Season to taste with salt, pepper, a pinch of dried savory or thyme or basil, and cook gently until heated through. Sharpen the sauce with a little herb or cider vinegar before serving, if liked.

Green beans in bacon rolls

Serves 4

6 peppercorns
salt
1 lb green beans, trimmed
3 tablespoons butter
2 shallots or 1 small onion, peeled and finely chopped
1–2 tablespoons chopped parsley
8 slices of bacon

Put the peppercorns in a pan with water to a depth of 2 inches and a little salt. Bring the water rapidly to a boil, add the beans and lower the heat once the water has returned to a boil. Cook the beans over gentle heat for 5–10 minutes, or until they are tender but still crisp. Rinse the beans briefly under cold running water and drain well.

Melt the butter over gentle heat and fry the shallots or onion until soft but not browned. Add the drained beans and parsley and toss until well coated with the butter and shallot or onion mixture. Keep hot.

Meanwhile fry the bacon slices in a non-stick skillet, turning once during cooking. Drain on paper towels, if necessary, and lay them on a work surface. Divide the beans between the slices and roll up each one.

Arrange on a serving dish and serve hot with roast lamb, broiled or fried steak or lamb or pork chops.

Cook's Tip

Frozen green beans are very good and can be used successfully in these recipes provided they are not overcooked. Remember that frozen beans have already been blanched and so require less cooking time than fresh beans.

Green bean purée

Serves 4

1½ lb green beans, trimmed and halved
¼ cup sour cream
2 tablespoons heavy cream
1 tablespoon butter
salt and freshly ground black pepper
pinch of dried savory
2 teaspoons chopped parsley
1 teaspoon chopped chervil

Bring a pan of salted water to a boil, add the beans and bring the water back to boiling point, then lower the heat. Cook the beans for 15 minutes, or until tender. Drain well and allow them to cool slightly. Purée the beans by processing them in a blender, food mill or food processor, then push them through a sieve to obtain a really fine purée.

Beat the sour cream into the bean purée with the heavy cream and the butter, then heat the mixture, stirring constantly, without allowing it to boil. Season to taste with salt, pepper and savory. Stir in half the chopped herbs and arrange the mixture on a heated serving dish. Sprinkle with the remaining herbs and serve with roast beef, veal, chicken, turkey breast or game birds.

Variations
Use ½ lb green beans and ½ lb shelled lima beans. Cook the beans together in a pan with a peeled onion, cut in quarters, added to the cooking water; or add a chopped clove of garlic or a generous squeeze of lemon juice to the cooking water. Remove the onion before puréeing the beans.

For a smoother, more delicate-tasting purée, use double the quantity of lima beans to that given above, and blanch them for a few minutes in boiling water before draining well, then removing the gray-green outer skins. Rinse the skinned beans in cold water before puréeing as above.

Vegetables

Carrot purée

Serves 4–6

1½ lb carrots, peeled and sliced
3 tablespoons long-grain rice, rinsed
  well to remove excess starch
pinch of salt
¼ cup butter
¼ cup heavy cream
freshly ground white pepper
pinch of sugar

Put the carrots in a pan with the rice
and water to cover, then add the salt
and half the butter and bring the
water to a boil. Lower the heat and
cook for about 15 minutes until the
carrots are soft and the rice is
cooked. Drain well and purée rice
and carrots by processing in a
blender, food mill or food processor.
Return the purée to the rinsed-out
pan and heat gently with the cream,
stirring constantly. Season with
pepper and sugar to taste. When
thickened, remove the pan from the
heat and beat in the rest of the
butter little by little until the purée
is light and fluffy. Adjust the
seasoning and serve hot.

Fennel purée

Serves 4

¼ cup butter
1 clove garlic, chopped
1½ lb fennel bulbs, trimmed and
  coarsely chopped
1 cup chicken stock or broth
½ cup heavy cream
pinch of salt
freshly ground white pepper
dash of lemon juice

Melt half the butter in a pan over
gentle heat and fry the garlic until
soft but not browned. Add half the
chopped fennel to the pan, pour in
the chicken stock, bring to a boil
then lower the heat and cook the
fennel until tender. Purée the
cooked fennel by processing in a
blender, food mill or food processor.
Return to the rinsed-out pan.
  Purée the raw fennel by grating as
finely as possible or using a blender,
food mill or food processor. Add to
the cooked purée in the pan and stir
in the cream over low heat.
Continue stirring until the purée is
thick and creamy, then remove the

pan from the heat and beat in the
rest of the butter, a little at a time.
  Season the purée with salt, pepper
and a little lemon juice and serve
hot.

Brussels sprout purée

Serves 4–6

1½ lb Brussels sprouts, cleaned and
  trimmed, with a cross cut in the
  base of each stalk
1 medium-size potato, peeled and
  quartered
salt
¾ cup heavy cream
¼ cup butter
freshly ground black pepper
pinch of grated nutmeg

Put the sprouts and potato in a pan
with salted water to cover; bring the
water to a boil and cook until
tender. Take out the potatoes with a
slotted spoon and set aside. Drain
the sprouts and rinse briefly under
cold running water. Drain
thoroughly then add the potatoes
and purée both together by
processing in a blender, food mill or

Vegetables

food processor, then push through a sieve for a very smooth purée.

Return the purée to the rinsed-out pan and stir in the cream over gentle heat. Continue stirring until the purée thickens. Beat in the butter, a little at a time, and season to taste with salt, pepper and nutmeg. Serve hot.

Cook's Tip

Vegetable purées are a delicious and unusual way of serving vegetables. Some such as root vegetables and peas naturally form quite a thick purée whereas others such as watercress or spinach form a thinner purée and therefore make an excellent basis for sauces. The secret of a smooth purée is making sure that all the vegetables are evenly cooked so cut them into pieces of equal size before cooking.

Summer vegetables

Serves 4–6

6 small artichokes, washed, trimmed, quartered and choke removed
juice of 1 lemon
3 tablespoons olive oil
2 medium-size onions, peeled and quartered
2 cloves garlic, crushed with a little salt
½ lb carrots, peeled and cut into julienne strips
1 medium-size kohlrabi, peeled and cut into julienne strips
¾ cup dry white wine
1 cup veal or chicken stock or broth
salt and freshly ground white pepper
4 sprigs fresh thyme or ½ teaspoon dried thyme

Sprinkle the prepared artichokes with lemon juice to prevent discoloration. Heat the oil in a pan and add the artichokes, onions, garlic, carrots and kohlrabi. Stir them as they cook to seal the vegetables without allowing them to brown — about 5 minutes. (If a less pronounced garlic flavor is required,

add the garlic 2 minutes before the end of the frying time.) Pour in the wine and stock, bring to a boil, then lower the heat, cover the pan and finish cooking the vegetables over low heat for 10–15 minutes. They should be tender, but still a little crisp. Season to taste with salt and pepper, then flavor with thyme.

Serve with broiled or fried meat, especially veal.

Variation

To make this into a satisfying main dish add a few small new potatoes and some peas to the mixture and increase the quantity of each vegetable, and both wine and stock, by half again. When the vegetables are cooked, add ½ lb cooked ham, cut in strips. Serve hot.

Vegetables

Baked fennel

Serves 4–6

1 cup clear beef stock or broth
½ cup dry white wine
¼ cup butter
salt and freshly ground white pepper
pinch of grated nutmeg
8 small fennel bulbs, wiped, trimmed
    and halved lengthwise
½ cup grated Parmesan cheese
2 tablespoons soft white breadcrumbs
parsley to garnish

Bring the stock to a boil in a pan with the wine and a third of the butter. Season to taste with salt, pepper and nutmeg. Lay the fennel in the pan, cut sides down, then cover and simmer gently for 15–20 minutes, or until the fennel is tender but still a little crisp.

Preheat the oven to 450°. Remove the fennel with a slotted spoon and lay, alternate sides down, in a heated baking dish. Keep hot.

Briskly boil the cooking liquid in the pan, until it is reduced by half, then pour over the fennel. Mix the Parmesan and breadcrumbs and sprinkle over the fennel. Dot with the rest of the butter and bake in the preheated oven for about 10 minutes, until the butter has melted and the top is lightly browned and crisp. Garnish with parsley.

Serve with broiled or fried meat, or as an accompaniment to any white fish dish.

Tip If the fennel bulbs still have their feathery, bright green leaves, trim these away, chop them and save them for sprinkling over the fennel before baking or use in a salad.

Variations
Mix strips of cooked ham with the cooked fennel before baking, or serve it with a tomato sauce. The dish can also be broiled under high heat to finish off the butter and crumbs instead of cooking in the oven. In this case, put the fennel and other ingredients in a flameproof gratin dish.

Fennel in white sauce Instead of dotting the rest of the butter (two thirds) on top, make a roux by cooking it with 3 tablespoons flour until straw-colored. Take the pan off the heat and stir in the cooking liquid. Replace the pan on the heat and cook, stirring constantly, for 5 minutes. Add ½ cup cream and any chopped green feathery leaves from the fennel. Add a pinch of garlic salt, if liked, or a few drops of Worcestershire sauce. Pour over the fennel in the heated baking dish. Sprinkle with the grated Parmesan cheese, omitting the breadcrumbs, and bake as above.

Kohlrabi in sour cream sauce

Serves 4

4 kohlrabi, each weighing about
    5 oz, peeled, trimmed and finely
    sliced
3 slender leeks, washed and thinly
    sliced
¼ cup butter
¾ cup sour cream
salt
pinch of sugar
pinch of cayenne (optional)
1 tablespoon chopped parsley

Cut away and reserve any small leaves from the kohlrabi when preparing them. Blanch the kohlrabi and leeks together in boiling salted water for 3 minutes, then rinse under cold running water, or plunge into a bowl of iced water to stop further cooking, and drain well. Melt the butter in a pan over gentle heat and, before it is colored, stir in the sour cream to make a thick, smooth sauce. Season to taste with the salt and sugar, then add the drained vegetables. Cover and cook over gentle heat for 10–12 minutes, or until the vegetables are cooked through but still slightly crisp. Adjust the seasoning, if necessary, and sprinkle with a little cayenne, if liked. Slice any reserved kohlrabi leaves and sprinkle over the vegetables, with the parsley, for serving.

This accompaniment goes well with delicately flavored meats such as chicken or veal, or with poached or baked fish.

Tip Kohlrabi can either be pale green — when grown in a greenhouse, or purplish — from the garden plot. The former is more delicate in flavor and can be served raw, in salads. Young kohlrabi need only to be scrubbed, not peeled, and thus retain more of the vitamins in the skin. Always use any young, tender leaves and shoots, as these, too, are rich in nutrients.

Variations
Use scallions instead of leeks. Trim and blanch them first, or soften in the melted butter. Snip any darker green parts from the tops of the shoots into small rings and scatter over the dish before serving. Chopped chives also make a good garnish.

Try mixing the sour cream with 2 tablespoons heavy cream for a milder-tasting sauce.

Substitute young carrots, thinly sliced, and young peas, for the leeks. Blanch carrots for 4–5 minutes (depending on how thinly they are sliced) before being added to the sauce. Cook frozen peas, if used, according to the directions on the package, then drain and rinse under cold running water before draining thoroughly and adding them to the vegetables cooking in the sauce.

Vegetables

Braised red cabbage

Serves 4

¼ cup butter or margarine
1 medium-size red cabbage, core
  removed and leaves finely
  shredded
1 small onion, peeled and grated
2 tart apples, peeled, cored and
  chopped
3 tablespoons red currant jelly
salt and freshly ground black pepper
2 tablespoons wine vinegar
1 bay leaf

Melt the butter or margarine in a
large saucepan, add the shredded
cabbage and stir briskly until coated
with the fat. Add the grated onion
and apples and stir to mix with the
cabbage. Add the red currant jelly,
season with salt and pepper and
sprinkle over the vinegar. Add
about 1 cup water and stir the
mixture. Put the bay leaf on top and
braise over low heat in a covered
pan for 30–40 minutes. Take out the
bay leaf and adjust the seasoning
before serving.

Cabbage braised in white wine

Serves 4

2 tablespoons butter
2 tablespoons oil
2 medium-size onions, peeled and
  chopped
1 medium-size white cabbage, core
  removed and leaves shredded
1 cup chicken stock or broth
¾ cup dry white wine
salt and freshly ground white pepper

Heat the butter and oil in a large
saucepan and cook the onion until
transparent. Add the shredded
cabbage and continue cooking for 5
minutes, stirring continuously. Pour
in the stock and wine and season to
taste. Cover the pan and cook for
5–10 minutes, then remove the lid
and cook gently until the cabbage is
tender and the liquid almost
evaporated. Serve with white meats
and poultry.

Savoy cabbage with bacon

Serves 4

1 medium-size Savoy cabbage, core
  removed and coarsely shredded
4 slices of bacon, diced
1 medium-size onion, peeled and
  chopped
1 clove garlic, peeled and crushed
salt and freshly ground pepper
pinch of grated nutmeg

Blanch the cabbage by bringing it to
a boil in a pan of salted water, then
draining well and rinsing under cold
running water. Meanwhile, cook the
diced bacon in a pan until the fat
runs, then add the onion and garlic.
Cook briskly in the bacon fat until
transparent, but not browned. Add
the drained cabbage, season with
salt, pepper and nutmeg, then cover
the pan and cook over low heat for
20–30 minutes, or until tender but
still a little crisp.
  Serve with dark or light roast
meat, or with broiled meats.

Old-fashioned Brussels sprouts

Serves 4

*1 lb Brussels sprouts, trimmed and
    stems cross-cut at the base*
salt and freshly ground black pepper
4 slices of bacon, finely diced
¼ cup butter or margarine
*1 medium-size onion, peeled and
    chopped*
1 slice of white bread, toasted
1 clove of garlic, halved
a little grated nutmeg

Cook the sprouts in boiling salted
water for 10–15 minutes.
Meanwhile, cook the bacon in a
skillet until the fat runs, then add
half the butter or margarine and
allow it to melt. Add the onion and
cook over medium heat until golden
brown. Meanwhile, rub both sides of
the toast with the cut garlic clove,
then cut the toast into neat, small
dice. Heat the remaining butter or
margarine in a separate skillet and
fry the bread dice, or croûtons, until
all the butter or margarine has been
absorbed and the croûtons are

evenly browned. Sprinkle with a
little salt and set aside.

Thoroughly drain the cooked
sprouts and add them to the bacon
and onion mixture, stirring well to
mix them together. Adjust the
seasoning, sprinkle with grated
nutmeg and sprinkle over the
croûtons for serving.

Brussels sprouts with chestnuts

Serves 4

1½ tablespoons sugar
2 cups hot chicken stock or broth
*½ lb chestnuts, blanched and peeled
    (see below)*
*1 lb Brussels sprouts, trimmed and
    stems cross-cut at the base*
salt
¼ cup butter
freshly ground black pepper
2 tablespoons soft breadcrumbs

Put the sugar in a pan and let it
caramelize gently over low heat,
without allowing it to burn. Remove
the pan from the heat, cover the
hand holding it with a dish towel

and carefully add the stock. Return
the pan to the heat and cook gently
until the caramel has dissolved. Add
the chestnuts and simmer for 25
minutes. Meanwhile, cook the
sprouts in boiling salted water for
10–15 minutes. Drain well.

Lift out the chestnuts from the
pan with a slotted spoon and keep
them hot. Reduce the remaining
stock by two-thirds, then replace the
chestnuts, with 3 tablespoons of the
butter and stir over gentle heat until
the chestnuts are coated with a
sticky brown glaze. Tip into a
heated serving dish with the sprouts.
Fry the breadcrumbs in the
remaining butter and spoon over the
sprouts before serving.

Tip To blanch and peel chestnuts,
make a crosswise cut in the base of
each and put them in a pan with
enough boiling water to cover.
Allow them to cook for 5–6
minutes, then drain and peel off
both outer and inner skins.

Vegetables

Baked potatoes

Serves 4

*4 large Idaho potatoes, scrubbed and
dried*
1–2 tablespoons oil
salt

Preheat the oven to 400°.

Cut a shallow cross on the surface
of each potato, brush with a little oil
and sprinkle with salt. Wrap each
potato in kitchen foil, making sure
each one is securely sealed. Do not
wrap the potatoes too tightly, as the
potato will swell a little as it cooks.
Bake the potatoes in the heated
oven for about 1 hour, or until one
feels soft right through when tested
with a fork or skewer.

Unwrap the potatoes and lightly
press each one to open out the cut
on top. Fill this with a tablespoonful
of sour cream for each potato and
sprinkle with snipped chives.
Alternatively, serve with a pat of
chilled butter.

Baked potatoes go well with most
broiled or fried meat, especially
steaks; try them with sausages or
broiled fish steaks.

Baked caraway potatoes

Serves 4

1 tablespoon kosher salt
2–3 tablespoons caraway seeds
*8 medium-size potatoes, scrubbed,
dried and halved*
¼ cup melted butter

Preheat the oven to 400°. Mix the
salt and caraway seeds together and
dip the cut surfaces of each halved
potato in the mixture. Set the
potatoes on a cookie sheet, spoon a
little melted butter over each and
bake them in the preheated oven for
30–35 minutes. Serve piping hot,
with roast pork and a crisp green
salad.

Fan potatoes

Serves 4

1½ lb medium-size potatoes, peeled
salt
paprika
6 tablespoons butter

Preheat the oven to 400°. Cut each
potato across in the thinnest possible
slices, without cutting right through
to the base. Gently separate the
slices so that the potato "fans" out.
Season by sprinkling lightly with salt
and paprika. Grease a baking dish
or pan with a little of the butter and
set the potatoes in it, uncut side
down.

Melt the rest of the butter and
pour it over the potatoes. Bake
them in the preheated oven for 45–
50 minutes, basting frequently as
they cook, until they are golden-
brown.

Serve with broiled, poached or
fried fish, game and steaks.

Variation
Sprinkle the fan potatoes with a
little grated Parmesan or Cheddar
cheese 10 minutes before the end of
the cooking time. Serve with freshly
ground black pepper.

Ardennes-style potatoes

Serves 4

4 equal-sized potatoes
½ cup diced lean cooked ham
2 tablespoons chopped chives
¼ cup butter
salt and freshly ground black pepper
½ cup grated Swiss or Cheddar cheese

Bake the potatoes following the
recipe above. Leave the oven set at
400°.

Unwrap each foil-baked potato
and cut a "lid" from the top of
each. Scoop out the inside, leaving a

½-in shell. Mash the cooked potato
until smooth and stir in the diced
ham, chives and butter. Sprinkle
inside the hollowed-out potato shells
with a little salt, then pile the
mixture back into each potato.
Sprinkle with cheese and bake for
10–15 minutes until the cheese is
melted and golden. Season with
pepper and serve with roast poultry
or game and baked or fried fish
steaks or fillets.

Anna potatoes

Serves 4

*1½ lb potatoes, peeled and very thinly
sliced*
6 tablespoons softened butter
salt
pinch of paprika

Preheat the oven to 400°. Rinse the
sliced potatoes in cold water to rid
them of excess starch, then dry them
well. Generously grease the inside of
a baking dish with some of the
butter. Arrange the sliced potatoes
in layered circles, with the edges
overlapping. Dot every second layer
with softened butter and sprinkle it
with salt and a little paprika.
Continue in this way until the
baking dish is filled. Season the top
layer and dot with the remaining
butter. Cover the dish with foil and
bake in the preheated oven for 40–
45 minutes. Test with a skewer —
the exact cooking time depends on
the type of the potatoes and the
thickness of the slices.

Unmold the potato "cake" onto a
heated dish and serve with calf or
lamb liver, veal cutlets or baked or
steamed fish.

Vegetables

Potato purée

Serves 4

1½ lb potatoes, peeled and cooked
about 1 cup hot milk
salt and freshly ground pepper
3 tablespoons butter or margarine
a little grated nutmeg

Drain the potatoes well and, if
necessary, return them to the pan
and toss over gentle heat until all
excess water has evaporated and
they are quite dry. Mash them
throughly or use a potato ricer. Beat
in the hot milk a little at a time and
season to taste with salt and pepper.
Add the butter or margarine piece
by piece, beating between each
addition until a light, fluffy purée is
formed. Season with a little nutmeg
before serving.

Variations
Special potato purée Use half the
given amount of milk, making up
the quantity with an equal amount
of cream. An egg yolk and up to 1
cup grated cheese may also be
beaten into the potato. For an extra
special finish, spread the potato in a
heated flameproof serving dish and
finish off under a preheated hot
broiler until the top bubbles and
turns a golden-brown. Onion
softened in a little butter or a
handful of mushrooms, sliced and
sautéed, also make tasty additions.

A little crushed garlic and/or
chopped fresh herbs in season lend a
distinctive touch. Or try beating in
some sour cream and one or two
chopped hard-cooked eggs for
flavor.

Duchesse potatoes Replace 2–3
tablespoons of the milk with light
cream and add an egg yolk to the
seasoned potato purée, as above.
Spoon the potato into a pastry bag
fitted with a vegetable tube. Grease
a cookie sheet and pipe out large
rosettes onto it, keeping them apart.
Bake in a preheated 400° oven for
about 15 minutes, or until the tops
are crisp and golden brown.

Potato nests or baskets Make the
purée as for Duchesse potatoes
(above) and spoon it into a pastry
bag fitted with a vegetable tube.
Pipe circles of potato, about the size
of the palm of your hand, onto a
greased cookie sheet. Decorate
around the edge of each one with
smaller rosettes, using up all the
potato. Bake as for Duchesse
potatoes. Serve on a heated serving
dish, filled with diced cooked
vegetables, or lightly scrambled egg.

Potato croquettes Beat 2 egg yolks
into the potato purée, then stiffen it
by beating in 2 tablespoons flour.
Shape the mixture into balls about
1-in. in diameter, or into small,
cork-shaped rolls. Dip these in
beaten egg and coat with dried
breadcrumbs. Deep fry in hot fat, a
few at a time, and drain on paper
towels.

Rösti

Serves 4

1½ lb potatoes, peeled
¼ cup butter
salt and freshly ground black pepper

Boil the potatoes for 15 minutes
only then drain and allow them to
cool. Shred or grate the potatoes,
using a coarse grater. Melt half the
butter in a heavy based skillet, add
the grated potato and season with
salt and pepper. Spread out the
potato into an even layer, pressing it
down with a fork or spatula to
flatten the "cake". Fry over medium
heat until golden-brown and crisp on
the underside, then slide it out onto
a plate, flip over the rösti and fry on
the other side, adding a little extra
butter, if necessary. Serve hot.

A classic Swiss dish, Rösti makes
the perfect accompaniment to veal
cutlets, but can also be served with
ragoûts, or broiled meat.

Tiny individual rösti are
sometimes made and served as
canapés.

Variations
Try mixing a little finely diced bacon
or blanched onion with the grated
potato. Flavor the rösti with a little
garlic, a few chopped fresh herbs, or
sprinkle with cheese (Swiss for
preference) and finish off under the
broiler.

Fried potatoes with onions

Serves 4

1½ lb potatoes, peeled and very thinly
    sliced
6 tablespoons oil
3 medium-size onions, peeled and
    sliced in thin rings
2–3 cloves of garlic, crushed with a
    little salt
salt and freshly ground white pepper
1–2 tablespoons chopped chives

Make sure the potatoes are dry by
patting with paper towels. Heat the
oil in a skillet and, when hot, fry the
sliced potatoes, turning them
constantly, for a minute or two
before adding the onion rings.
Continue frying, stirring and turning

constantly; the potatoes should take
15–20 minutes depending on
thickness. Five minutes before the
end of the cooking time, mix in the
garlic and season to taste with salt
and pepper. Arrange on a heated
serving dish and sprinkle with the
chives.

These fried potatoes make a
savory accompaniment to fried eggs,
bacon, sausages, or fried or baked
fish.

Tip For really thinly sliced potatoes,
use a mandoline or food processor.

Salads
for all Seasons

Salads

Dandelion salad

Serves 4

¼ lb slices of bacon, finely chopped or
   diced
1 medium-size onion, peeled and
   finely chopped
2 cloves of garlic, peeled and crushed
   with a little salt
2 slices white bread, finely diced
1 lb dandelion leaves, picked over,
   washed and dried

Dressing
2 hard-cooked eggs, halved
¼ cup dry sherry vinegar or wine
   vinegar
1 teaspoon prepared English mustard
salt and freshly ground black pepper

Fry the bacon in a heavy-based
skillet over medium heat, stirring
constantly until the fat runs and the
bacon is lightly browned and crisp.
Add the onion and garlic with the
bread dice and continue frying until
both the onion and the bread are
golden brown, adding a little extra
fat if necessary. Set aside to drain
on paper towels.
   Remove the yolks from the eggs
and push through a fine-meshed
sieve, then beat to a creamy
consistency with the dry sherry or
wine vinegar and mustard. Season to
taste with salt and pepper. Finely
chop the egg whites.
   Arrange the dandelion leaves in a
large bowl or serving dish and pour
over the dressing. Gently reheat the
bacon mixture and spoon it over the
salad. Garnish with the chopped egg
whites.

Variations
This recipe also works well with
finely shredded raw spinach instead
of dandelion leaves. And for those
who like a contrast between a cold
salad and a hot dressing, arrange the
salad leaves on the dish, then stir
the egg-yolk dressing into the bacon
and crouton mixture. Pour this hot
dressing over the salad, add the egg
whites and serve at once.

Avocado salad

Serves 4

½ lb fresh asparagus spears, cooked
   and drained or 1 (10½-oz) can of
   asparagus spears, drained
1 (8-oz) can palm hearts, drained
   and thinly sliced
2 tablespoons capers, drained
3 ripe avocados
juice of 1 lemon
¾ cup plain yogurt
salt and freshly ground white pepper
pinch each of sugar and cayenne
1 small bunch garden cress

Slice the asparagus spears into
2-in lengths and put them in a salad
bowl with the palm hearts and
capers. Halve two of the avocados,
remove the seeds and peel. Thinly
slice the flesh and sprinkle with
lemon juice to prevent discoloration.
Add them to the salad bowl.
   For the dressing, halve, seed, peel
and purée the third avocado with
the rest of the lemon juice and the
yogurt. Season to taste with salt,
pepper and sugar, then add a
sprinkling of cayenne and stir
thoroughly to mix.
   Rinse the cress in cold water and
strip off the leaves. Reserve about a
third for the garnish and stir the rest
into the dressing. Arrange the salad
in the bowl, pour over the dressing
and sprinkle with the reserved cress.

Note Serve the salad as soon as
possible after making otherwise the
avocados may turn brown.

Variations
For a stronger flavor, add 2 scallion
stalks. Either cut these into thin
slices, or cut each into 2-in lengths
and cut halfway down the stalk,
making cross cuts so that the cut end
of each looks like a brush. Soak
them in iced water so the ends curl
outwards, before draining and
adding to the salad.
   Try adding a few coarsely
chopped shelled walnuts or
hazelnuts to the dressing for a
contrast in texture, and to
complement the slightly nutty flavor
of the avocados.

Green pea salad

Serves 4

2¼ cups cooked peas
1 (5-oz) can whole kernel corn,
   drained
1 medium-size green pepper,
   deseeded and finely chopped
1 medium-size red pepper, deseeded
   and finely chopped
2 celery stalks, washed and thinly
   sliced
1 tablespoon chopped parsley
1 head of Belgian endive, washed
   and separated into leaves

Dressing
2 tablespoons herb or cider vinegar
salt and freshy ground pepper
pinch of cayenne
pinch of sugar
3 tablespoons olive oil or 2
   tablespoons olive oil and 1
   tablespoon walnut oil

Combine all the vegetables except
the endive and stir in the parsley.
Season the vinegar with salt and
pepper, and sprinkle in a little
cayenne to taste. Add the pinch of
sugar, then whisk in the oil, drop by
drop, until the mixture thickens.
Pour the dressing over the salad
ingredients and chill for
15–20 minutes.
   Line a salad bowl with the endive
leaves and pile the salad on top.

Cook's Tip

Nut oils are ideal for giving a
simple salad dressing an unusual
flavor. Walnut, hazelnut and almond
are those most commonly available
and should be used to replace some
or all of the olive or vegetable oil
used in a dressing. The amount
required will depend on the strength
of the oil and individual taste so
experiment until you find the right
combination of flavors.

Salads

Radiccio salad

Serves 4

2–3 heads of radiccio (red lettuce),
    washed, trimmed and torn into
    strips
1 red pepper, deseeded, cored and
    cut into thin rings
2 red onions, peeled and cut into thin
    rings
1 small bunch radishes, trimmed,
    washed, drained and sliced
½ small bunch garden cress to garnish

Dressing
2 tablespoons red wine vinegar
salt and freshly ground black pepper
3–4 tablespoons oil
1 clove of garlic, peeled and crushed
    with a little salt

Mix together the radiccio, pepper
and onion rings in a bowl and
arrange the sliced radishes on top.

For the dressing, season the
vinegar with salt then add plenty of
freshly ground black pepper. Whisk
in the oil, drop by drop, until the
mixture thickens. Add the garlic and
pour the dressing over the salad.
Toss lightly. Rinse and snip the
leaves from the cress and sprinkle
them over the salad.

Serve at once, before the leaves
lose their crispness.

Note Radiccio is a red-leaved, white-
stemmed salad plant with crisp
leaves, similar to lettuce in taste. It
is very popular in Italy and is
becoming increasingly available in
the U.S. as its attractive leaves are a
popular addition to many salads.

Variations
Add 2–3 tomatoes, peeled,
deseeded and sliced. For a main
course at lunch, add strips of cold
cooked beef and 2 sliced hard-
cooked eggs.

Red bean salad

Serves 4

1 (16-oz) can red kidney beans,
    rinsed and drained
1 red pepper, deseeded and diced
2 ripe tomatoes, peeled, deseeded
    and diced
1 red onion, peeled and diced

Dressing
1 tablespoon wine vinegar or cider
    vinegar
salt and freshly ground black pepper
3 tablespoons olive oil
dash of hot pepper sauce
1 clove of garlic, peeled and crushed
    with a little salt

Garnish
2 sprigs fresh thyme
2 sprigs fresh basil

Put the beans in a salad bowl with
the diced pepper, tomatoes and
onion and mix the ingredients well.

For the dressing, season the
vinegar with a little salt and plenty
of freshly ground black pepper.
Whisk in the oil a little at a time.
Add the pepper sauce and garlic.
Pour the dressing over the salad and
toss lightly. Cover the salad and chill
for 20 minutes.

Before serving, adjust the
seasoning and garnish with sprigs of
thyme and basil.

Tip If fresh thyme and basil are not
obtainable, sprinkle ½ teaspoon each
of dried thyme and basil into the
dressing with the garlic.

Beet salad

Serves 4

¾ lb cooked beets, cut in julienne
    strips
1 small tart apple, peeled, coarsely
    grated and sprinkled with the juice
    of 1 lemon

Dressing
1–2 tablespoons prepared
    horseradish
¾ cup plain yogurt
salt and freshly ground black pepper
pinch of sugar

Mix together the beets and apple in
a salad bowl.

For the dressing, beat the
horseradish into the yogurt and
season well with salt and pepper,
then add a pinch of sugar. Pour over
the beet and apple mixture and stir
well. Cover and chill for 15–20
minutes to allow the flavors to
mingle.

Adjust the seasoning before
serving.

Variation
Substitute 3–4 tablespoons sour
cream for half the yogurt in the
dressing, and substitute finely grated
fresh celeriac for up to one third of
the beets.

Cook's Tip

Spread a piece of moistened
grease-proof paper over the
chopping board before slicing beet
to prevent the juice staining the
board.

Salads

Potato salad

Serves 4

1½ lb small potatoes, cooked in their
   skins
2 medium-size onions, peeled and
   finely chopped
salt and freshly ground pepper
2 tablespoons oil
¼ lb slices of bacon, chopped
¼ cup herb vinegar

Garnish
2 tablespoons finely chopped dill or
   parsley
2 tablespoons chopped chives

Drain the potatoes, rinse under cold
running water then, holding each in
turn on a fork, peel while still hot
and slice them. Put them in a bowl
and add half the chopped onion.
Season with salt and pepper.

Heat the oil in a pan and briskly
fry the bacon until cooked, then
remove the bacon from the pan with
a slotted spoon and set aside.

Fry the rest of the onion in the
hot fat and oil until transparent but
not browned.

Return the bacon to the pan and
mix with the cooked onion. Pour
this mixture with the vinegar, into
the potato salad, cover the bowl and
leave to stand for 10 minutes for the
flavors to mingle.

Adjust the seasoning if necessary.
Serve with the chopped herbs
sprinkled over.

Tip It is important to use general
purpose potatoes such as Norgold
Russet and Red Pontiac for salads,
as floury varieties such as Russet
Burbank, or Idaho, may disintegrate
when cooked and sliced.

Special potato salad

Serves 4–6

1½ lb small potatoes, cooked,
   drained, then peeled and sliced
1 medium-size onion, peeled and
   finely chopped
1 apple, peeled, cored and thinly
   sliced, then sprinkled with the juice
   of ½ lemon
¼ lb cooked ham, cut in strips
½ small cucumber, thinly sliced
1 small dill pickle, thinly sliced or
   chopped
2 tablespoons cocktail onions, halved
small bunch of radishes, trimmed,
   washed and sliced
2 hard-cooked eggs, chopped to
   garnish

Dressing
3 tablespoons mayonnaise (page 112)
3 tablespoons plain yogurt
1–2 teaspoons prepared Dijon-style
   mustard
1 tablespoon herb or cider vinegar
1 teaspoon juice from the dill pickle
   jar
salt and freshly ground black pepper
pinch of paprika

Mix together the potatoes, onion,
apple, ham, cucumber, dill pickle,
the cocktail onions and radishes and
turn into a salad bowl.

For the dressing, beat together the
mayonnaise and yogurt, then beat in
the mustard, vinegar and pickle
juice. Season to taste with salt,
pepper and paprika and stir it into
the salad. Cover the bowl and chill
for 30 minutes. Adjust the seasoning
before serving and garnish with
hard-cooked egg. This salad goes
well with cold roast chicken.

Variations
Slices of your favorite continental
sausage can be substituted for the
cooked ham. Vary the other
ingredients according to taste: add 4
or 5 canned artichoke hearts, cut in
quarters, or 4 stalks of celery,
washed and chopped, or 1 small
leek, blanched and sliced, or ½ cup
stuffed olives, drained and sliced.

Potato salads are always improved
by a sprinkling of fresh, leafy herbs
or parsley just before serving. Sliced
mushrooms whether raw or lightly
blanched also make a good addition
to a potato salad.

If you substitute fish or shellfish
— pieces of smoked fish or shelled,
cooked shrimp — for the meat, add
a tablespoon of prepared
horseradish to the dressing, with
plenty of chopped parsley.

Tip Really small new potatoes can
be left unpeeled. Choose ones of an
even size for the best appearance in
the finished dish.

Cook's Tip

Always cook potatoes for a salad
until just tender but no more so that
they slice well. Remember to mix all
the ingredients together very gently
so that the potato slices do not
break up.

Salads

Chicken salad

Serves 4

1 head of Iceberg lettuce, washed and
 torn into strips
3 stalks of celery, washed and thinly
 sliced
4 cooked chicken pieces, skinned and
 flesh cut into chunks
½ bunch garden cress, washed and
 snipped
2 ripe pears, peeled, cored and
 sliced, then sprinkled with juice of
 ½ lemon
2 tablespoons coarsely chopped
 salted peanuts to garnish

Dressing
¾ cup plain yogurt
2 tablespoons sour cream
a little extra lemon juice (optional)
salt and freshly ground white pepper
pinch each of sugar, cayenne and
 paprika

Put the lettuce in a bowl with the
celery and chicken. Sprinkle over
the snipped cress and add the pears.
 For the dressing, stir the yogurt

into the sour cream and add a little
extra lemon juice, if liked. Season to
taste with salt and pepper, sugar,
cayenne and paprika. Pour the
dressing over the salad, toss gently
once or twice and sprinkle the
peanuts over the salad before
serving.

Variation
Substitute canned or fresh peaches
or pineapple chunks for the ripe
pears.

Summer beef salad

Serves 4

½ lb boneless sirloin steak, fried in a
 little oil, then seasoned and left to
 cool
½ lb cooked green beans, cut in
 2-in lengths
1 cup thinly sliced button mushrooms
1 shallot, peeled and thinly sliced
1 large head radiccio (red) or Iceberg
 lettuce, washed and leaves
 separated
a little chopped lemon balm
 (optional) to garnish

Dressing
salt and freshly ground black pepper
2 tablespoons wine vinegar
¼ cup oil
½ teaspoon prepared Dijon-style
 mustard
1 tablespoon chopped parsley
1 tablespoon chopped tarragon

Cut the steak into thin strips and
mix with the beans, mushrooms and
shallot. Line a salad bowl with
radiccio or lettuce leaves and tear
the rest into strips. Mix the torn
leaves with the rest of the salad
vegetables and put these into the
salad bowl.
 For the dressing, whisk salt and
pepper into the vinegar to season it
to taste, then whisk in the oil a little
at a time. Stir in the mustard and
chopped herbs and pour the dressing
over the salad, garnishing with
lemon balm, if liked.

Salads

Mixed pepper salad

Serves 4–6

½ lb cooked tongue or beef, cut in
   thin strips
2 red peppers, deseeded and sliced
1 green pepper, deseeded and sliced
1 large Bermuda onion, peeled and
   sliced
1 small fennel bulb, washed, trimmed
   and thinly sliced
½ small head of romaine lettuce,
   washed and torn into thin strips
2 tomatoes, peeled and chopped
3 hard-cooked eggs, halved
2 tablespoons tarragon vinegar or
   white wine vinegar
1 teaspoon prepared Dijon-style
   mustard
¼ cup oil
salt and freshly ground black pepper
½ teaspoon paprika
pinch of cayenne
2 teaspoons capers
1 tablespoon snipped chives
1 tablespoon chopped parsley

Put the meat into a salad bowl and
add the prepared vegetables. Toss
them to mix lightly. Remove the
yolks from the hard-cooked eggs and
finely chop the whites. Sieve the
yolks, then beat them into the
vinegar with the mustard. Whisk in
the oil, drop by drop, then season
with salt, pepper, paprika and
cayenne to taste and pour the
dressing over the salad. Add the
capers, chives and parsley and toss
well. Garnish with chopped egg
white.

Zucchini and cheese salad

Serves 4–6

½ cup dry white wine
¼ cup olive oil
3 medium-size zucchini, wiped,
   trimmed and thinly sliced
salt and freshly ground black pepper
2 medium-size onions, peeled and
   sliced into rings
1 green pepper, deseeded and cut
   into thin rings
¼ lb lean cooked ham, cut into strips
2 ripe tomatoes, cut into eighths
2 tablespoons white wine vinegar
¼ lb mild cheese such as Monterey
   Jack, crumbled or diced
shredded lettuce to garnish (optional)

Bring the wine to a boil in a pan
with the olive oil and add the sliced
zucchini. Season with salt and
pepper and allow them to cook for 3
to 5 minutes, until cooked but still
slightly crisp. Lift out the zucchini
slices, set them aside and leave to
cool, then reduce the cooking liquid
in the pan by about two-thirds by
boiling rapidly. Set the pan aside,
reserving the cooking liquid.

Put the onion rings in a colander
and pour boiling water over them to
soften them slightly. Allow to cool.

Put the pepper, ham and tomatoes
into a bowl and stir to mix them
together. Add the cooled zucchini
and the onion rings and mix the
ingredients again.

Beat the vinegar into the cooled
cooking liquid then pour it over the
salad. Sprinkle over the cheese and
garnish with shredded lettuce.

147

Salads

Chicory and grapefruit salad

Serves 4

1 head of chicory, washed and thinly sliced
1 large grapefruit, peeled and cut into neat segments
1 shallot or small onion, peeled and finely chopped
½ cup roughly chopped walnuts

Dressing
¾ cup plain yogurt
1 teaspoon walnut or olive oil
salt and freshly ground black pepper
pinch each of sugar and ground ginger
1–2 teaspoons brandy

Put the chicory in a bowl with the grapefruit and onion, toss gently, then add the nuts. For the dressing whisk the yogurt with the oil and season it well with salt, pepper, sugar and ginger. Stir in enough brandy to add a little extra piquancy, then pour the dressing over the salad. Toss the salad lightly and serve immediately.

Winter salad with chicken livers

Serves 4

½ lb chicken livers, trimmed
3 tablespoons butter or oil
salt and freshly ground black pepper
small bunch (about ¼ lb) corn salad (lamb's lettuce), rinsed and dried
2 small heads of Belgian endive, wiped, trimmed and thinly sliced
1 head radiccio (red lettuce), trimmed and leaves separated (optional)
1 small leek, very thinly sliced, then washed and dried

Dressing
2 tablespoons white wine vinegar
salt and freshly ground black pepper
¼ cup olive oil

Pat the chicken livers with paper towels to remove any excess moisture. Melt the butter, or heat the oil, in a pan and fry the livers briskly on all sides for about 3 minutes, or until cooked. Lift out with a slotted spoon and leave to drain on paper towels. Season with salt and pepper.

Whisk the vinegar with salt and pepper to taste, then whisk in the oil, a little at a time.

Pour the dressing into a large salad bowl, add all the salad ingredients except the chicken livers and toss them in the dressing. Thinly slice the cooked chicken livers and arrange on top, then spoon a little of the dressing from the bottom of the bowl over the livers before serving.

Tip This winter salad also goes well with thin slices of rare roast beef, cut into strips, or poultry, cut into shreds. Try adding half an onion, peeled and grated or very finely chopped, to the dressing, or crush a clove of garlic with a little salt for a stronger flavor, and add this to the dressing.

Salad frisée

Serves 4

½ *small head of chicory, washed, dried and torn into bite-sized pieces*
1 heart of fennel, wiped, trimmed and sliced
1 red pepper, deseeded and sliced
1 green pepper, deseeded and sliced
2 onions, peeled and cut into thin rings
1 cup thinly sliced button mushrooms, sprinkled with 1 – 2 tablespoons lemon juice
2 hard-cooked eggs, cut into eighths
2 tablespoons chopped parsley

Dressing
2 tablespoons white wine vinegar
½ *teaspoon prepared English mustard*
salt and freshly ground black pepper
pinch of sugar
1 – 2 cloves of garlic, crushed with a little salt
¼ *cup olive oil*

Mix all the salad ingredients in a large bowl, adding the chopped parsley, then make the dressing. Whisk together the vinegar and mustard, then add salt, pepper and sugar, stirring well until the salt and sugar have dissolved. Add the garlic and whisk in the oil a little at a time. Pour the dressing over the salad and toss lightly. Serve immediately.

Salade niçoise

Serves 4 – 6

1 lb small potatoes, cooked in their skins, then peeled and sliced or diced
¾ *lb cooked green beans, drained and refreshed in cold water*
2 large ripe tomatoes, peeled, deseeded and thinly sliced
8 green olives, pitted and sliced
8 ripe olives, pitted and sliced
1 shallot, peeled and finely diced
1 (1¾-oz) can anchovies, rinsed and drained
2 tablespoons capers

Dressing
3 tablespoons red wine vinegar
salt and freshly ground black pepper
pinch of sugar
5 tablespoons olive oil

Mix together all the salad ingredients in a large bowl, then make the dressing. Whisk the vinegar with the salt, pepper and sugar, then whisk in the oil a little at a time. Pour it over the salad, cover and chill for 30 minutes before serving.

Cook's Tip

A (7-oz) can of tuna fish, drained and flaked, can be added to the salad to make it into a light luncheon dish. Hard-cooked eggs, peeled and cut into eighths, make a good addition as do zucchini, sliced and lightly cooked.

Salads

Rice salad

Serves 4

1 cup long-grain rice, cooked and
  drained
1 Bermuda onion, peeled and finely
  chopped
1 red pepper, deseeded and diced
1 green pepper, deseeded and diced
2 dill pickles, drained and finely
  sliced
1 apple, peeled, cored and diced,
  then sprinkled with lemon juice
½ lb continental sausage (e.g.
  Mortadella or salami), skinned and
  sliced
10 ripe olives, drained and pitted

Dressing
2 tablespoons wine or cider vinegar
salt and freshly ground pepper
1 teaspoon paprika
1 clove of garlic, peeled and crushed
  with a little salt
2 tablespoons chopped parsley
1 tablespoon chopped chives
2 tablespoons mayonnaise (page 112)
1 teaspoon tomato paste (optional)
¾ cup plain yogurt

To serve
few large lettuce leaves
extra chopped chives

Mix together all the salad
ingredients in a large salad bowl and
leave, covered, to chill while making
the dressing. Whisk the vinegar with
a generous seasoning of salt and
pepper until the salt dissolves.
Whisk in the paprika, add the garlic
and stir in two-thirds of the parsley
and chives. Mix in the mayonnaise,
tomato paste (if using) and yogurt.
Stir gently to mix all the dressing
ingredients and adjust the seasoning
— it should be piquant and a little
sharp.
  Mix the dressing into the salad,
cover and chill for about 1 hour.
Line four individual serving plates
with lettuce leaves and top with the
salad. Garnish with the remaining
parsley and chives.

Variations
Try adding a small can of corn
kernels, well drained, to the salad,
or 2 – 3 tablespoons leftover cooked
peas. Sliced fresh button mushrooms
make a good variation, and a few
capers or cocktail onions add extra
piquancy.

Oriental rice salad

Serves 4

1 cup long-grain rice, cooked with
  saffron and curry flavoring (see
  Note below)
4 dried Chinese mushrooms, soaked
  in tepid water for up to 1 hour and
  sliced
1 (10½-oz) can bamboo shoots,
  drained and sliced
6 oz bean sprouts, rinsed and drained
small bunch scallions, washed and
  sliced into thin rings

Dressing
3 tablespoons rice wine (sake) or dry
  sherry
1 tablespoon soy sauce
2 tablespoons wine vinegar
freshly ground white pepper
½ teaspoon hot chili sauce (optional)
1 clove of garlic, peeled and crushed
  with a little salt
pinch each of ground ginger and
  sugar
5 tablespoons oil
salt (optional)

Pile the rice in a bowl, then drain
and add the mushrooms. Mix in the
bamboo shoots, bean sprouts and
most of the scallion and set aside
while making the dressing.
  For the dressing, stir the rice wine
or sherry with the soy sauce and
vinegar, then add a generous
sprinkling of pepper. Add the chili
sauce, if using, then the garlic,
ginger and sugar. Whisk in the oil, a
little at a time. Adjust the
seasoning, adding a little salt, if
necessary, although the soy sauce
and hot seasoning may make the
sauce quite salty enough for most
tastes.
  Stir the dressing into the salad,
cover and let stand for about 30
minutes. Adjust the seasoning again,
if necessary, and serve sprinkled
with the reserved scallion.

Note Use 3 saffron strands, or a
large pinch ground saffron to flavor
the cooking water for the rice, and
from ½ – 1 tablespoon curry powder,
depending on individual taste.
Turmeric can be substituted for the
more expensive saffron as it will
color the rice although, of course,
the flavor will be rather different —
spicy rather than aromatic.

Cold meat and rice salad

Serves 4 – 6

1 cup long-grain rice, cooked,
  drained and cooled
½ lb lean cooked meat (pork, veal or
  chicken), cut into neat cubes
  (about 2 cups)
1 small leek, sliced into thin rings,
  then washed and drained
2 canned pineapple rings, drained
  and cut into chunks
1 orange, peeled and segmented with
  all white pith and membrane
  removed
1 tablespoon mango chutney
1 canned pimiento, drained and
  finely diced
a few lettuce leaves
1 small bunch of watercress, washed
  and drained (optional)

Dressing
1 – 2 tablespoons pineapple juice
¾ cup heavy cream, lightly whipped
pinch of chili powder
salt and freshly ground pepper
pinch of cayenne

Pile the rice into a bowl, add the
meat, leek, and pineapple and mix
into the rice. Cut each orange
segment across into three and stir
into the salad. Add the chutney and
pimiento and mix all these
ingredients together well. Cover and
set aside while making the dressing.
  Stir the pineapple juice into the
cream, add the chili powder and
season to taste with salt, pepper and
cayenne. Pour the dressing over the
uncovered salad.
  Turn the salad carefully in the
dressing, cover the bowl and let
stand for about 30 minutes before
adjusting the seasoning and serving.
Serve on indvidual plates, lined with
a few lettuce leaves. Garnish with
watercress, if liked.

Tip Rice salads are good for serving
at buffet parties as they need to
stand for a while for the flavors to
mingle and stay fresher longer. They
are also convenient for taking on
picnics.

Salads

Scandinavian mushroom salad

Serves 4

1 small head of lettuce, washed and
  leaves separated
2 cups thinly sliced button
  mushrooms, sprinkled with 2
  tablespoons lemon juice

Dressing
¾ cup heavy or whipping cream
juice of ½ lemon
salt and freshly ground pepper
pinch each of sugar and mustard
  powder
½ onion, peeled and grated
½ small bunch garden cress, snipped,
  or small bunch fresh dill, finely
  chopped

Divide any large lettuce leaves into
two and use them to line 4
individual plates. Arrange a portion
of mushrooms on top of each.

For the dressing, whip the cream
with the lemon juice and season
with salt and freshly ground pepper.
Add the sugar and mustard powder
and stir in the onion. Spoon a
portion on each plate and sprinkle
with cress, or dill. Serve
immediately.

Tip Parsley may be used instead of
dill, though it is the dill which adds
the Scandinavian touch to this
simple salad.

Radish salad

Serves 4

2 bunches radishes, trimmed and
  thinly sliced, then spread out and
  sprinkled with salt
2 tart apples, peeled, cored and
  thinly sliced, then sprinkled with
  lemon juice
1 small cucumber, wiped and very
  thinly sliced

Dressing
2 oz Stilton or other blue cheese,
  mashed or crumbled
½ cup sour cream
3 tablespoons plain yogurt
salt and freshly ground pepper
dash of wine vinegar
pinch of sugar

Thoroughly drain the radishes and
pat dry with paper towels. Mix with
the apple and cucumber and arrange
in a salad bowl or dish.

For the dressing, mash the cheese
with the sour cream and yogurt,
then season well with salt and
pepper and continue beating until
the mixture is smooth. Whisk in the
vinegar and add a pinch of sugar.
Adjust the seasoning, if necessary
and pour the dressing over the
salad. Serve immediately, tossing the
salad at the table.

Fish and vegetable salad

Serves 4

½ head of Iceberg lettuce, washed and torn into strips
1 lb white fish fillets, poached
¾ cup cooked peas
1 cup thinly sliced button mushrooms, sprinkled with a little lemon juice
2 hard-cooked eggs, cut lengthwise into eighths
1 (10½-oz) can asparagus spears, drained

Dressing
½ cup sour cream
¾ cup plain yogurt
salt and freshly ground white pepper
pinch of cayenne
dash of Worcestershire sauce
1 – 2 tablespoons chopped dill or parsley

Line a salad bowl with the lettuce. Pat the cooked fish dry with paper towels and break it into large flakes. Place these in the salad bowl, add the peas, mushrooms, eggs and asparagus spears. Cover and set aside while making the dressing.

Whisk together the ingredients for the dressing and pour over the salad before serving.

Curried fish salad with fruit

Serves 4

1 lb white fish fillets, poached, cooled and drained
1 medium-size onion, peeled and chopped
1 apple, peeled, cored and diced, then sprinkled with a little lemon juice
1 orange, peeled and segmented
1 banana, cut in slices and sprinkled with a little lemon juice
2 canned pineapple rings, drained and cut into chunks
salt and freshly ground pepper
a few leaves of lettuce, washed and drained
2 tablespoons roasted salted peanuts

Dressing
5 tablespoons light cream
¾ cup plain yogurt
1 tablespoon mango chutney
salt and freshly ground pepper
1 teaspoon curry paste
pinch each of sugar, ground cinnamon, paprika and cayenne

Pat the fish dry with paper towels and break into large flakes. Place these in a salad bowl with the onion and apple. Cut each orange segment into two and add to the salad. Put in the banana and pineapple and stir very gently to mix the ingredients. Sprinkle with salt and pepper.

For the dressing, stir the cream into the yogurt, add the mango chutney, season to taste with salt and pepper, then add the curry paste, sugar, cinnamon, paprika and cayenne.

Mix together all the ingredients for the dressing and stir this gently into the salad. Serve on individual plates lined with lettuce leaves and sprinkle each portion with salted peanuts.

Salads

Oriental chicken salad

Serves 4

*4 dried Chinese mushrooms, soaked
  in tepid water for up to 1 hour*
*1 (2½-lb) chicken, cooked, skinned
  and cut up or 4 cooked chicken
  pieces, skinned*
*1 small leek, trimmed and sliced into
  thin rings, then washed and
  drained*
½ lb bean sprouts, rinsed and drained
*1 (10½-oz) can bamboo shoots,
  drained and cut into thin strips*
*8 – 10 leaves of crisp lettuce or
  Chinese cabbage (bok choy)*
1 tablespoon chopped chives

Dressing
2 tablespoons soy sauce
¼ cup rice wine (sake) or dry sherry
salt and freshly ground pepper
*pinch each of ground ginger and
  sugar*
2 tablespoons oil

Drain the mushrooms, pat dry with
paper towels and slice. Cut the
chicken meat into neat bite-sized
pieces, discarding the bones (use
these for stock). Put the chicken
pieces into a bowl with the
mushrooms and leek, then add the
bean sprouts and bamboo shoots.
Stir to mix the ingredients lightly,
then set aside while making the
dressing.

   For the dressing, stir the soy sauce
into the rice wine or sherry, then
season lightly with salt (the soy
sauce may already be salty enough)
and generously with pepper, ginger
and sugar. Whisk in the oil, a little
at a time. Pour the dressing over the
salad ingredients, toss gently, then
cover the bowl and leave to
marinate for 15 – 20 minutes.

   Meanwhile, line a salad bowl with
the lettuce leaves. Adjust the
seasoning of the salad, arrange it on
the lettuce and garnish with chopped
chives before serving.

Variation
If a package of Chinese egg noodles
is obtainable, cook about ¼ lb in
boiling salted water, drain them,
allow to cool and cut into 1-in
lengths. Add them to the salad and
let stand for a few minutes to absorb
the flavor from the dressing.

Chicken and corn salad

Serves 4

*1 (2½-lb) chicken, cooked, skinned
  and cut up or 4 cooked chicken
  pieces, skinned*
*1 (11½-oz) can whole kernel corn,
  drained*
*1 red pepper, deseeded and finely
  chopped*
*1 green pepper, deseeded and finely
  chopped*
*2 ripe tomatoes, peeled, deseeded
  and finely chopped*
*1 Bermuda onion, peeled and finely
  chopped*
salt and freshly ground white pepper
*1 small bunch garden cress, washed
  and snipped*

Dressing
2 tablespoons mayonnaise (page 112)
¾ cup plain yogurt
juice of ½ lemon
salt and freshly ground white pepper
*pinch each of paprika, cayenne and
  sugar*

Cut the chicken meat into bite-sized
pieces, discarding the bones (use
these for stock). Place in a bowl or
dish with the corn, peppers, tomato
and onion, and stir to mix. Season
with salt and pepper and mix again.

   For the dressing, whisk the
mayonnaise with the yogurt and
lemon juice, then season to taste
with salt and pepper and the spices.
Add a pinch of sugar to lighten the
taste.

   Pour the dressing over the salad
and toss all the ingredients well,
then cover and chill for 20 – 30
minutes. Adjust the seasoning just
before serving and sprinkle with
snipped cress.

Tip A little chopped garlic, or a
good pinch of garlic salt in the
dressing complements the flavor of
the salad. For a really spicy
dressing, add a dash of hot pepper
sauce, or 1 – 2 teaspoons tomato
paste and extra salt and paprika.

Chicken and cucumber salad

Serves 4

*1 (2½-lb) chicken, cooked, skinned
  and cut up or 4 cooked chicken
  pieces, skinned*
*1 small cucumber, wiped and thinly
  sliced*
*2 cups thinly sliced button
  mushrooms, sprinkled with 2
  tablespoons lemon juice*
*1 small bunch dill or parsley, washed
  and finely chopped with a few
  sprigs reserved for garnish*

Dressing
¾ cup plain yogurt
¼ cup sour cream
¼ cup light cream
*2 cloves of garlic, peeled and crushed
  with a little salt*
salt and freshly ground black pepper
1–2 teaspoons white wine vinegar

Cut the chicken meat into bite-sized
pieces, discarding the bones (use
these for stock). Put the chicken
into a bowl with the cucumber
slices, reserving a few for garnish.
Add the mushrooms and chopped
dill or parsley. Set aside.

   For the dressing, stir the yogurt
with the sour cream and light cream,
add the crushed garlic, then season
to taste with salt, pepper and
vinegar.

   Pour the dressing over the salad
and toss until all the ingredients are
well coated, then cover the bowl and
let the salad chill for 20–25 minutes.
Adjust the seasoning and garnish
with the reserved cucumber slices
and dill or parsley sprigs for serving.

   This salad is best served while still
chilled.

Variation
A few halved or sliced pitted ripe
olives add a delicious flavor to this
salad.

Salads

Zucchini salad

Serves 4–6

½ cup olive oil
juice of ½ lemon
¾ cup dry white wine
¾ cup water
salt and freshly ground black pepper
1½ lb small zucchini, wiped, trimmed
and thinly sliced
1 onion, peeled and thinly sliced
2 cloves of garlic, peeled and crushed
with a little salt
pinch each of dry mustard and sugar
2 ripe tomatoes, peeled and roughly
chopped
½ cup roughly chopped walnuts
2 slices dry white bread, crusts
removed, and cut into dice
1–2 tablespoons chopped parsley

Heat 1 tablespoon of the oil in a
thick-based pan, add the lemon
juice, wine and water and season
with salt and pepper. Once the
liquid has come to a boil, add the
zucchini, and when the liquid
returns to a boil, lower the heat and
cook the sliced zucchini for 2–3
minutes, until tender but still a little
crisp. Lift out the zucchini with a
slotted spoon, drain well on paper
towels and leave in a salad bowl to
cool. Reduce the cooking liquid in
the pan by boiling rapidly until
about half remains. Take the pan off
the heat, measure out about 3
tablespoons of the cooking liquid
into a bowl and discard the rest.

Beat 2 tablespoons of the oil into
the cooking liquid, then add the
onion, garlic, dry mustard and
sugar. Season with salt and pepper,
and pour over the sliced zucchini in
the salad bowl. Add the tomatoes
and walnuts and turn all the
ingredients lightly to coat with the
liquid.

Heat the rest of the olive oil in a
heavy-based skillet and fry the bread
cubes on all sides until an even,
golden brown, adding an extra clove
of garlic, peeled and crushed with a
little salt, if liked.

Pour the croûtons and oil over the
salad in the bowl, sprinkle with
parsley and serve immediately.

Note Add a few stuffed green olives,
sliced into rings, for a variation in
flavor.

Mixed vegetable salad

Serves 4–6

1 small cauliflower, trimmed, washed
and separated into florets
4 sprigs broccoli, trimmed, washed
and separated into florets, stems
chopped into 1-in slices
1 small kohlrabi, peeled and cut into
julienne strips
2 carrots, peeled and cut into julienne
strips
¼ lb cooked green beans
½ lb cooked asparagus spears,
trimmed if fresh and cut into
1-in lengths
¾ cup cooked peas
1 cup thinly sliced button
mushrooms, sprinkled with 1–2
tablespoons lemon juice
1–2 tablespoons chopped chervil or
parsley

Dressing
juice of 1 lemon
salt and freshly ground white pepper
¾ cup sour cream
1 teaspoon prepared Dijon-style
mustard
1–2 cloves of garlic, peeled and
crushed with a little salt
1 small onion, peeled and grated
2 tablespoons chopped mixed herbs
(parsley, basil, thyme, chives)

Blanch all the uncooked vegetables
except the mushrooms for a few
minutes in boiling salted water, then
drain and rinse under cold running
water to set the colors and prevent
further cooking. Allow to cool. Trim
the beans into equal lengths and
make the dressing.

Stir the lemon juice with salt and
pepper until the salt dissolves. Mix
into the sour cream, then add the
mustard, garlic and onion and mix
well. Stir in the mixed herbs.

Combine all the vegetables in a
bowl with the dressing, then cover
the bowl and leave to stand for
15–20 minutes. Adjust the seasoning
and sprinkle with the chopped mixed
herbs before serving.

This salad makes a good
appetizer, or goes particularly well
with ham as a main course.

Shrimp and artichoke salad

Serves 4–6

½ lb corn salad (lamb's lettuce),
washed and dried
6 canned artichoke hearts, drained
and quartered
3 hard-cooked eggs, sliced into
eighths
¾ cup thinly sliced button
mushrooms, sprinkled with 1–2
tablespoons lemon juice
1 cup peeled shrimp
salt and freshly ground pepper

Garnish
1 tablespoon chopped dill or parsley
1 tablespoon chopped chives

Dressing
2 tablespoons herb or cider vinegar
salt and freshly ground black pepper
pinch of celery salt
dash of Worcestershire sauce
¼ cup oil

Put the corn salad in a bowl with the
artichoke hearts, eggs, mushrooms
and shrimp. Season lightly with salt
and pepper and set aside while
making the dressing.

Combine the vinegar with salt and
pepper and a pinch of celery salt,
whisking until the salts dissolve.
Add the Worcestershire sauce, then
beat in the oil a little at a time.

Pour the dressing over the salad,
turning once so the ingredients are
evenly coated, then sprinkle with dill
or parsley and chives and serve at
once.

This salad makes an excellent
appetizer, light lunch dish or side
dish.

Variation
This salad is also excellent made
with fresh spinach. The leaves
should be thoroughly washed and
dried then torn into strips.

Salads

Mediterranean cheese salad

Serves 4

½ cucumber, wiped and thinly sliced
1 red pepper, deseeded and cut in
thin rings
1 green pepper, deseeded and cut in
thin rings
1 medium-size onion, peeled and cut
in thin rings
2 ripe tomatoes, peeled, deseeded
and quartered
¼ cup stuffed green olives, drained
and halved crosswise
¼ cup ripe olives, pitted and halved
6 oz Gorgonzola or Roquefort
cheese, crumbled
freshly ground black pepper
1 tablespoon chopped basil or
parsley

Dressing
1 tablespoon wine vinegar
salt and freshly ground black pepper
1–2 cloves of garlic, peeled and
crushed with a little salt
4–5 tablespoons olive oil

Combine the cucumber, peppers,
onion, tomatoes and olives in a bowl
and sprinkle over the cheese. Stir to
mix well and season with pepper,
then add the chopped herbs and
lightly mix them in.
  For the dressing, season the
vinegar with a little salt and freshly
ground black pepper, then add the
garlic and whisk in the oil a little at
a time. Pour this over the salad and
toss and serve it at once.

Dutch cheese salad

Serves 4

½ lb small potatoes, cooked, drained
and cooled, then peeled
½ lb Gouda cheese, rind removed
2 red onions, peeled and sliced
¼ lb cooked tongue, cut in thin strips
2 dill pickles, drained and cut in thin
strips
1 apple, peeled, cored and sliced then
sprinkled with a little lemon juice
salt and freshly ground pepper

Dressing
¾ cup sour cream
salt and freshly ground pepper
dash of Worcestershire sauce
1–2 teaspoons prepared Dijon-style
mustard
1 anchovy fillet, rinsed well and
finely chopped
1 tablespoon tarragon vinegar or
cider vinegar
1 tablespoon chopped chives

Cut the potatoes and cheese into
small pieces and place in a bowl
with the onion, tongue strips, pickle
and apple and season with salt and
pepper.
  Beat the sour cream with a little
salt and pepper, the Worcestershire
sauce, mustard, anchovy and
vinegar, then stir in the chives. Pour
the dressing over the salad and turn
the salad ingredients lightly in the
dressing, taking care not to break
the potatoes, cheese or tongue
strips. Cover and chill for about 1
hour, then adjust the seasoning and
serve.

Spiced summer fruit salad

Serves 4

juice of 1 lemon
2 tablespoons whiskey
1 tablespoon orange liqueur
½ lb ripe strawberries, hulled and
  halved
2 peaches or nectarines, peeled,
  halved, pits removed and flesh
  thinly sliced
1 tablespoon bottled green
  peppercorns, drained (optional)
small sprig of fresh tarragon
  (optional)
1 crisp lettuce heart (Iceberg),
  divided into 4
¾ cup whipping or heavy cream
pinch of cayenne

First, combine the lemon juice, whiskey and orange liqueur, then add the strawberries, peaches or nectarines and peppercorns, if using. Turn the fruit so it is coated with the liquid, add the tarragon, if using, then chill for 30 minutes.

Meanwhile, line 4 individual dishes with small lettuce leaves and stiffly whip the cream with the cayenne. Arrange a portion of fruit in each dish and top with a spoonful of cream before serving.

Note Instead of lining the dishes with lettuce leaves, the little sprigs from the heart of the lettuce can be left whole and added as a garnish.

Fresh fruit salad

Serves 4

1 lb mixed soft fruit in season
  (apples, pears, peaches,
  strawberries, melon, grapes)
about ½ cup sugar
juice of 1 lemon
¼ cup rum, brandy or a fruit brandy
  (cherry or apricot)

Pick over, clean and prepare the fruit as appropriate (e.g. cut melon into balls, deseed grapes if necessary, hull and halve strawberries). Sprinkle with sugar to taste and lemon juice, then pour over the rum, brandy or liqueur. Cover the dish and chill for 20–30 minutes before serving.

Tropical fruit salad

Serves 4

1 small fresh pineapple, peeled,
  cored and cubed
1 mango, peeled, quartered, pitted
  and sliced
2 Chinese gooseberries (kiwi fruits),
  peeled and cut across in very thin
  slices
1 banana, peeled, sliced and
  sprinkled with a little lemon juice
6 fresh or preserved kumquats,
  wiped (if fresh) or drained (if
  preserved), then halved lengthwise
2 teaspoons sugar
½ cup Marsala
pinch of ground ginger

Combine the pineapple chunks, mango, gooseberries, banana and kumquats in a bowl. Add the sugar to the Marsala and stir well before adding the ginger. Pour the dressing over the fruit and chill for 15–20 minutes before serving.

Rice
and
Pasta

Rice and Pasta

Rice

To cook rice, say the Orientals, is as difficult for Westerners as it is for them to make good tea, because for both one needs a little peace and quiet. And they aren't far wrong, for whoever cooks rice too fast (that is to say over too great a heat) cannot be surprised when all the grains stick together and the rice ends up mushy. So here are two simple, foolproof ways of cooking rice so you'll never again break into a panic because the rice just won't work. You'll get the best results if you use long-grain rice for savory dishes, short round grain rice for milk puddings and most other desserts.

Rice Indian-style

Serves 4

1 cup long-grain rice
10 cups water
1 tablespoon salt
6 tablespoons butter

Preheat the oven to 350°.
   Wash and drain the rice as for Rice Chinese-style. Put it in a large deep pan with the water and salt. Bring to a boil and cook rapidly for 6 minutes over high heat, then drain off the water.
   Transfer the rice to a warmed casserole. Mix in the butter, put on the lid and continue cooking for 25 minutes in the heated oven. Serve at once.

Variations
Increase the butter to ½ cup. Fry 1 chopped onion and 1 cup chopped mushrooms in it, then mix these into the cooked rice. Or mix a pinch of saffron with the melted butter. Curry powder, ground ginger, chopped blanched almonds, pistachio nuts and raisins all make tasty additions.

Rice Chinese-style

Serves 4

1⅓ cups long-grain rice
water
1 teaspoon salt

Wash the rice in a strainer under running cold water until the water runs clear, stirring the rice around all the time with your fingers or a spoon. Shake in the strainer to drain thoroughly, then put into a large, ideally non-stick, pan. Cover with water to barely twice the amount of rice in the pan, salt it and cook over high heat till the grains have absorbed all the water.
   Cover the pan with a tight-fitting lid and continue cooking over gentle heat for 20 minutes more. Do not stir the rice during this time. Serve as soon as it is ready.

Cheese risotto

Serves 4

$\frac{1}{4}$ cup butter
2 small onions, peeled and chopped
1$\frac{1}{3}$ cups long-grain rice, washed and
   drained
$\frac{1}{2}$ cup dry white wine
2$\frac{1}{2}$ cups chicken stock or broth
small pinch of saffron
$\frac{1}{2}$ cup grated Parmesan cheese
$\frac{1}{2}$ cup grated Swiss cheese
salt

Heat half the butter in a deep
skillet. Add the onions and cook till
soft and transparent. Add the rice
and cook till transparent also,
stirring all the time.
   Slowly pour in the wine and when
it has been completely absorbed,
pour in all but 6 tablespoons of the
stock
   Cover the pan and cook the rice
for 10 minutes over a very gentle
heat. Stir in the saffron, dissolved in
the remaining stock, cover the pan
again and cook 10 minutes longer.
Just before serving, stir in the
cheeses and the rest of the butter.
Season to taste with salt.

This risotto can be served with
salads or to accompany veal cutlets,
broiled steaks or chops.

Variation
To make the risotto into a main
dish, fry diced lamb or pork in the
fat (or olive oil if you like) before
frying the onions and rice; add
chopped deseeded peppers and
peeled, deseeded, diced tomatoes.

Pilaff
Pilaff, or more correctly pilau, is the
Turkish version of risotto. It is made
with 2 tablespoons butter or
margarine and 3 tablespoons olive
oil to 1$\frac{1}{3}$ cups long-grain rice. Garlic
is added with the onions and the
cheese is omitted.

Chili pilaff
After the onions and garlic have
been softened in the fat, cook 1 cup
sliced mushrooms in it until the
liquid has evaporated. Add the rice
and cook it in chicken stock as
above, then add $\frac{2}{3}$ cup raisins and $\frac{1}{4}$
cup tomato paste. Season to taste
with cayenne or chili powder.

Lamb pilaff
Trim off all the fat from 1 lb
boneless lamb, and cut into small
dice. Heat the fat as above, adding a
little olive oil if necessary, and seal
the meat in it. Put in the onions and
cook with a little garlic, and rice as
above, mixing in diced deseeded
peppers, chopped tomatoes, and
cheese to taste.

Chicken liver pilaff
Cook the rice as for Cheese risotto
above but substitute extra stock for
the wine. Dice $\frac{1}{2}$ lb chicken livers
and fry them in the butter with 2
diced apples for about 4 minutes.
Stir into the rice at the end of the
cooking time.

Rice and Pasta

Spaghetti with various sauces

Serves 4

1 lb spaghetti
1–2 tablespoons salt
large dash of olive oil

Bring to a boil a generous quantity of water in a large saucepan. Add the salt and slide the spaghetti gradually into the water. Cook for about 12 minutes till 'al dente' or retaining some bite. About 2 minutes before the end of the cooking time, add the oil.

When cooked, drain the spaghetti in a large colander, return it to the pan and steam-dry for a moment. It can then be refreshed quickly with cold water to prevent it sticking together but this shouldn't be necessary.

Tomato and basil sauce

Serves 4

1 (29-oz) can peeled tomatoes, drained and juice reserved
1 onion, peeled and finely chopped
2 cloves of garlic, peeled and finely chopped
¼ cup olive oil
pinch of dried oregano
1 tablespoon chopped basil or 1 teaspoon dried basil
salt and freshly ground black pepper

Chop the tomatoes finely or crush with a potato masher. Gently cook the onion and garlic in the oil until soft and transparent. Pour over the reserved tomato liquid. Add the tomato pulp, the oregano and half the basil. Season to taste with salt and pepper and cook rapidly, uncovered, to a thick creamy consistency. Adjust the seasoning and sprinkle with the remaining basil. Serve with grated Parmesan cheese separately.

Note To make this sauce more piquant, flavor it with a mashed anchovy fillet, or a little anchovy paste, and/or season it with a pinch of grated nutmeg. It will be especially delicious if made with fresh tomatoes, although not so red in color, in which case add a little tomato paste, cooked for a few minutes with the onions and garlic.

Blue cheese cream sauce

Serves 2–4

1 tablespoon butter
½ lb blue cheese, mashed with a fork
1½ cups heavy cream
freshly ground black pepper
pinch of grated nutmeg
salt

Melt the butter, without browning, in a wide saucepan or a skillet. Add the cheese and cream and simmer until thick, stirring all the time. Season to taste with plenty of pepper, nutmeg and only a very little salt as the cheese is salty.

Serve the sauce with the cooked pasta and plenty of freshly ground black pepper. Or toss the pasta quickly in the sauce, spoon onto a serving plate and then season with pepper.

Bolognese sauce

Serves 4

2 tablespoons butter
4 slices of bacon, diced
1 onion, peeled and finely chopped
1 medium-sized carrot, peeled and finely chopped
1 celery stalk, finely chopped
1 tablespoon olive oil
¾ lb ground beef, lamb or veal
1–2 tablespoons tomato paste
½ cup stock or broth
½ cup red wine
½ cup milk or cream
salt and pepper
large pinch of dried oregano

Heat the butter in a large skillet. Add the bacon and vegetables and cook for about 10 minutes until lightly browned, stirring from time to time. Transfer them to a large saucepan.

Heat the olive oil in the skillet, add the ground meat and cook rapidly, stirring constantly, until it is browned and crumbly; add to the saucepan and heat through thoroughly.

Stir in the tomato paste, stock and wine. Bring to a boil, lower the heat, cover and simmer for a least 45 minutes. If possible, continue to cook very gently for another ½–1 hour, stirring from time to time to prevent it from sticking and burning.

Stir in the milk or cream and cook, uncovered, for a few minutes.

Season to taste with salt, pepper and oregano and serve very hot with the cooked pasta.

Note There are many variations of this sauce, which the Italians call *ragu alla bolognese*. It can be made with chopped mushrooms, chicken livers sautéed in butter, or chopped parsley may be added. Peeled canned tomatoes may be used instead of or as well as the tomato paste, and extra flavor added with garlic, chili or cayenne. But for a really exclusive and expensive bolognese, add a small chopped truffle.

Variation
Try this simple but quite delicious way of flavoring spaghetti. Fry several sliced cloves of garlic till golden in a little olive oil. Add a couple of fresh chili peppers, seeded and cut into fine rings. Toss the cooked drained spaghetti in the flavored oil and grind plenty of black pepper over. A sprinkling of fresh basil leaves can be added as the spaghetti is brought to the table.

Cook's Tip

For a change try these recipes using wholewheat spaghetti—it has a delicious flavour and an interesting nutty texture. Other types of wholewheat pasta such as rings or macaroni are also suitable.

Rice and Pasta

Gnocchi alla romana

Serves 3–4 as an accompaniment

1 cup milk
1 cup water
½ teaspoon salt
⅔ cup farina
2 egg yolks
6 tablespoons butter
1¼ cups grated Parmesan or Swiss cheese

In a large pan, bring the milk and water to a boil. Add the salt. Pour the farina in a thin stream into the boiling liquid stirring all the time, and continue stirring over gentle heat for 10 minutes while it cooks and thickens.

Stir in the egg yolks. Remove from the heat and leave until cool enough to handle. Using the back of a tablespoon, press the mixture out to a thickness of about ½ in on a plate or tray that has been rinsed with cold water. Let it rest for 1 hour. Then cut out small rounds or crescents with a small plain cookie cutter, or cut into squares. Preheat the oven to 450°.

Grease a large shallow baking dish

with a little of the butter. Put the unshaped paste trimmings in first, then cover with the shaped pieces, overlapping them to form a neat pattern. Sprinkle each layer with a little grated cheese and finish the top layer with the rest of the cheese. Dot the remaining butter all over the top and cook in the heated oven for 12–15 minutes. Serve hot with stews, goulash, or roast game birds.

Potato dumplings Piedmontese-style

Serves 3–4 as an accompaniment

2 lb potatoes, well scrubbed
¼ cup butter
salt
1 cup flour
2 eggs, lightly beaten
1 quart salted water
2 cups milk
½ cup grated Parmesan cheese

Boil the potatoes in their skins. Quickly refresh them with cold water then peel. Mash them thoroughly, then beat in 1 tablespoon of the butter and season with salt to taste. Stir them over a

low heat to dry them out a little, then leave until cool enough to handle. Tip them into a bowl and knead in the flour and eggs.

Using 2 teaspoons, form the potato mixture into little dumplings. Heat the salted water and milk together in a large pan until barely simmering. Put in the dumplings and cook gently in the simmering liquid for 6–8 minutes; do them in several batches if necessary. Lift out with a slotted spoon and drain on paper towels. Put in a warm serving dish. Melt the rest of the butter and pour it over the dumplings. Sprinkle with Parmesan.

Serve with fried liver or liver ragoût, roast lamb, or beef olives.

Variation
Reduce the amount of potatoes to 1 lb. Use 2 egg yolks instead of whole eggs, and add 1 (8-oz) package cream cheese to the potato mixture. Shape as above. These dumplings need 5–6 minutes cooking only. Finish by topping with the flaked butter and grated cheese and brown under a hot broiler.

Pasta with ham and egg

Serves 3–4 or 6 as an appetizer

*¾lb bow-shaped pasta (use a mixture
  of green and white shapes if you
  can get them)
2 quarts boiling salted water
3 tablespoons olive oil
½ cup finely diced cooked ham
4 eggs
¼ cup heavy cream
½ cup grated Parmesan cheese
freshly ground black pepper*

Cook the pasta in the boiling salted
water in a large uncovered pan for 8
minutes; then add 2 tablespoons of
the oil to prevent the pasta sticking
together, and cook about 4 minutes
more or until the pasta is 'al dente'.

Meanwhile, gently fry the ham in
the remaining oil till browned. Beat
the eggs with the cream and cheese,
adding black pepper to taste.

Drain the cooked pasta well and
pour at once into a warmed dish.
Quickly stir in the egg mixture,
spoon over the ham and serve with
more grated Parmesan cheese if you
wish.

Serve on its own as an appetizer,
or with broccoli, green beans, or
fennel sautéed in butter, as an
inexpensive main course.

Green noodles with peas

Serves 3–4 or 6 as an appetizer

*¾lb green ribbon noodles
2 quarts boiling salted water
2 tablespoons olive oil
¾ cup heavy cream
1 1-lb package frozen peas, cooked
  and drained
salt
freshly ground black pepper*

Cook the noodles in the boiling
salted water in a large pan,
uncovered, for 10 minutes, then add
the oil to stop the noodles sticking
together, and cook for about 5
minutes more till 'al dente'.

In another pan, heat the cream
and boil it rapidly, uncovered, until
reduced to about two-thirds. Add
the peas and drained noodles and
bring to a boil again. Season to taste
with salt and pepper. Serve at once,
as the cream is quickly absorbed by
the noodles.

This is an ideal accompaniment to
roast meats, fried veal cutlets or
pork chops.

Note The cream can be flavored with
a little garlic or chopped basil or
chervil if liked.

Variation
The addition of ½ cup chopped
cooked ham makes this an excellent
appetizer. Serve sprinkled with
chopped parsley.

Rice and Pasta

Lasagne

Serves 6

20 sheets (about ½ lb) lasagne
¼ cup oil
1 large onion, peeled and finely
  chopped
1 cup wiped and chopped
  mushrooms
2 carrots, peeled and finely chopped
2 cloves of garlic, peeled and crushed
½ lb ground beef
1 (16-oz) can tomatoes
salt and freshly ground black pepper
pinch of cayenne
½ teaspoon dried basil
½ teaspoon dried oregano
1 cup frozen peas

For the sauce
5 tablespoons butter
½ cup chopped cooked ham
6 tablespoons flour
2½ cups milk
pinch of grated nutmeg
¼ cup chopped parsley

To finish
½ lb mozzarella cheese, cubed
½ cup grated Parmesan cheese
6–8 ripe olives, pitted and halved

Preheat the oven to 350°.

Cook the lasagne for 8–10 minutes in boiling salted water to which a tablespoon of the oil has been added. Drain, refresh under cold water and lay out to dry on sheets of paper towels or a clean dish towel.

Heat the remaining oil in a saucepan and add the onion, mushrooms and carrots. Cook gently, stirring from time to time, until the onion is transparent but not brown. Add the garlic and the meat and continue cooking until the meat is brown and crumbly. Pour in the tomatoes with their liquid and season to taste with salt, pepper, cayenne and the herbs. Simmer gently for 30–45 minutes, stirring occasionally to prevent sticking.

Meanwhile cook the peas for a few minutes in a little boiling salted water. Drain, then refresh with cold water. Melt all but 1 tablespoon of the butter in a saucepan and fry the

ham for a few minutes. Sprinkle in the flour and continue cooking for 1–2 minutes. Add the milk a little at a time, stirring continuously, to make a thick sauce. Season to taste with salt, pepper and nutmeg. Remove from the heat and stir in the parsley.

Grease an oblong baking dish (about 6 × 10 in) and cover the bottom with a layer of lasagne. Spread over some meat mixture and pour over a little of the white sauce. Scatter over equal amounts of peas, mozzarella and Parmesan. Continue to build layers in this way, adding the olives to the top layer with the peas and cheese. Dot with the remaining butter and bake in the heated oven for 25–30 minutes until golden brown and bubbling.

Serve with a fresh green salad, tossed in an Italian dressing of oil, vinegar and mustard. A light Italian red wine goes very well with lasagne.

Note This dish is even more attractive if you use green lasagne (lasagne verde) and is also tastier as fresh spinach juice is used in the manufacture of green lasagne. If you cannot obtain green lasagne you can use ½ lb fresh spinach with the white lasagne. Wash it well, blanch for a few minutes in boiling water and refresh with cold water. Drain well, squeezing out excess moisture and place in layers over the white lasagne before spreading over the meat mixture.

Variation
Try adding some corn, quartered artichoke hearts or strips of tomato or pepper to the dish. Replace the ripe olives with stuffed green ones for a milder flavor.

Cook's Tip

Lasagne makes an ideal dish for a large informal buffet party. It can be assembled in advance, then frozen. Either use a dish which is both oven- and freezer-proof or line the dish with foil. When the lasagne is frozen lift the foil out of the dish and fold it tightly to make a sealed parcel.

Defrost the lasagne overnight at room temperature. If you have removed it from the dish, unwrap the foil parcel while still frozen and replace it in the original dish for defrosting and reheating. Before serving, place in a moderately hot oven (350°) for 30–40 minutes or until heated through and golden and bubbling on top.

Egg Dishes

Egg Dishes

Poached eggs

Serves 2–4

2 quarts water
2 teaspoons salt
1 tablespoon vinegar
4 fresh eggs

Bring the water to a boil with the salt and vinegar then reduce the heat so that it simmers steadily. Break the eggs one at a time into a ladle and slide them quickly into the water. Cook for about 3–5 minutes until the whites are set and the eggs are cooked to taste. Carefully lift them out using a slotted spoon, transfer to a warmed serving dish and trim the edges to neaten the eggs. Serve immediately.

Tip Eggs used for poaching must be as fresh as possible as slightly stale ones will be more apt to fall apart during cooking.

Note Poached eggs are delicious served with a variety of sauces. Try them with Mustard or Horseradish sauce (see page 111) or Mushroom or Mock béchamel (see page 108). For an unusual variation serve the Tomato and basil sauce on page 164, made thinner by stirring in a little red wine or sour cream just before serving.

Poached eggs with vegetable purée

Serves 4

4 cups shredded cabbage, sliced carrots or chopped broccoli
¾ cup boiling chicken stock or broth
1 (3-oz) package cream cheese
1 tablespoon butter
2 tablespoons sour cream
salt and pepper
pinch of nutmeg
1 tablespoon chopped parsley
1 tablespoon chopped dill or chives
4 eggs

Prepare the vegetables and cook them in the stock in a covered pan until they are tender — about 5–15 minutes depending on their type. Strain them, reserving any stock for use in soups or casseroles, then purée in a blender or food processor. Beat in the cream cheese, butter and sour cream and season to taste with salt, pepper and a little nutmeg. Stir in the chopped herbs and divide the vegetable purée between four individual, warmed serving dishes. Keep hot while you poach the eggs, following the instructions above. Make a hollow in the mixture and place a poached egg on each. Serve immediately.

Poached eggs Olivet

Serves 4

½ quantity Béchamel sauce (page 108)
2 tablespoons butter
4 shallots, peeled and finely chopped
1 clove of garlic, peeled and crushed
1 lb fresh sorrel or spinach, washed, trimmed and dried
salt and pepper
¼ cup heavy cream
4 eggs

Make the Béchamel sauce according to the recipe instructions and keep it hot. Melt the butter in a saucepan, add the shallots and garlic and cook until soft but not browned. Add the sorrel or spinach, cover the pan and cook it over low heat for about 10 minutes. Chop the cooked vegetables or purée in a blender or food processor. Season the purée generously. Whip the cream until stiff and fold it into the sorrel or spinach, then divide the mixture between four individual serving dishes and keep warm while you poach the eggs according to the instructions above. Pour the sauce around the vegetable mixture and top with a poached egg. Serve immediately.

Poached eggs Beaugency

Serves 4

½ quantity Béarnaise sauce (page 122)
4 canned artichoke hearts
1 tablespoon butter
4 cooked scallops or button mushroom caps
4 eggs
1 tablespoon chopped parsley

Make the sauce according to the recipe instructions. Heat the artichoke hearts in their liquid but do not let them boil. Melt the butter, add the drained scallops or mushroom caps and heat through gently for 2–3 minutes. Drain the artichokes and place them on individual, warmed serving dishes or one large dish. Poach the eggs according to the instructions above. Pour the sauce over the artichoke hearts and top each with a poached egg. Garnish with the scallops or mushrooms and sprinkle the chopped parsley over. Serve immediately.

Cook's Tip

Special egg poaching pans can be obtained or you can use greased plain pastry cutters set in a frying pan filled with boiling water to help poached eggs keep their shape. It is sometimes necessary to trim the edge of the egg a little to obtain a neat shape.

Egg Dishes

Scrambled eggs

Serves 4

8 eggs
¼ cup light cream
salt and freshly ground white pepper
¼ cup butter
1 tablespoon chopped chives
*   (optional)*

Whisk the eggs with the cream and seasoning to taste until the ingredients are thoroughly combined and frothy. Melt three-quarters of the butter in a non-stick or heavy-based saucepan over gentle heat, swirling it around the sides of the pan. Do not allow it to overheat. Pour the eggs into the pan and cook them, stirring continuously, over gentle heat until they are just set and very creamy. Remove the pan from the heat immediately and quickly stir in the remaining butter.

Serve the eggs at once — the heat of the pan continues to cook the eggs so they should not be left in it for too long. Sprinkle the scrambled eggs with chopped chives, if using.

Tip For a lower calorie content substitute milk for the cream.

Variations
Scrambled eggs with bacon Chop ¼ lb slab bacon and fry it gently in the pan until the fat runs. Add 2 tablespoons butter before pouring in the egg mixture, then cook as above.

Scrambled eggs with herbs Any finely chopped, fresh herbs are suitable for this dish, for example, parsley, thyme, sage, lemon balm, tarragon, rosemary or chives. Add small quantities of the herbs to the beaten eggs before cooking.

Scrambled egg Antoine Cook the bacon as above and add 2 tablespoons chopped mixed fresh herbs and 1 tablespoon chopped capers to the beaten eggs as they are poured into the pan. Pour Noisette butter sauce (see page 110) over the cooked eggs before serving.

Scrambled eggs with shrimp Finely chop 3 slices of bacon and sauté this with ¼ cup peeled and deveined shrimp in 1 tablespoon of the butter. Remove this mixture from the pan and keep it hot. Cook the eggs as above, then stir in the shrimp mixture and 2 tablespoons chopped parsley. Serve immediately.

Scrambled eggs jardinière

Serves 4

1½ cups peeled and thinly sliced
*   carrots*
½ lb green beans, trimmed
salt
1 cup frozen peas
6 tablespoons butter
½ lb shallots or pearl onions, peeled
1 quantity Scrambled eggs (see
*   above)*
1 cup grated sharp Cheddar cheese

Cook the carrots and green beans separately in boiling salted water for about 10 minutes or until cooked to taste then drain well. Cook the peas according to the instructions on the package and drain. Keep the

vegetables warm. Melt two-thirds of the butter in a skillet and fry the shallots or pearl onions, seasoning them lightly first, until golden brown. Meanwhile make the scrambled eggs according to the instructions above, then stir in the grated cheese until it melts.

Spoon the scrambled eggs into a serving dish and arrange the cooked vegetables, including the onions, around them. Dot the remaining butter over the peas, beans and carrots and serve with warm French bread as an accompaniment.

Plain omelette

Serves 1

2 large or 3 small eggs
salt and pepper
2 teaspoons water
2 tablespoons butter

Beat the eggs with the seasoning and water until the yolks and whites are just amalgamated. Melt the butter in an omelette pan over high heat then pour in the egg mixture. Lift the edge of the omelette as it sets and tilt the pan to allow the uncooked egg to run onto the pan and set. The underside of the omelette should be golden brown and the top just set. Carefully fold the omelette in half or roll it up and slide it onto a warmed serving plate.

Tip When making a filled omelette it is essential that the filling is prepared and hot before the eggs are cooked. Spoon the filling over half the omelette and fold the other half over to cover. Serve as above. Fricassée of chicken or veal, lightly cooked vegetable or cooked fish or shrimp are all ideas for fillings.

Omelette fines herbes

Serves 1

2 large or 3 small eggs
pinch of salt
2 teaspoons light cream or milk
1 teaspoon chopped parsley
1 teaspoon chopped chives
1 teaspoon chopped chervil
2 tablespoons butter

Mix the eggs with the salt, cream or milk and the herbs. Melt the butter in an omelette pan, pour in the egg mixture and cook as for the Plain omelette. Fold the omelette in half and serve immediately.

Variations
Pour the egg mixture over lightly cooked mushrooms, chopped onion or crispy fried chopped bacon or ham and cook as above. The omelette may be filled with a little grated Swiss cheese.

Egg Dishes

Savory soufflé crêpes

Makes 6

1¼ cups all-purpose flour
pinch of salt
3 eggs, separated
1¼ cups water
a little grated lemon rind (optional)
butter for frying

Sift the flour and salt into a bowl and make a well in the center. Add the egg yolks and gradually beat in the water, incorporating the flour to make a fairly thick batter. Stir in the lemon rind, if used, and allow the batter to stand for 15 minutes. Beat the egg whites until stiff and fold them into the batter.

Melt a little butter in a medium-sized skillet, pour in enough of the batter to make a thin layer over the bottom and cook until golden brown on the underside and lightly set on top. Carefully flip it over using a spatula and cook until golden on the other side. Keep the crêpes warm until they are all cooked then fill and serve.

Note This basic recipe for soufflé crêpes can be enriched by the addition of milk or cream and up to 3 tablespoons melted butter can be folded into the batter.

Steak and kidney filling

Enough for 6 crêpes

½ lb lamb kidneys, halved, cored and sliced
¾ lb steak, trimmed and cut in thin strips
juice of ½ small lemon
¾ cup thinly sliced mushrooms
2 tablespoons butter
2 tablespoons oil
1 onion, peeled and finely chopped
1 clove of garlic, peeled and crushed
¾ cup light cream
salt and freshly ground black pepper
dash of Worcestershire sauce
2 tablespoons chopped parsley

Soak the kidneys in cold water for 30 minutes. Drain well and dry the pieces carefully, then mix with the steak. Sprinkle the lemon juice over the mushrooms and allow to stand for 10 minutes.

Melt the butter with the oil in a skillet. Add the onion and garlic and cook until soft but not browned. Stir in the steak and kidney mixture and cook until browned, stirring occasionally to prevent burning. When the meat is cooked, add the mushrooms and cook for 2–3 minutes. Add the cream, seasoning and a little Worcestershire sauce and heat it through without allowing the mixture to boil. Finally stir in the parsley. Divide the mixture between the crêpes, fold them over and serve immediately.

Variations
Melt 2 tablespoons butter in a saucepan and sauté 1 finely chopped onion until soft but not browned. Add the juice of 1 lemon and about 6 tablespoons dry white wine. Stir in 1 cup cooked and flaked smoked haddock (finnan haddie) or smoked eel, or ¾ cup finely diced cooked chicken meat. Heat through gently for 5 minutes then mix in 2 tablespoons heavy cream. Remove from the heat at once and season to taste before serving.

Vegetable filling

Enough for 6 crêpes

1 medium-sized eggplant, thinly sliced
salt
2 tablespoons olive oil
1 tablespoon butter
1 large onion, peeled and sliced
1 zucchini, cut into thin strips
2 ripe tomatoes, peeled, deseeded and roughly chopped
1 clove of garlic, peeled and crushed
5 tablespoons red wine
freshly ground black pepper
1 teaspoon chopped mixed herbs
1 teaspoon green peppercorns
a few basil leaves to garnish (optional)

Place the eggplant in a colander, sprinkle with salt and leave to stand for 15 minutes then rinse and dry throughly. Heat the oil and butter together in a skillet, add the prepared vegetables and garlic and cook until soft but not browned. Pour over the wine and season with a little pepper, then stir in the herbs and peppercorns and cook for 5 minutes. Divide the filling between the soufflé crêpes and fold them in half. Garnish with the basil leaves, if using. Serve immediately.

Variation
Sweet soufflé crêpes These crêpes are also delicious with a sweet filling. Try a sweetened fruit purée such as apricot flavored with a little orange rind or apple purée flavored with cinnamon. Alternatively spread the crêpes with a little jam before folding over and serve dusted with sugar.

Egg Dishes

Stuffed eggs

Stuffed eggs can be served as an appetizer or as a snack and they are ideal for serving as part of a cold buffet.

Columbus eggs

1 boneless chicken breast, cooked, skinned and finely chopped
2 anchovy fillets, chopped
2 tablespoons capers, finely chopped
1 small onion, peeled and grated
8 hard-cooked eggs
1 tablespoon chopped parsley
¾ cup mayonnaise
1 teaspoon prepared mustard
sprigs of dill or parsley to garnish

Mix the chicken, anchovy fillets, capers and onion together. Halve the eggs lengthwise, remove the yolks and sieve them into the chicken mixture. Stir in the chopped parsley and spoon this mixture into the whites. Beat the mayonnaise and mustard together and place it in a pastry bag fitted with a small star tube. Garnish the eggs with rosettes of the mayonnaise mixture and sprigs of dill or parsley.

Russian eggs

8 hard-cooked eggs
¼ cup butter
juice of ½ lemon
½ (3½-oz) jar black lumpfish caviar

Halve the eggs lengthwise, remove the yolks and sieve them. Cream the butter with the lemon juice and sieved yolks until soft then spoon it back into the whites. Garnish each with a little caviar.

Pâté-stuffed eggs

8 hard-cooked eggs
¼ lb pâté de foie gras or liver pâté
salt and freshly ground white pepper
3 tablespoons grated Parmesan cheese
¼ cup butter

Halve the eggs lengthwise and scoop out the yolks. Beat the pâté with the yolks and seasoning and use this mixture to fill the egg whites. Sprinkle the Parmesan cheese over the top and dot each with a little of the butter. Place the stuffed eggs under a hot broiler until lightly browned. Serve immediately.

Shrimp-stuffed eggs

8 hard-cooked eggs
½ lb peeled shrimp, deveined
¼ cup butter
salt and freshly ground white pepper
¾ cup heavy cream
parsley sprigs to garnish

Halve the eggs lengthwise and remove the yolks. Reserve 16 shrimp for garnish and chop the remainder very finely. Cream the butter with the yolks, seasoning and chopped shrimp until soft. Fill the egg whites with this mixture. Whip the heavy cream until stiff and place in a pastry bag fitted with a small plain tube. Pipe a cream border around the stuffed eggs, then top with the reserved shrimp and parsley sprigs.

Eggs in brine

1 quart water
3 tablespoons salt
2 small onions
8 hard-cooked eggs in their shells

Boil the water with the salt and the onions, with their skins, for 10 minutes. Allow the liquid to cool then strain and reserve it. Crack the eggs but do not remove their shells, then place them in an earthenware crock or canning jar. Pour the cooled brine over the eggs to cover them completely. Cover the crock or jar and leave for about 3 days. Do not allow the eggs to steep for more than 5 days.

Serve the eggs from the crock or jar with fresh wholewheat or pumpernickel bread. The eggs should be shelled, halved and seasoned with mustard, Worcestershire sauce or hot pepper sauce.

Tip To make a spicier brine a little fresh ginger root may be added. Use about 1 inch of ginger and add 1 teaspoon peppercorns, ½ teaspoon mustard seeds and 2–3 bay leaves.

Coddled eggs

An egg-coddler is a small decorative china or glass vessel with a lid which is traditionally used for lightly cooking eggs. Most coddlers are big enough for 2 eggs or 1 egg plus additional flavorings.

Place a small pat of butter inside the coddler and place in a pan of simmering water until the butter has melted. Swirl the butter around the sides and drop in the egg. Put the lid on the coddler and simmer the water for 8–10 minutes until the egg is just set.

Variations
Spinach egg Lightly season 2 tablespoons drained, cooked, chopped spinach with salt, pepper and nutmeg. Stir in a little heavy cream. Put half this mixture in the greased coddler. Drop in the egg and cover with the remaining spinach. Cook as above. A little chopped, cooked ham may also be stirred into the spinach, if liked.

Cheese egg Beat 1 tablespoon finely grated Cheddar cheese with 2 tablespoons heavy cream and use in place of the spinach mixture above. Season with a pinch of paprika.

Tuna egg Use 2 tablespoons drained, flaked tuna fish instead of the spinach mixture and omit the nutmeg.

Bacon egg Chop 2 slices of lean bacon and fry lightly. Place half in the bottom of the egg coddler then put in the egg and sprinkle the rest of the bacon over the top before cooking as above. Chopped cooked ham or tongue can be used in this way without frying first.

Soufflés and Bakes

Soufflés and Bakes

Gratin dauphinois

Serves 4

2 lb potatoes, peeled and thinly sliced
2 cloves garlic, halved
salt and freshly ground white pepper
freshly grated nutmeg
1¼ cups milk
1¼ cups light cream
1 egg, beaten
1 cup grated Swiss cheese
¼ cup butter

Preheat the oven to 400°.

Rinse the sliced potatoes under running water and pat them dry on paper towels. Rub the inside of a gratin or baking dish with the cut cloves of garlic. Grease the dish and layer the potatoes in it, seasoning each layer with salt, pepper and nutmeg. The potatoes should come to about ½ in below the rim of the dish.

Heat the milk and cream together until just lukewarm. Stir in the egg and two-thirds of the grated cheese then slowly pour this mixture over the potatoes, allowing it to run between the layers. Sprinkle the remaining cheese over the top, dot with the butter and bake for 50–60 minutes or until the potatoes are cooked and the top is crisp and golden brown.

Note Instead of half milk and cream, this dish may be enriched by using all cream.

Leek and potato gratin

Serves 4

1½ lb potatoes, peeled and thinly sliced
1 large leek, thinly sliced and washed
2 tablespoons butter
1–2 cloves garlic, crushed
2 egg yolks
1 cup light cream
salt and freshly ground white pepper
pinch of cayenne
¾ cup grated cheese

Preheat the oven to 400°.

The potatoes should be sliced very thinly — a mandoline or slicing attachment to a food processor or mixer will make this easier. Rinse the slices and dry them on paper towels. Separate the leek slices into rings and dry them thoroughly. Grease a baking dish thickly with the butter and layer half the potatoes in it. Arrange the leek and garlic evenly over them and then top with the remaining potatoes. Whisk the egg yolks and cream together and season thoroughly with salt, pepper and a little cayenne. Pour this mixture over the potatoes and sprinkle the cheese evenly over the top.

Bake for 45–50 minutes until golden brown. Serve immediately — this dish is particularly good with roast lamb or game.

Note For extra flavor layer a thinly sliced green pepper with the potatoes and leeks and sprinkle Parmesan cheese over the top instead of the grated cheese. The gratin would then be ideal for a supper or light luncheon dish.

Quick potato gratin

Serves 4

¼ cup butter
2 onions, peeled and sliced into rings
1 clove garlic, crushed
½ cup chopped cooked ham
2 tablespoons chopped parsley
salt and freshly ground white pepper
pinch of freshly grated nutmeg
generous pinch of caraway seeds
1 lb boiled potatoes, cooled and sliced
¾ cup sour cream
1 egg, beaten
½ cup grated sharp Cheddar cheese

Preheat the oven to 400°.

Melt the butter in a skillet, add the onion slices, separated into rings, and cook them, turning frequently, until they are golden brown. Add the garlic and toss well then mix in the ham and parsley. Season to taste with salt, pepper, nutmeg and caraway seeds. Remove the pan from the heat and carefully mix in the potatoes. Spoon this mixture into a baking dish.

Whisk the sour cream into the egg and stir in half the cheese. Pour the egg mixture over the potatoes, sprinkle the remaining cheese evenly over the top and bake for about 20 minutes until golden brown. Serve immediately. Quick potato gratin goes particularly well with broiled steak.

Soufflés and Bakes

Oven-baked kohlrabi

Serves 6

1 lb kohlrabi
¼ cup butter
2–3 onions, peeled and sliced
½ slab bacon, cut in strips
2 tablespoons chopped chives
2 tablespoons chopped parsley
salt and freshly ground black pepper
1 lb potatoes, peeled and thinly sliced
1 lb tomatoes, peeled and sliced
1¼ cups milk
½ cup sour cream
1½ cups grated Swiss cheese
2 eggs, beaten
freshly grated nutmeg

Preheat the oven to 400°.
    Trim any leaves and stalks from the kohlrabi, then peel and slice thinly. Melt half the butter in a skillet, add the onion and cook the slices until soft but not browned. Add the bacon, herbs and seasoning and stir the ingredients together. Remove the pan from the heat.
    Layer the potatoes, kohlrabi and tomatoes in a well-greased baking dish together with the onion mixture, ending with a layer of potatoes. Heat the milk and sour cream together to just lukewarm then gradually stir in the cheese, standing the saucepan over low heat until the cheese melts. Do not allow the mixture to boil. Remove the saucepan from the heat and stir in the beaten eggs. Season with nutmeg and a little salt and pepper, then pour the mixture over the layered vegetables and dot with the remaining butter.
    Bake for 45–50 minutes until the vegetables are cooked and the top layer of potatoes is crisp and golden. Serve immediately with French bread or as an accompaniment to broiled chops or steaks.

Variation
Broccoli may be substituted for the tomatoes. Divide the broccoli into florets and blanch it in boiling water for a few minutes. Layer it with the other ingredients, pour over the sauce and bake as above. Smoked chicken or turkey may be substituted for the bacon.

Cook's Tip

Turnips can be used in this recipe if kohlrabi cannot be obtained as they have a similar flavor. Choose small young turnips and prepare as in recipe above. Turnip tops can be cooked separately as a green vegetable.

Moussaka

Serves 4

4 medium-size eggplants, trimmed
  and sliced
salt
about ½ cup flour
olive oil for frying
2 large onions, peeled and finely
  chopped
1½ lb ground lamb
2 cloves garlic
1 lb tomatoes, peeled and chopped
¼ cup red wine
2 tablespoons tomato paste
¼ cup chopped parsley
freshly ground black pepper
generous pinch of ground cinnamon
1 cup light cream
2 eggs, beaten
1 cup finely grated cheese
freshly grated nutmeg

Place the eggplants in a colander, sprinkle generously with salt and leave them to stand for 15–20 minutes.

Preheat the oven to 350°. Rinse the eggplants then pat dry on paper towels and dust them lightly with the flour. Heat the oil in a skillet and fry the eggplant slices, a few at a time, for about 1 minute on each side then drain them on paper towels. Add more oil to the pan if necessary, and heat it between batches so that the eggplant slices brown quickly.

Add the chopped onion to the remaining oil in the skillet and cook it with the ground lamb, stirring frequently, until lightly browned. Stir in the garlic and tomatoes, red wine and tomato paste and cook the mixture for 5 minutes. Add the parsley and season the meat mixture with salt, pepper and a little cinnamon.

Layer the eggplant and meat together in a baking dish, ending with eggplant on top. Lightly whip the cream with the eggs and stir in the cheese. Season with a little nutmeg and pour the egg mixture over the moussaka. Bake in the preheated oven for about 1 hour until the egg mixture is set and golden brown on top. Serve immediately with a crisp green salad.

Variation

Sliced, cooked potatoes or sliced zucchini can be layered in the moussaka together with the eggplant and lamb. Béchamel sauce (page 108) may be poured over the moussaka instead of the custard mixture. Ground beef or pork may be substituted for the lamb.

Cook's Tip

If preparing onions makes you weep, try putting them in cold water for half an hour before peeling them. Alternatively peel onions under running water and remember not to lean over the board whilst chopping them.

Soufflés and Bakes

Layered cottage pie

Serves 4

¾ *cup finely diced salami*
2 onions, peeled and chopped
1 lb ground beef
3 tablespoons tomato paste
1 teaspoon dried oregano
salt and freshly ground black pepper
1½ lb potatoes, peeled
¾ *cup hot milk*
1 cup grated Cheddar cheese

Fry the salami in a thick-based saucepan, over a moderate heat, until the fat runs. Remove the salami with a slotted spoon. Add the onion to the fat in the pan and fry until golden. Remove a little of the onion and reserve. Add the ground beef and fry until brown and crumbly. Return the salami to the pan and cook for a further 5 minutes over a moderate heat. Drain all excess fat from the pan and stir in the tomato paste and oregano. Season well to taste then cover the pan and cook over a low heat for 20 minutes.

Meanwhile cook the potatoes in boiling salted water until tender. Drain then mash well and push through a ricer to make a smooth purée. While still hot, beat in the milk and some extra seasoning. Stir in ¾ cup of the grated cheese. Preheat the oven to 400°.

Grease a 1-quart baking dish and layer the meat and potato mixtures in it, ending with a layer of potato. Sprinkle with the remaining cheese. Bake for 20 minutes in the preheated oven or until golden.

Variations
The salami can be replaced with 8 oz chopped slab bacon and minced cooked beef can be used to replace the fresh beef mince. Try adding 1 green pepper, deseeded and chopped or 4 oz mushrooms, wiped and sliced to the mince mixture.

Baked Chinese cabbage

Serves 4

1¼ cups Béchamel sauce (page 108)
1 cup grated Swiss cheese
salt and freshly ground white pepper
freshly grated nutmeg
2 eggs, separated
1 large Chinese cabbage (bok choy), shredded and washed
¼ *lb slab bacon, cut in strips*

Preheat the oven to 400°. Make the Béchamel sauce according to the recipe instructions. Stir two-thirds of the cheese into the sauce and season it with salt, pepper and nutmeg. Beat in the egg yolks. Stiffly beat the egg whites and fold them into the sauce.

Layer the shredded Chinese cabbage with the bacon and sauce in a buttered baking dish, ending with a layer of sauce on top. Sprinkle the remaining cheese over and bake for 30–40 minutes. If the top of the dish becomes too brown during cooking cover it loosely with a piece of foil. Serve immediately.

Jack's cherry pudding

Serves 6

6 tablespoons butter
½ cup sugar
4 eggs, separated
1 teaspoon ground cinnamon
grated rind of ½ lemon
few drops vanilla extract
¼ cup Kirsch or sherry
⅓ cup chopped blanched almonds
¼ cup soft white breadcrumbs
8 slices white bread
1 lb Bing cherries, pitted
confectioners' sugar to dust

Preheat the oven to 350°.

Cream the butter with the sugar and egg yolks. Add the cinnamon, lemon rind, vanilla extract, Kirsch or sherry and stir in the chopped almonds. Beat the egg whites until stiff and fold them into the mixture.

Grease a 7½-cup soufflé dish and sprinkle the breadcrumbs into it, tilting it to ensure that they coat the sides. Layer the bread, cherries and creamed mixture in the dish, ending with the creamed mixture on top. Bake for 50–60 minutes. Dust with confectioners' sugar before serving.

Cream cheese soufflé

Serves 4–6

½ cup chopped tenderized prunes
6 tablespoons dry white wine
¼ cinnamon stick
2 cloves
6 tablespoons butter
½ cup sugar
3 eggs, separated
3 tablespoons heavy cream
3 tablespoons farina
4 (3-oz) packages cream cheese
¼ cup ground hazelnuts

Sauce
5 egg yolks
6 tablespoons sugar
2 tablespoons lemon juice
1 cup dry white wine

Mix the prunes with the wine, cinnamon and cloves and leave to soak for a few hours.

Preheat the oven to 375°. Reserve about 1 tablespoon of the butter and beat the remainder with the sugar, egg yolks and cream. Gradually beat in the farina and cream cheese. Beat the egg whites until stiff and fold them into the cheese mixture

together with the drained prunes. Grease a 7½-cup soufflé dish and coat it with half the hazelnuts. Pour in the soufflé mixture and sprinkle with the remaining hazelnuts. Dot with the reserved butter and bake for 20 minutes, then reduce the temperature to 350° and cook for a further 30 minutes.

Make the sauce about 10 minutes before the soufflé is ready. Beat the egg yolks with the sugar and lemon juice, gradually adding the wine. Stand the bowl over a saucepan of hot water and beat the mixture, preferably using an electric beater, until it thickens. Serve the hot sauce with the soufflé immediately it is removed from the oven.

Soufflés and Bakes

Rhubarb pudding

Serves 4–6

*1 lb rhubarb, trimmed and cut into
  1-in lengths*
*¼ cup raspberry syrup or strawberry
  syrup*
¾ lb frozen strawberries
½ cup + 2 tablespoons sugar
2 eggs, separated
1 teaspoon vanilla extract
¾ cup flour
½ cup cornstarch
grated rind ½ lemon
1 egg white
pinch of salt
confectioners' sugar to dust

Put the rhubarb in a saucepan with
the raspberry or strawberry syrup.
Heat gently until the juice runs,
bring to a boil and simmer for 5
minutes then allow to cool. Sprinkle
the strawberries with ¼ cup of the
sugar and leave to thaw.
  Preheat the oven to 350°. Beat the
egg yolks with the remaining sugar
and vanilla extract until thick and
creamy. Sift together the flour and
cornstarch and fold into the egg yolk
mixture. Drain the strawberries and
rhubarb and gradually fold the juice
into the mixture together with the
lemon rind. Beat all the egg whites
with the salt until stiff and fold into
the egg yolk mixture.
  Grease a 7½-cup soufflé dish with
butter. Put the rhubarb and
strawberries in the bottom of the
dish and cover with the sponge
mixture. Bake the pudding in the
preheated oven for 1 hour. If the
pudding browns too quickly cover
with foil towards the end of the
cooking time. Dust while still hot
with confectioners' sugar and serve
immediately.

Variations
Flavor the rhubarb with 2
tablespoons red currant jelly instead
of the raspberry or strawberry syrup.
The strawberries can be omitted and
the quantity of rhubarb increased to
1½ lb; replace the syrup with the
grated rind and juice of 1 orange,
adding a little extra sugar, if
necessary.

Sauce sabayon I

3 egg yolks
pinch of salt
3 tablespoons vanilla sugar
1 cup medium dry white wine
1 teaspoon Kirsch

Beat the egg yolks with the salt and
sugar in a bowl over a saucepan of
hot water until foamy. Gradually
whisk in the wine and continue to
whisk until the sauce thickens
slightly. Lastly, whisk in the Kirsch
and continue whisking the mixture,
off the heat, until the sauce has
cooled. Serve the sauce
immediately.

Sauce sabayon II

6 egg yolks
pinch of salt
1 teaspoon lemon juice
2 tablespoons vanilla sugar
½ cup medium-dry sherry or Marsala

Whisk the egg yolks with the salt
and lemon juice in a bowl over a
saucepan of hot water. Gradually
whisk in the sugar. Continue
whisking, slowly pouring in the
sherry or Marsala, until the sauce is
slightly thickened. Serve
immediately.

Cook's Tip

.To make your own vanilla sugar
break a vanilla bean in half and mix
it thoroughly into ½ cup sugar. Spoon
the sugar and the vanilla bean into a
jar and cover it with a tight-fitting
lid. Keep the sugar for 1–2 weeks
before using. Shake the jar
occasionally during this storage time
to allow the vanilla flavor to mingle
with the sugar.

Soufflés and Bakes

Cheese soufflé

Serves 4

3 tablespoons butter
1¾ cups grated Swiss cheese
6 tablespoons flour
1 cup milk
salt and freshly ground white pepper
pinch of freshly grated nutmeg
4 eggs, separated
½ teaspoon lemon juice

Preheat the oven to 350°.

Grease a 1-quart soufflé dish with a little of the butter and sprinkle a little of the cheese around the inside of it. Melt the remaining butter, add the flour and cook it over low heat, stirring continuously, for 3 minutes. Gradually stir in the milk and bring the sauce to a boil, then reduce the heat and cook it, stirring continuously, until it is thick and smooth. Season the sauce with salt, pepper and nutmeg and remove the saucepan from the heat. Stir in the egg yolks and most of the remaining cheese, reserving about 2 tablespoons for garnish. Allow to cool until just warm.

Beat the egg whites and lemon juice until they are very stiff and quite dry. Fold a little of the whites into the sauce, then fold in all the remaining whites and spoon the mixture into the prepared dish. Sprinkle the reserved cheese on top and bake the soufflé for 40–45 minutes until well risen and golden brown. Serve immediately.

Raspberry soufflé

Serves 6

½ lb raspberries
½ cup sugar
4 egg yolks
1 tablespoon vanilla sugar (page 188)
  or few drops of vanilla extract
6 tablespoons cornstarch
5 egg whites
pinch of salt
1 teaspoon lemon juice
confectioners' sugar to dust

Preheat the oven to 375°.

Purée the raspberries with 2 tablespoons of the sugar in a blender then press the purée through a sieve to remove the seeds. Whisk the remaining sugar with the egg yolks and vanilla sugar or vanilla extract until pale and creamy then fold in the cornstarch. Beat the egg whites with the salt and lemon juice until they are stiff and dry then carefully fold them into the yolk mixture. Lastly, fold in the raspberry purée and spoon the mixture into a greased 7½-cup soufflé dish. Bake the soufflé for 15 minutes then increase the oven temperature to 400° for a further 10–15 minutes. Dust the hot soufflé with confectioners' sugar, wrap a napkin around the dish for a professional look, and serve it immediately.

Alaska surprise

Serves 6

½ lb strawberries
½ cup + 2 tablespoons sugar
16 ladyfinger cookies
2 tablespoons Framboise liqueur or
  Kirsch
4 egg whites
1 teaspoon lemon juice
⅓ cup ground almonds
1 pint vanilla ice cream

Trim, wash and hull the strawberries then halve and sprinkle 2 tablespoons of the sugar over them. Arrange the cookies over the bottom of an 8-in tart pan, cutting some to fill in the gaps and form an even base. Arrange the strawberries on top and sprinkle the liqueur over them. Beat the egg whites with the lemon juice until they are very stiff and dry. Beat the remaining sugar in and continue to beat until stiff and glossy. Divide the whites into two equal portions and fold the ground almonds into one half. Cut the ice cream into slices and lay it on top of the strawberries, then cover it with the almond meringue. Place the remaining meringue in a pastry bag fitted with a star tube and, working quickly, cover the top of the dessert with piped meringue. Cover the top completely, right up to the edge of the dish. Brown the meringue in a preheated 450° oven for about 2 minutes until the meringue peaks are lightly browned. Serve immediately.

Perfect
Desserts

Desserts

Bavaroise

Serves 4

1 vanilla bean
1¼ cups milk
pinch of salt
1½ envelopes unflavored gelatine
2 tablespoons hot water
4 egg yolks
1 cup confectioners' sugar, sifted
1¼ cups heavy cream

Break the vanilla bean, place it in a saucepan with the milk and a pinch of salt and bring slowly to a boil. Dissolve the gelatine in 2 tablespoons hot water. Beat the egg yolks with the confectioners' sugar until frothy then gradually strain the milk over them, beating continuously. Place the bowl over a saucepan of hot water and continue beating until the custard thickens slightly. Do not overcook or the custard will curdle.

Stir the dissolved gelatine into the custard and allow to cool until it begins to set. Whip the cream until stiff and fold it into the bavaroise then spoon it into a 1-quart mold and chill until set. Just before serving, unmold and decorate with whipped cream.

Bavaroise with gooseberries

Serves 4

½ lb gooseberries, washed and trimmed
½ cup sugar
1 cinnamon stick
4 cloves
½ cup white wine
1½ teaspoons unflavored gelatine
2 tablespoons hot water
1 quantity bavaroise (see left)
¾ cup heavy cream, whipped
a few fresh gooseberries for decoration (optional)

Cook the gooseberries with the sugar, cinnamon, cloves and white wine for about 20–25 minutes in a covered saucepan over medium heat. Remove the cinnamon and cloves and purée the fruit in a blender then press it through a sieve to remove the seeds. Dissolve the gelatine in the hot water then stir it into the gooseberry purée.

Prepare the bavaroise according to the recipe instructions and pour half of it into a 1-quart mold or glass serving dish. Chill it quickly until just set then carefully spoon the gooseberry purée over the layer of bavaroise. Chill the gooseberry purée until just set then spoon the remaining bavaroise over the top. Chill until the layers are quite set then unmold the bavaroise, if it is in a mold, and decorate it with whipped cream and a few fresh gooseberries.

Note A little gin may be added to the gooseberry purée or 1 teaspoon juniper berries can be substituted for the cinnamon stick and cloves.

Cook's Tip

Always make sure that gelatine is completely dissolved before adding to another mixture. Do not let the gelatine boil or become overheated as it will become stringy.

Bavaroise with red and black currants

Serves 4

½ lb red currants
½ lb black currants
½ cup sugar
3–4 tablespoons crème de cassis (black currant liqueur)
½ (2-cup) package raspberry-flavored gelatine
1 quantity bavaroise (see left)

Wash, trim and dry the currants, reserving a few red currants for decoration. Sprinkle them with sugar, then leave them to stand for 30–40 minutes until most of the sugar has dissolved. Pour over the liqueur and stir the currants to dissolve the remaining sugar and mix well. Dissolve the gelatine in ¾ cup hot water then stir it into the fruit and leave it until half set.

Meanwhile, make the bavaroise according to the recipe instructions and spoon half of it into a 5-cup mold or glass serving dish. Chill it until just set. Spoon the currant mixture on top and chill again until just set. Finally top with the remaining bavaroise and chill until quite set. Unmold onto a serving dish (if the bavaroise is set in a mold) and decorate with the reserved red currants.

Variation
Substitute your favorite jam or preserve for the jellied currant mixture. Spoon a thin layer of it over the bavaroise base, top with the second half of the bavaroise and chill thoroughly. Unmold just before serving and decorate with fresh fruit in season. A mixture of crumbled macaroons and raisins steeped in rum or brandy is delicious layered with the bavaroise instead of the currants.

Alternatively, layer drained canned or bottled fruit with the bavaroise and sprinkle a little coarsely grated chocolate over the finished dessert.

Desserts

Figs with raspberry purée

Serves 4

8 ripe figs, peeled and halved
$\frac{1}{4}$ cup Kirsch
$\frac{3}{4}$ lb raspberries
1 tablespoon lemon juice
$\frac{1}{4}$ cup sugar
$\frac{3}{4}$ cup whipping cream
1 tablespoon vanilla sugar (page 188)
2 tablespoons confectioners' sugar

Arrange the figs in individual serving dishes and sprinkle the Kirsch over them. Leave them in the refrigerator for about 1 hour. Meanwhile purée the raspberries with the lemon juice and sugar in a blender then sieve to remove the seeds. Whip the cream with the vanilla and confectioners' sugars then spoon it over the chilled figs and top each serving with raspberry purée. Serve with wafer cookies.

Variation
Vanilla or chocolate ice cream can be served with the figs, either with the whipped cream or instead of it. Alternatively the Kirsch-flavored figs can be served in meringue nests then topped with the cream and raspberry purée.

Apricots flambé

Serves 4

$\frac{1}{2}$ cup white wine
1-in piece cinnamon stick
$\frac{1}{4}$ vanilla bean
3 tablespoons sugar
12 large, ripe apricots
2 tablespoons butter
$\frac{1}{2}$ cup flaked almonds
$\frac{1}{4}$ cup Kirsch

Heat the wine with the cinnamon, vanilla and sugar. Then cover the pan and allow it to simmer for 10 minutes. Blanch the apricots in boiling water for a minute, then drain, peel, halve and pit them. Remove the cinnamon and vanilla bean from the wine. Add the apricots and poach them gently for about 5 mintues. Remove them from the wine and pat them on paper towels. Melt the butter, add the apricot halves and almonds and cook for a few minutes until the almonds are lightly browned. Pour over the warmed Kirsch, set it alight and serve immediately with a little of the cooking wine.

Tip Serve these apricots with vanilla or chocolate ice cream. They are also good with crêpes.

Variation
Peaches flambé Use four large ripe peaches instead of the apricots and replace the vanilla bean with a strip of thinly pared lemon rind.

Farina fritters

Serves 4

2 cups milk
pinch of salt
3 tablespoons sugar
2 tablespoons butter
1 cup farina
⅓ cup ground almonds
2 eggs
grated rind of 1 orange
⅔ cup dry white breadcrumbs
6 tablespoons butter for frying

Bring the milk to a boil with the salt, sugar and butter. Sprinkle in the farina and ground almonds and stir for 10 minutes over low heat until thickened. Remove the pan from the heat and blend a little of the farina in a small bowl with one of the eggs and the orange rind. Return this mixture to the pan, stir well and allow it to stand for 10 minutes.

Rinse a 9 × 13-in jelly roll pan with cold water and spread the farina evenly over it. Leave it in the refrigerator until quite firm then use a wet knife to cut it into squares.

Beat the second egg and dip the farina squares first in the egg then in the breadcrumbs to coat.

Fry these fritters in the butter until they are crisp and golden brown, turning once to ensure even browning. Drain them carefully on paper towels and serve them immediately with canned or bottled fruit or seasonal fresh fruit. Alternatively sweeten and purée the fruit or serve warmed jam with the fritters.

Rice pudding

Serves 4

2½ cups milk
pinch of salt
¼ cup butter
1 vanilla bean, split
thinly pared rind of ½ lemon
¼ cup sugar
3 tablespoons short-grain rice
a little freshly grated nutmeg

Heat the milk slowly in a heavy-based saucepan with the salt, half the butter, vanilla bean, lemon rind and sugar. As soon as the milk reaches boiling point, remove it from the heat and leave to infuse for 10 minutes. Strain the milk, return it to the pan, add the rice and bring it to a boil stirring occasionally. Reduce the heat to the lowest setting, cover the pan and cook the rice for about 50–60 minutes. Stir the pudding occasionally to ensure that it does not stick.

Pour the rice into a warmed serving dish. Melt the remaining butter in a saucepan and pour it over the pudding together with a generous sprinkling of nutmeg. The butter should be stirred into the pudding just before it is eaten to enrich the rice.

Desserts

Mocha charlotte

Serves 6

2 envelopes unflavored gelatine
¼ cup hot water
5 eggs, separated
6 tablespoons sugar
1 tablespoon instant coffee, dissolved
   in 2 tablespoons hot water
grated rind and juice of 1 orange
¼ cup orange liqueur
4 (1-oz) squares semisweet chocolate
4 oz sweet chocolate
2 tablespoons water
6 tablespoons butter
1¼ cups heavy cream, whipped
28 ladyfinger cookies

Decoration
a little chocolate sprinkles
coarsely grated orange rind

Dissolve the gelatine in the hot water. Whisk the egg yolks with the sugar until pale and creamy. Whisk the coffee into the yolks together with the orange rind and juice and 1 tablespoon of the orange liqueur. Stir in the dissolved gelatine. Melt the semisweet and milk chocolate with the cold water and butter in a bowl over a saucepan of hot water. Stir it lightly to ensure that the ingredients are well blended then carefully fold it into the yolk mixture. Beat the egg whites until stiff then fold them into the mixture followed by half of the whipped cream.

Moisten the cookies with the remaining liqueur and use them to line a 7½-cup charlotte mold or straight-sided deep dish. Fill it with the mocha cream and top with any remaining cookies. Chill until set then unmold and decorate with the remaining cream, piped in swirls, a little chocolate sprinkles and a little coarsely grated orange rind.

Yogurt charlotte

Serves 8

Sponge cake
3 eggs
6 tablespoons sugar
¾ cup flour
a little confectioners' sugar
⅓ cup raspberry jam, warmed

Cream
3 eggs, separated
½ cup + 2 tablespoons sugar
2 envelopes unflavored gelatine
3 tablespoons hot water
grated rind and juice of 1 lemon
½ cup dry white wine
1 cup plain yogurt

Decoration
¾ cup heavy cream, whipped
3 tablespoons chopped pistachio nuts

Preheat the oven to 425°.
   Line and grease a 9 × 13-inch jelly roll pan. Beat the eggs with the sugar until pale, thick and creamy. Sift the flour over the egg mixture and carefully fold it in. Pour the mixture into the prepared pan and smooth it out evenly. Bake for 5–7 minutes until well risen and golden brown.

   Lay a sheet of wax paper on a clean dish towel and sprinkle it with the confectioners' sugar. Turn the cake out onto the paper. Working quickly, remove the lining paper and trim the edges of the cake then spread the warmed jam over it. Roll up the cake using the paper and dish towel to help form a neat roll. Leave it to stand, wrapped in the towel for a minute. Remove the roll to a wire rack and allow to cool then slice it thinly.

   To make the yogurt cream, beat the egg yolks with the sugar until pale and creamy. Meanwhile dissolve the gelatine in the hot water. Stir the lemon rind and juice, wine and yogurt into the egg yolks and whisk thoroughly. Stir in the dissolved gelatine and leave the mixture until it begins to set. Beat the egg whites until they are stiff, but not too dry, then fold them into the cream. Line a 7½-cup mold with the jelly roll slices and pour the cream into the middle. Chill until set then unmold and decorate with piped whipped cream and the pistachio nuts.

Tip The yogurt cream can be set in a mold without the jelly roll slices or a purchased jelly roll may be used to save time.

Desserts

Raspberries Romanoff

Serves 4

1 lb raspberries
½ cup confectioners' sugar
3 tablespoons orange liqueur
1¼ cups heavy cream
1 tablespoon vanilla sugar (page 188)

Wash and dry the raspberries and remove any stalks. Sprinkle two-thirds of the confectioners' sugar over and leave them to stand for 15–20 minutes. Reserve 12 of the best raspberries for decoration then pour the orange liqueur over the remainder and leave them to stand for 1–2 hours.

Whip the cream with the remaining confectioners' sugar and vanilla sugar. Layer the raspberries and cream in sundae glasses (piping the cream if liked) ending with a layer of cream. Decorate with the reserved raspberries.

Tip Port can be used to flavor the raspberries instead of the liqueur and strawberries or blackberries may be used instead of raspberries.

Peaches with fresh fig cream

Serves 4

4 firm ripe peaches
¼ cup Kirsch
4 ripe figs
3 tablespoons sugar
1 teaspoon lemon juice
1¼ cups heavy cream

Decoration
1 cup wild or Alpine strawberries
¼ cup flaked almonds

Blanch the peaches in boiling water for 1–2 minutes then peel and halve them, removing the pit. Arrange them in a large serving dish or individual dishes, sprinkle over the Kirsch and leave to stand for 1–2 hours. Peel, quarter and purée the figs in a blender or food processor with the sugar and lemon juice. Whip the cream until stiff then stir it into the fig purée.

Pipe the fig cream in large swirls into the halved peaches. Hull, wash and dry the strawberries and use to decorate the peaches together with

the almonds. Serve with almond macaroons or other sweet cookies.

Variation
Pineapple with fresh fig cream Halve a small fresh pineapple lengthwise and scoop out the flesh, leaving the skin intact. Discard the hard parts of the core and chop the flesh. Return the flesh to the hollowed-out shell and sprinkle with Kirsch or rum. Decorate the pineapple with Alpine strawberries or raspberries and the piped fig cream.

Cherry gelatine

Serves 4–6

2 envelopes unflavored gelatine
1 (16-oz) can red or Bing cherries,
  pitted
2–3 tablespoons sugar
pared rind of $\frac{1}{2}$ small lemon
$1\frac{1}{4}$ cups rosé wine
juice of 1 lemon
3 tablespoons Kirsch
$\frac{3}{4}$ cup heavy cream
2 tablespoons vanilla sugar (page
  188)
2 tablespoons pistachio nuts

Dissolve the gelatine in 2
tablespoons hot water in a basin
over a saucepan of hot water. Drain
the cherries, reserve the syrup and
heat $\frac{3}{4}$ cup of it with the sugar and
lemon rind. Stir it thoroughly then
remove from the heat and leave it to
stand for 5 minutes before removing
the lemon rind.
  Stir the dissolved gelatine, wine
and lemon juice into the syrup
together with the Kirsch. Allow it to
set very lightly then stir in the
cherries and pour it into a $2\frac{1}{2}$-cup
mold. Chill the cherry gelatine until

set then unmold it onto a serving
dish. Whip the cream with the
vanilla sugar until stiff and decorate
the gelatine with swirls of whipped
cream and pistachio nuts.

Variation
The gelatine can be set in individual
molds. Try serving the gelatine with
scoops of your favorite ice cream.
Sauce Sabayon (page 188) or
Zabaglione (page 204) can also be
served as accompaniments. Other
canned fruits, for example
raspberries or strawberries, can be
used instead of the cherries.

Cook's Tip

To unmold the gelatine, dip the
mold briefly into hot water then
place a plate over the top of the
mold and invert the mold sharply.
Give a couple of vigorous shakes
and the gelatine should drop onto
the plate.

Desserts

Blackberry and apple soup

Serves 4

5 tablespoons dry white wine
¾ cup sugar
2 apples, peeled, cored and sliced
1 quart water
thinly pared rind of 1 lemon
2 cloves
1-in piece cinnamon stick
2 lb blackberries
1 egg white
pinch of salt
¼ cup cornstarch

Heat the wine and sugar together, stirring continuously until the sugar has dissolved. Add the apples and cook them gently for 5 minutes. Remove and reserve the apple slices. Add the water, lemon rind and spices to the pan together with the blackberries and simmer them, covered, for about 20 minutes. Sieve the mixture and return the liquid to the pan.

Beat the egg white with the salt until stiff. Dissolve the cornstarch in a little of the liquid, add it to the pan and cook it, stirring continuously, over low heat until it boils. Cook for 2–3 minutes, return the apples to the soup then remove it from the heat. Drop teaspoonfuls of the egg white onto the hot soup, cover the pan and allow the egg white to set in the steam from the soup for 15 minutes.

Remove the "snowballs" carefully from the soup with a slotted spoon, pour the soup into a serving bowl and carefully float the snowballs back on top. Allow to cool and chill thoroughly before serving.

Fruity milk whip

Serves 6

½ lb mixed soft fruits (plums,
  gooseberries, cherries, peaches,
  strawberries, raspberries, red
  currants or blackberries)
½ cup sugar
2 teaspoons unflavored gelatine
2 cups milk
¾ cup plain yogurt
½ teaspoon vanilla extract
pinch of salt
¾ cup heavy cream

Wash or wipe the fruit and prepare it as appropriate, slicing any large fruits. Mix them together in a bowl and sprinkle half the sugar over them. Leave them to stand for about 30 minutes. Meanwhile dissolve the gelatine in 2 tablespoons hot water.

Dissolve the remaining sugar in the milk and stir in the yogurt, vanilla extract and salt. Whisk the gelatine into the milk mixture then chill it until it begins to set. Whisk the half-set gelatine thoroughly to incorporate as much air as possible. Whip the cream and fold it into the milk whip then transfer the mixture to a serving bowl and chill it thoroughly. Top the whip with the prepared fruit and serve it immediately.

Note The amount of sugar may vary with the ripeness and quality of the fruit.

Chocolate flakes, small macaroons or cinnamon sugar may be used to top the whip instead of the fruit and a little brandy, rum or other liqueur may be added to the milk mixture.

Cook's Tip

Fruit soups make an unusual and refreshing end to a rich meal. The fruit used can be varied according to season. Black cherries, red currants and raspberries would all be suitable in this recipe instead of the blackberries and apples.

Fruit soups should be served with plain sweet cookies.

Desserts

Zabaglione

Serves 4

5 egg yolks
6 tablespoons sugar
1 tablespoon vanilla sugar (page 188)
grated rind and juice of ½ lemon
½ cup Marsala
a few purple grapes for decoration

Whisk the egg yolks with the sugar and vanilla sugar until very pale and creamy. Stand the bowl over a saucepan of hot water, add the lemon rind and juice and Marsala and whisk the mixture until thickened. Pour into individual dishes or glasses and decorate with a few grapes. Serve immediately.

Variations
Zabaglione is nearly always served hot as soon as it is made. Other fresh fruits besides grapes may be served with it. For an unusual contrast put a scoop of ice cream or sherbet in the bottom of the glass before pouring in the hot cream. Serve at once before the ice cream has melted.

Note Marsala is a full-bodied dessert wine from Sicily which is gradually regaining popularity all over the world. It is available in varying grades of sweetness; the best one to choose for Zabaglione is Marsala all'uovo (Marsala with egg) which is creamy and sweet.

Orange cream

Serves 4

2 teaspoons unflavored gelatine
1¼ cups freshly squeezed orange juice
2 egg yolks
6 tablespoons sugar
1¼ cups heavy cream
3 tablespoons orange liqueur
1 orange

Dissolve the gelatine in 2 tablespoons hot water. Warm the orange juice, stir in the gelatine and leave it to cool. Whisk the egg yolks with the sugar until thick and creamy then stir it into the orange juice just as it begins to set. Whip the cream with the orange liqueur until it is stiff and fold it into the jellied mixture. Spoon the orange cream into individual serving dishes or glasses.

Grate the rind from the orange and peel it, removing all the white pith. Cut it into thin slices and use them to decorate the creams then sprinkle the grated orange rind over the top.

Tip To make a light and airy orange cream, fold in 2 stiffly beaten egg whites after the cream.

Variations
Freshly squeezed grapefruit or lemon juice may be substituted for the orange juice in which case the quantity of sugar should be adjusted to taste. Blood oranges taste particularly good in this dessert.

Honey ice cream with Chinese gooseberry purée

Serves 4

2 eggs
3 egg yolks
2 tablespoons vanilla sugar (page 188)
1¼ cups light cream
½ cup milk
½ cup clear honey, warmed
5 Chinese gooseberries (kiwi fruit)
¼ cup Kirsch

Whisk the eggs, extra egg yolks and vanilla sugar until pale and thick. Heat the cream and milk together and pour gradually into the eggs, whisking continuously. Gradually whisk in the honey then leave the mixture to cool. Pour it into a large freezer container and place it in the freezer until it is half frozen. Remove the ice cream from the freezer and whisk it thoroughly to remove any ice crystals. Return it to the freezer and repeat the whisking process once more then allow the ice cream to freeze until firm.

Peel the gooseberries and reserve one for decoration. Purée the remaining fruit in a blender with the Kirsch. Serve scoops of ice cream in individual dishes decorated with slices of the reserved gooseberry. Pour a little fruit purée over each serving.

Tip Honey ice cream can also be served with blackberry purée. About 1 lb ripe blackberries should be puréed with sugar to taste then pressed through a sieve. The purée may be flavored with a little Kirsch and a few whole blackberries used for decoration.

Desserts

Champagne orange sherbet

Serves 4

½ cup + 2 tablespoons sugar
1¼ cups freshly squeezed orange juice
juice of 1 lemon
1¼ cups well-chilled champagne or
*   sparkling white wine*
1 egg white, stiffly beaten
1 cup hulled and halved strawberries

Dissolve the sugar in the orange juice over low heat. Add the lemon juice and allow the syrup to cool. Pour it into a large freezer container and chill it in the freezer for 30 minutes. Gradually whisk in the champagne or sparkling wine and return the sherbet to the freezer until it is half frozen. Whisk it thoroughly and fold in the stiffly beaten egg white then return the sherbet to the freezer and leave it until frozen, whisking once or twice to prevent ice crystals from forming. Spoon the sherbet into individual dishes and decorate with the strawberries.

Note This sherbet may be served in small quantities to refresh the palate between the courses of a main meal. It may also be served in small quantities in champagne glasses, topped up with champagne.

Coffee parfait

Serves 6

½ cup + 2 tablespoons sugar
⅓ cup water
¼ cup instant coffee
1 tablespoon hot chocolate powder
¼ cup boiling water
¾ cup heavy cream
4 egg yolks
1 tablespoon coffee or chocolate
*   liqueur*
candy coffee beans to decorate

Dissolve the sugar in the water over low heat then bring it to a boil and remove it from the heat. Dissolve the coffee and hot chocolate in the boiling water. Whip the cream with the coffee and chocolate mixture until stiff. Whisk the egg yolks in a

bowl over a saucepan of hot water then gradually whisk in the sugar syrup in a slow stream until the mixture is very pale and creamy. Continue whisking until it is quite cold, adding the liqueur drop by drop. Fold in the whipped cream, pour the parfait into individual freezerproof molds and freeze for several hours. Unmold and decorate with the candy coffee beans.

Blackberries Astoria

Serves 4

4 large tart apples, peeled, cored and
*   sprinkled with lemon juice*
½ cup white wine
¼ cup sugar
½ teaspoon ground cinnamon
¾ lb blackberries, washed and dried
⅓ cup apricot jam, warmed and
*   sieved*
3 tablespoons Kirsch
¼ cup sliced almonds
1 tablespoon butter
¾ cup heavy cream
3 tablespoons confectioners' sugar
2 tablespoons vanilla sugar (page
*   188)*

Stand the apples in a saucepan, pour
over the wine and sprinkle the sugar
and cinnamon over them. Cover the
pan and cook the apples gently for
about 10 minutes. Remove them
from the pan, arranging them on
individual plates or dishes, and leave
them to cool.

Mix the blackberries with the jam
and Kirsch and divide this between
the apples then chill them
thoroughly for about 30 minutes.
Lightly fry the sliced almonds in the
butter until golden. Drain them on
paper towels. Whip the cream with
the confectioners' sugar and vanilla
sugar until stiff and spoon it over
the apples. Decorate with the sliced
almonds.

Blueberry ice cream

Serves 4

1 lb fresh blueberries or blackberries
½ cup sugar
2 eggs, separated
1 tablespoon lemon juice
2 tablespoons black currant liqueur
¾ cup heavy cream
¼ lb blueberries or blackberries,
*   trimmed, washed and dried to*
*   decorate*

Wash, trim and dry the blueberries
or blackberries and mix them into
the sugar then leave to stand for 30
minutes. Whisk the egg yolks with
the lemon juice in a bowl over a
saucepan of hot water and whisk in
all the juice from the fruit. Continue
whisking until the mixture is thick
and creamy, then remove it from the
heat, add the liqueur and continue
whisking till cool. Chill it thoroughly
then whisk both the egg whites, and
cream separately until they are stiff
and fold them into the blueberry
cream. Freeze the ice cream in a
large freezer container, whisking
occasionally to prevent ice crystals
forming, until it is firm. Serve the
ice cream, scooped into tall glasses,
decorated with the whole fruit.

Desserts

Guelph pudding

Serves 4

6 tablespoons cornstarch
pinch of salt
1¼ cups milk
1 vanilla bean
½ cup sugar
4 eggs, separated
2 tablespoons lemon juice
1¼ cups dry white wine

Mix the cornstarch with the salt and a little of the milk until smooth and creamy. Heat the remaining milk to boiling point with the vanilla bean, remove it from the heat and allow it to cool for a few minutes. Strain the milk into the cornstarch mixture, stirring continuously. Return it to the pan, stir in half the sugar and bring the mixture slowly to a boil, stirring continuously. Remove it from the heat and allow to cool to lukewarm, stirring frequently. Beat the egg whites until stiff and fold them into the sauce then divide it between four individual dishes.

Whisk the egg yolks with the remaining sugar in a bowl over a saucepan of hot water, gradually adding the lemon juice and wine until the mixture is cooked and thickened — do not allow it to overcook or it will curdle. Remove from the heat and continue whisking until it is quite cold. Divide the custard between the dishes, forming an even layer over each of the cornstarch bases. Chill lightly before serving.

Note The cornstarch base may be made up to a day in advance and chilled ready for use. The base can also be made using flavored dessert powder.

Steamed bread pudding

Serves 6

4 slices of stale white, crustless bread,
*   cubed*
¾ cup crumbled macaroons
1½ cups crumbled pumpernickel
*   (optional)*
¾ cup hot milk
½ cup + 2 tablespoons butter
½ cup sugar
4 eggs, separated
2 tablespoons vanilla sugar (page
*   188)*
grated rind and juice of 1 orange
3 tablespoons orange liqueur
½ cup finely chopped or ground
*   almonds*
pinch of salt

Mix the bread, macaroons and pumpernickel together and pour over the hot milk then leave the mixture to soak for 10 minutes.

Meanwhile, cream the butter with the sugar then beat in the egg yolks and vanilla sugar, and orange rind and juice. Add the liqueur, chopped or ground almonds and stir in the soaked ingredients.

Beat the egg whites with the salt until they are stiff then fold them into the pudding. Turn the mixture into a well greased 1-quart round steaming or kugelhopf mold and cover it first with a piece of pleated, greased parchment paper and then loosely with foil, sealing it well around the rim of the mold. Boil or steam the pudding for 1½ hours then carefully remove it from the pan or steamer, uncover and unmold it onto a warmed plate. Remember to check the level of the water in the saucepan during cooking and add more boiling water when necessary. Sauce Sabayon (page 188) goes very well with this pudding.
Alternatively, serve cream whipped with a little vanilla sugar and orange liqueur as an accompaniment to the pudding.

Tip Pistachio nuts, hazelnuts or walnuts may be used instead of the almonds and a few raisins may be added to the pudding. These may be first soaked in a little brandy or rum for extra flavor. Small scoops of ice cream make a refreshing contrast to this warming winter pudding.

Entertaining
Menus for Celebration Meals

Entertaining

Dinner party menu

Serves 6

Baked oysters
Stuffed sirloin steak
Neapolitan potato balls
Asparagus (see page 122)
Filled pineapple

Baked oysters

3 dozen fresh oysters with tightly shut
* shells (others are inedible)*
¼ cup butter
1 cup soft breadcrumbs
2 tablespoons chopped parsley
2 tablespoons Pernod
freshly ground white pepper

Open the oysters. Hold one oyster firmly and insert a strong rigid knife, preferably an oyster knife, between the two shells just beside the hinge. Twist the knife sharply to open the shell. Run the knife under the oyster to remove it from the shell. Reserve any liquid that runs out and discard the shell. Prepare all the oysters in this way.

Preheat the oven to 450°. Grease a baking dish with some of the butter and coat it with a few of the breadcrumbs.

Mix the rest of the breadcrumbs with the parsley. Sprinkle half the oysters with half the Pernod and some of the reserved oyster liquid then season with pepper, cover with half the breadcrumb mixture and dot with flakes of butter. Repeat with the remaining ingredients. Bake for 10 minutes in the heated oven then serve at once with French bread and a dry white wine.

Note If you prefer you can serve the oysters on the half shell. After opening them loosen them on their half shells and place on a cookie sheet covered with salt. Sprinkle with lemon juice and a few breadcrumbs and dot with butter. Brown under a broiler, preheated to its hottest setting.

Stuffed sirloin steak

1½-lb piece boneless sirloin steak
¼ cup oil
1 medium-size onion, peeled and
* chopped*
½ cup ground lean beef
salt and freshly ground black pepper
pinch paprika
pinch dried thyme
½ cup finely chopped lean cooked
* ham*
1 cup finely chopped button
* mushrooms*
1 tablespoon chopped parsley
1 tablespoon chopped chervil
* (optional)*
1 egg, beaten
2 tablespoons butter

Trim the steak and cut a pocket in one side with a sharp knife. Heat 2 tablespoons of the oil in a saucepan and fry the onion until soft but not browned. Add the ground beef and fry until brown and crumbly. Season to taste with salt, pepper, paprika and dried thyme. Stir in the ham and mushrooms and continue to cook until the liquid from the mushrooms has evaporated. Add the parsley and chervil, if using, and remove from the heat. Allow the mixture to cool then mix with beaten egg to bind.

Stuff the pocket in the steak with the meat mixture and sew up the opening with fine string or secure with wooden toothpicks. Heat the oil in a large skillet and cook the steak to seal on all sides. Remove from the pan and rub the steak with salt and pepper. Melt the butter in the oil and return the steak to the pan. Cook the steak for 20 to 25 minutes then allow to rest for a few minutes before carving. Remember to remove the string or toothpicks before serving with Neapolitan potato balls and asparagus. A full-bodied red wine goes well with this dish.

Neapolitan potato balls

6 oz small pasta rings
1 lb potatoes, peeled
3 tablespoons butter
½ cup flour
¾ cup light cream
½ cup chopped cooked ham
2 tablespoons chopped parsley
salt
little grated nutmeg
oil for deep frying

Cook the pasta rings in plenty of boiling salted water until just tender. Drain and refresh with cold water. Cook the potatoes in boiling salted water until tender then drain, mash well and put through a ricer to make a smooth purée. Blend the butter and flour together and add, a little at a time, to the hot potato. Mix well and stir in the cream. Add the ham and parsley and season to taste with salt and nutmeg.

Form the potato mixture into balls about 1½-inches across and roll them firmly in the pasta rings. Heat the fat to 360° and fry the potato balls for 3–4 minutes or until golden brown.

Filled pineapple

1 ripe pineapple, halved lengthwise
* and core removed*
2 tablespoons Kirsch
2 tablespoons maraschino liqueur
* (optional)*
½ lb raspberries
1–2 tablespoons granulated or vanilla
* sugar*
1 cup halved purple grapes, seeds
* removed*
1 pint vanilla ice cream

Remove the flesh from the pineapple with a melon baller or teaspoon and place with any juice that collects in a bowl. Reserve the shells. Sprinkle the pineapple flesh with the Kirsch and maraschino, if using, and leave in a cool place or refrigerator for about 2 hours.

Meanwhile purée the raspberries by pushing through a sieve and sweeten to taste with sugar or vanilla sugar.

Drain the liquid from the pineapple and mix with the raspberry purée. Arrange the pineapple with the grapes in the reserved pineapple shells and chill. Just before serving top with slices of ice cream and pour over the raspberry sauce.

Tip To test whether a pineapple is ripe pull one of the inner leaves from the top of the pineapple. If it comes away easily the pineapple is ripe.

Entertaining

Dinner party menu

Serves 6

Stuffed artichokes
Beef Wellington
Zucchini salad (page 156)
Mocha mousse

Stuffed artichokes

6 small artichokes, trimmed and
  chokes removed
3 shallots, peeled and chopped
2 tablespoons butter
3 tablespoons chopped parsley
½ cup chopped lean cooked ham
3 hard-cooked eggs, chopped
1 bunch garden cress, snipped
salt and freshly ground black pepper
12 slices of bacon
2 tablespoons oil
1¼ cups dry white wine
1 tablespoon tomato paste
1¼ cups sour cream

Wash the artichokes and leave
upside down to drain. Fry the
shallots in the butter until soft but
not browned then stir in the parsley,
ham, eggs and cress. Season to taste
with salt and pepper. Use this
mixture to stuff the artichokes.

Wrap 2 slices of bacon around
each artichoke and secure with
wooden toothpicks. Heat the oil in a
skillet and seal the artichokes all
over. Transfer to a large saucepan
or flameproof casserole. Pour over
the white wine, tomato paste and
half the sour cream. Cover tightly
and simmer for 35–40 minutes.
Arrange the artichokes on a serving
dish. Beat the rest of the sour cream
into the cooking liquid and pour this
sauce over the artichokes. Serve
with fresh white bread.

Beef Wellington

1¾-lb piece beef tenderloin
6 tablespoons butter
salt and freshly ground black pepper
2 onions, peeled and finely chopped
1½ cups thinly sliced mushrooms
½ lb lamb liver, trimmed and diced
1 teaspoon dried marjoram
1 teaspoon dried thyme
2 tablespoons chopped parsley
2 tablespoons soft white breadcrumbs
2 tablespoons Madeira
1 egg yolk, beaten, to glaze
1 (¾-lb) package frozen puff pastry,
  thawed

Trim the beef and wipe with paper
towels. Melt 2 tablespoons butter in
a large skillet, then sear the meat all
over for 10 minutes. Remove from
the pan, allow to cool and rub all
over with salt and pepper. Melt half
the remaining butter in a small pan
and cook the onions until soft, but
not colored. Add the mushrooms
and cook gently, stirring from time
to time, until all the liquid from the
mushrooms has evaporated.
Meanwhile sauté the diced liver in
the rest of the butter until browned
on all sides. Combine the liver,
onion and mushroom with the herbs,
breadcrumbs and Madeira and
season to taste.

Preheat the oven to 400°. Roll out
the pastry on a floured surface to a
rectangle large enough to wrap
around the meat and spread with
two-thirds of the mushroom mixture.
Place the beef on top of this and top
with the rest of the filling. Fold the
pastry over to enclose the meat
completely, dampening the edges
with a little water to make a good
seal. Place the "package" on a
dampened cookie sheet so that the
joins are tucked underneath and
brush with egg yolk. Bake in the
heated oven for 50 minutes.

Serve with Spiced cranberry sauce
(page 115) and a mixed salad.

Mocha mousse

6 (1-oz) squares semisweet chocolate
2 oz sweet milk chocolate
4 eggs, separated
2 teaspoons instant coffee
½ teaspoon vanilla extract
1 teaspoon lemon juice
1¼ cups whipping cream
1 tablespoon coffee liqueur or brandy
2 drops almond extract
candy coffee beans to garnish
  (optional)

Break up the chocolate and place in
a bowl over a pan of hot, but not
boiling, water. Leave until melted
then remove from the pan. Beat the
egg yolks with the coffee powder
and vanilla extract until creamy.
Add to the melted chocolate and
mix well.

Beat the egg whites with the
lemon juice until stiff. Whip the
cream and reserve about one-third
for garnish. Fold the remaining
cream into the chocolate mixture
and flavor with liqueur or brandy
and almond extract. Finally fold in
the egg whites. Pour into a serving
dish and allow to set in the
refrigerator. Just before serving,
decorate with the reserved cream
and candy coffee beans.

Cook's Tip

A fresh young artichoke should
have tightly packed leaves of a good
fresh green colour. Avoid any whose
leaves are beginning to spread out
and show the purplish center.

Entertaining

Cold buffet party

Serves 12

A cold buffet party is one of the easiest and most pleasant ways of entertaining a large number of people. All the work can be done in advance, leaving the hostess free to enjoy the time with her guests.

The recipes given below are sufficient for a full scale buffet meal, but you may also like to add or substitute some of your favorite recipes from the preceding chapters.

Cold tomato soup

3 tablespoons butter
1 large onion, peeled and chopped
3–4 cloves garlic, peeled and crushed
3 tablespoons flour
2 teaspoons paprika
6 (16-oz) cans tomatoes, drained and juice reserved
1 chicken bouillon cube, crumbled
pinch of sugar
freshly ground black pepper
1¼ cups whipping cream
¼ cup sliced almonds
¼ cup chopped chives

Melt the butter in a large saucepan and use to fry the onion and garlic until soft but not browned. Sprinkle over the flour and paprika and stir until absorbed. Add the tomato liquid, stirring all the time and bring to a boil. Simmer for 5 minutes. Meanwhile chop the tomatoes roughly then add them to the pan. Season with the bouillon cube, sugar and pepper to taste, bring back to a boil and simmer for 10 minutes. Purée the mixture in a blender or food processor, in batches if necessary, then allow the soup to cool completely.

Lightly whip the cream and stir it into the soup. Just before serving, garnish with the sliced almonds and chives.

Variation
Add a dash of Worcestershire or hot pepper sauce to the soup for a really spicy flavor. Alternatively a few tablespoons of vodka or gin may be added for an unusual flavor.

Palmito cocktail

1 (16-oz) can palm hearts (palmitos), drained and cut into strips
¾ cup sour cream
¾ cup plain yogurt
1 tablespoon tomato paste
2 tablespoons orange juice
1 tablespoon brandy
salt
cayenne
pinch of sugar
½ lb very thinly sliced smoked ham
crushed black peppercorns to garnish

Arrange the palm hearts in a deep dish. Beat together the sour cream, yogurt, tomato paste, orange juice and brandy to make a dressing. Season to taste with salt, cayenne and sugar. Roll up the slices of ham and arrange on the dish with the palm hearts. Pour over the dressing and garnish with a few crushed black peppercorns.

Jumbo shrimp Chantilly

1 lb peeled jumbo shrimp, deveined
3 tablespoons lemon juice
¾ cup heavy cream
¾ cup mayonnaise (see page 112)
2–3 tablespoons dry sherry
pinch each of salt, cayenne, paprika and sugar
dash of Worcestershire sauce
dash of white wine vinegar
2 tablespoons green peppercorns, drained, to garnish

Rinse the shrimp quickly and sprinkle with the lemon juice. Divide between individual serving dishes. Whip the cream until stiff

and fold into the mayonnaise. Stir in the sherry and season to taste with salt, cayenne, paprika, sugar, Worcestershire sauce and vinegar. Spoon the dressing over the shrimp and garnish with green peppercorns.

Lettuce and ham salad

3 small heads of Iceberg lettuce, washed
2 cups thinly sliced button mushrooms
6 stalks celery, washed and sliced
2 red peppers, deseeded, washed and chopped
½ lb lean cooked ham, cut in strips
1 bunch radishes, washed, trimmed and sliced
1¼ cups mayonnaise (see page 112)
¾ cup plain yogurt
1 shallot, peeled and finely chopped
salt and white pepper
pinch of cayenne
pinch of sugar

Garnish
6 anchovy fillets, soaked in water, drained and halved
2 tablespoons capers, drained
2 tablespoons chopped parsley

Cut the hearts from the lettuces from the top and remove and discard any hard core. Separate the inner leaves and ease apart the leaves of the lettuce shells to form rosette shapes.

Shred the reserved inner leaves and mix with the mushrooms, celery, peppers, ham and radishes. Beat the mayonnaise and yogurt well together and add the finely chopped shallot. Season to taste with salt, pepper, cayenne and sugar.

Pile the ham and salad mixture into lettuce cases and pour over the dressing. Garnish with the anchovies, capers and chopped parsley.

Trout in aspic

1 quart fish stock (made from scraps of fish)
½ cup dry white wine
2 large carrots, roughly chopped
2 stalks celery, roughly chopped
1 onion, peeled and quartered
10 peppercorns
salt
6 trout, cleaned
1 egg white
1 egg shell, crushed (optional)
2 envelopes unflavored gelatine

Garnish
1 cooked carrot, very thinly sliced
sprigs of parsley

Put the fish stock, wine, carrots, celery, onion and peppercorns in a large pan and bring to a boil. Simmer for 10 minutes then season with salt. Put in the trout and let them simmer very gently for 15 minutes. Lift the fish out of the pan, taking care not to break up the flesh. Rub off the skin but leave the head and tail intact. Leave the trout to cool.

Meanwhile strain the stock and reduce to half its original quantity by boiling rapidly. Beat the egg white and stir into the broth with the crushed egg shell, if using. Bring the stock to a boil and as soon as the froth rises to the top remove the pan from the heat. Reduce the heat and simmer very gently for 10 minutes. Line a fine strainer with scalded cheesecloth or a clean dishtowel and pour the broth through. Dissolve the gelatine in 3 tablespoons of hot water, add to the strained stock and leave to cool.

As soon as the aspic becomes syrupy spoon a thin layer over the bottom of a large serving platter and lay the fish on it. Coat them with the rest of the aspic and allow to cool. Garnish with the carrot and parsley.

The main roast

The choice of main meat dish is naturally a matter of personal taste, but as it is to be eaten cold it is best to choose a lean cut. Cold stuffed breast of veal (page 220) makes an excellent party dish as does Austrian boiled beef (page 78) or roast chicken or turkey. For a large party choose two different roasts.

The cheese board

It is a good idea to include at least one of each of each type of cheese: a hard cheese (for example sharp Cheddar, Monterey Jack), a blue cheese (Stilton, Roquefort), a soft cheese (Brie, Camembert, Bel Paese) and a cream cheese such as one with herbs added.

As with all party food the presentation is most important. Decorate the cheese board according to the time of year with fruit (grapes, apples, pears, fresh or diced figs), celery leaves or stalks, radish roses, tomato or parsley.

To go with the cheese have a basket of different types of bread along with crackers and bread sticks.

The dessert

The dessert can be chosen from the recipes in the chapter beginning on page 192.

A light mousse made in individual dishes is a good choice or simply serve a selection of delicious fresh fruit to eat by itself or to dip into cream or Caramel sauce, the recipe for which is given below. This goes particularly well with strawberries, Chinese gooseberries, peaches, apricots and orange or mandarin segments.

Caramel sauce

1½ cups sugar
1¼ cups milk
¾ cup light cream
½ teaspoon ground cinnamon
pinch grated nutmeg
2 tablespoons brandy or Cointreau

Place the sugar in a heavy-based saucepan and allow to caramelize over a low heat. Remove from the heat as soon as it is all golden, cover the hand holding the pan with a dish towel and add the milk in a thin stream. Dissolve the caramel in the milk over a low heat. Remove the pan from the heat and stir in the cream. Flavor to taste with cinnamon, nutmeg and brandy or Cointreau.

Cook's Tip

When planning a meal for a large number of people remember that, as a general rule, the more people that are present the less food is needed per head. This applies particularly to accompaniments such as rice, bread and green salad. For example if you are feeding 20 people allow 2 oz rice per person but if you are feeding 40 allow only 1½ oz.

Entertaining

Dinner party menu

Serves 6

Snail Salad
Stuffed breast of veal
Glazed carrots (see page 125)
New potatoes
Champagne peaches

Snail salad

2 tablespoons butter
24 canned snails, drained
2 shallots, peeled and chopped
2 (16-oz) cans artichoke hearts,
*   drained and quartered*
⅓ cup white wine
2 tablespoons vinegar
3 tablespoons oil
salt and freshly ground white pepper
2 tablespoons chopped parsley
lettuce leaves

Melt the butter in a saucepan and fry the snails with the shallots until the shallots are soft but not browned. Add the artichoke hearts with the wine, vinegar and oil. Season with salt and pepper to taste, cover the pan and cook gently for 5 minutes. Allow the mixture to cool then chill.

Sprinkle with parsley and garnish with lettuce leaves before serving.

Stuffed breast of veal

2½-lb piece boned breast of veal
3 hard-cooked eggs, chopped
3 tablespoons chopped fresh mixed
*   herbs*
½ cup chopped cooked ham
1 cup soft white breadcrumbs
salt and freshly ground white pepper
2½ cups veal or chicken stock or
*   broth*
2 cups white wine
2 large carrots, scraped and chopped
2 stalks celery, washed and chopped
1 onion, peeled
4 cloves
1 bay leaf
6 peppercorns

Trim the meat and wipe with paper towels. Mix together the egg, herbs, ham and breadcrumbs and season to taste with salt and pepper to make the stuffing. Lay the meat on a flat surface and spread with the stuffing. Roll up the meat and tie with fine string.

Heat the stock and wine together in a large saucepan. Put in the carrots and celery, the onion, stuck with the cloves, the bay leaf and the peppercorns. Lower in the veal and bring to a boil. Skim, cover and simmer for 1½ hours. Drain the meat and leave to rest for 5 minutes before carving. Strain the stock and skim off any fat. Boil rapidly until well reduced and pour a little over the sliced meat before serving. Pass the rest separately. Serve with the glazed carrots and boiled new potatoes, sprinkled with parsley.

Champagne peaches

6 small peaches
1 bottle champagne or sparkling
*   white wine*

Wash the peaches and prick the skins all over with a fork. Place each peach in a rounded glass and top up with champagne or sparkling wine.

Index

Index